FOREST SCHOOL

FOR GROWN-UPS

FOREST SCHOOL

FOR GROWN-UPS

EXPLORE THE
WISDOM OF THE WOODS

RICHARD IRVINE

ILLUSTRATED BY PAUL OAKLEY

CHRONICLE BOOKS
SAN FRANCISCO

First published in the United States in 2022 by Chronicle Books LLC

Copyright © UniPress Books Ltd, 2022

Library of Congress Cataloging-in-Publication Data available.

ISBN 978-1-7972-1528-0

Manufactured in China

Produced by UniPress Books Ltd

Design: Fogdog.co.uk
Project editor: John Andrews
Feature writer and proofreader: Tracey Kelly
Indexer: Marie Lorimer

Neither the publisher nor the author bear responsibility for the results of any project or activity described in this book or for the reader's safety during participation. Caution and common sense are recommended at all times.

10 9 8 7 6 5 4 3 2 1

CONTENTS

INTRODUCTION

What is "forest school"? It means different things to different people in different countries, but at its heart forest school is an educational philosophy that places a high value on play and nurtures creativity and curiosity, putting the needs of the participants before the demands of a school curriculum. It should revolve around frequent visits to forests, woodlands, and other wild places to build familiarity, community, and care for the planet. The ideas behind forest school emerged from the progressive, communitarian forest cultures of Scandinavia and northern Europe, and in the past twenty years those ideas have put down roots all around the globe, including North America.

Forest school looks much further than a one-off trip to the forest. It's about getting to know an outdoors place well and having time there to settle in and learn from it. People sometimes talk about "forest school activities," but the term is really a misnomer. Inspired by the natural world around them and other members of the community, participants might choose to learn about absolutely anything that catches their interest—and this book aims to fill you with the same inspiration. There are no badges to collect or awards to win. You have permission to play, explore, improvise, and experiment, and to make your own path through a forest of ideas and learning.

WHY FOREST SCHOOL FOR GROWN-UPS?

The forest school model started as a form of early years' education outdoors but has adapted and evolved to be shared across a wide variety of ages and types of group. Often, adults accompanying young people to forest school ask if there's anything like this for grown-ups, and the answer is usually "No." Nonetheless, grown-ups are still part of the forest school community, and they want to play, make, and explore without necessarily being a "responsible adult." If that's what you would like to do but aren't sure where to start, then *Forest School for Grown-Ups* is for you. If you love forests, coasts, and wild places and want to spend more time in them, then there's plenty here to enrich your experience. If you need a little space with just the trees for company, then this book will also help you make the most of the peace and renewal that time in the woods can offer.

You don't need to become a wilderness guide or expert bushcraft instructor to feel at home in the forest in all seasons. The information and ideas on these pages will help you become more comfortable outdoors and better able to improvise, using what you know and what you can find in nature. This book was written not as a manual for forest school practitioners working with groups of adults but instead to provide inspiration for everyone who enjoys time in the woods—including outdoor educators.

NEW ADVENTURES

For all those who love being among the trees, *Forest School for Grown-Ups* offers a broad range of topics that aim to fascinate and inspire, from natural history, animal behavior, and ancient crafts to outdoor living skills, creative projects, and forest fun and games. It's not an exhaustive or comprehensive guide to living wild; whole tomes have been written about the smallest of details on some of these pages. But wherever your initial interest lies, this book will ignite that spark and help kindle a passion before you head off to find your own path, armed with new skills, local knowledge, and boundless curiosity. The forest school ethos values intrinsic motivation to learn about what intrigues you, leading you to seek answers to your own questions rather than accumulate knowledge for its own sake. You'll be much more likely to persist and learn when it's something you really want to do, and you can see how new experiences will lead to new possibilities.

Any one of the following pages could be a jumping-off point for a world of discovery, an absorbing new hobby, or a journey toward unexpected expertise. All learning involves uncertainty, and forest school embraces taking appropriate risks, whether they are physical, social, or psychological. It's easy to stay in our comfort zones and become slowly risk-averse, but a life well lived needs adventure, surprise, unpredictability, and spontaneity—so stray off the path, go out in the rain, climb a tree, but most of all, risk trying something new.

I wish you great adventures, new discoveries, and much learning about the forest—and yourself. As the great American writer and defender of the wilderness Edward Abbey (1927–89) said:

> *May your trails be crooked, winding, lonesome, dangerous,*
> *leading to the most amazing view. May your mountains rise into and above the clouds.*
> *May your rivers flow without end, meandering through pastoral valleys tinkling with bells,*
> *past temples and castles and poets' towers into a dark primeval forest . . . where*
> *something strange and more beautiful and more full of wonder than your*
> *deepest dreams waits for you.*

From spring through to winter, things can change dramatically in the forest for plants, trees, and animals. How we define the seasons, however, is not a clear-cut matter. Some prefer to use the neat packages of the meteorological calendar with four three-month seasons, where spring runs from March to May, summer June to August, fall September to November, and winter December to February. When it comes to the changing patterns of the forest, though, the astronomical calendar makes more sense, with each season bookended by a milestone in Earth's orbit around the Sun. The equinoxes—the dates when day and night are equal—and the solstices, which mark the longest and shortest days, relate directly to the amount of solar energy hitting the hemisphere and so define annual rhythms of plant growth and animal behavior.

Much like other animals, humans have habits and activities that are strongly linked to the seasons. This might relate to available resources—making the most of food gluts and preparing for times of shortage—but also to energy conservation, where activity is greatest when the most food is available but slows down in the colder, darker months. It's easy to forget or ignore these seasonal patterns if you live in a house with a furnace and electric lights and get your food from the grocery store. A conscious decision to be more aware of seasonality brings new understandings of ourselves, our ancestors' lives, and our species' connection to the land around us. Taking part in seasonal activity and marking the passing of different phases of the year will help you see the world (and your part in it) in new and potentially profound ways, anticipate and recognize patterns and changes as they happen, and feel comforting familiarity in the chronological story of the woods where one thing—usually—follows another.

1

THE FOREST YEAR

CLIMATE CHANGE
AND FORESTS

The climate of Earth has varied over time because of changes in the planet's orbit around the Sun and the actions of volcanoes and meteors on its atmosphere. Our current climate crisis, however, originates in the Industrial Revolution and results from humans burning fossil fuels, such as coal, oil, and gas, adding excess greenhouse gasses, particularly carbon dioxide and methane, to the atmosphere. These gases act like a blanket, trapping heat and changing global weather patterns.

Forests play a critical role in regulating the atmosphere and weather patterns. Trees transpire and exchange gases with the atmosphere, releasing oxygen and moisture and absorbing rainfall and carbon dioxide. In fact, it was the evolution of green plants over millions of years that created the conditions that sustain life today. Those plants also give us some protection from excessive use of fossil fuels, with forests globally taking up and storing about a third of the carbon dioxide that humans currently generate from energy production, manufacturing, and transportation.

Sadly, our demand for timber and desire to clear forest for agricultural land have led to an alarming rate of deforestation. That reduced area of forest cover means that less carbon is absorbed, while forest soils disturbed by felling, and the trees and other plant matter that rot or burn, release more carbon. The result is that deforestation alone now accounts for more than 10 percent of greenhouse gas emissions. This doesn't mean that we can't use wood, but we need to be much more mindful about how we use it, where it comes from, and how we can reforest previously felled areas.

A CHANGING PLANET

Disturbances to forests, such as fires, storms, pests, and diseases, occur naturally and are important in creating diverse habitats and variation in species and forest structure. Climate change, however, makes these disruptive incidents more frequent and potentially more extreme, meaning that if there's not enough time for regrowth or if the scale of the affected area is too big, then woodland recovery may not be possible, and the land could change to a non-forest ecosystem.

In 2021, the far-eastern Siberian province of Sakha (also known as Yakutia) suffered an unprecedented drought, which led to out-of-control wildfires that raged for months across more than 3.5 million acres (1.4 million hectares)—bigger than all the other wildfires in the world at the time combined. The impacts on human health and the economy were devastating, and the resulting huge release of carbon dioxide added even more greenhouse gases to the atmospheric system. Some forest scientists claim that increased atmospheric carbon will lead to greater tree growth rates and that longer growing seasons will mean that more carbon is recaptured by forests. The data, however, is contested and inconclusive.

TAKING ACTION

We can all play our part in protecting and healing the planet by leading more sustainable lifestyles, but mitigating or lessening the effects of climate change is a key global concern best addressed by large-scale intergovernmental agreements. It will also be necessary for communities to adjust to the current and future impacts as average global temperatures are already at least 1.8 degrees Fahrenheit (1 degree Centigrade) above the level in preindustrial times.

Foresters are adapting to climate change by building in resilience with new mixes of species that might be better suited to changing climates. In the case of food crops, this might mean planting soft fruits and olives farther north than before as the range of these trees extends. Uncertainty means that diversity in new planting is the key to ensuring that at least some of the future forests survive and thrive in the decades ahead. This will be important for wildlife, the timber economy, and food production, as well as for the carbon that the new trees will accumulate as timber.

It's easy to feel overwhelmed and helpless in the face of climate change, but there's a place for hope. Natural regeneration of woodland and sensitive planting can have a positive impact on locking up carbon, moderating climate, and bridging habitats as species are forced to migrate to more favorable areas. We need plenty of new forests in the right places for climate, people, and wildlife. More trees, please!

TREES AND CARBON OFFSETTING

The simple premise of carbon offsetting is that we can all take measures to reduce the amount of carbon dioxide we generate—our carbon "footprint"—in activities such as taking a flight or a car journey. The most widely propagated measure is to plant trees, and a profusion of companies, trusts, and charities have sprung up to meet this demand. Guilt-free holidays? What's not to like?

But before committing to an offset scheme, it's important to do your research. Find out where the new trees are being planted. Are they grown cheaply in the global south, perhaps on land needed for agriculture to feed local populations? Are the trees genuinely additional to what would have been planted anyway, or is a forestry company or landowner just increasing their income on their regular new planting? Trees don't develop at the same rate each year and need to grow for around twenty years to take up the amount of carbon that most schemes claim. They may not stay in the ground for long enough to store the carbon released by your airplane trip, or they might die from fire, drought, or disease and become additional contributors to atmospheric carbon. More forests are needed, but planting new ones on its own won't make up for releasing fossil stores of carbon. We need to reduce our use of fossil fuels first and think about taking fewer of those flights and road trips rather than simply attempting to cancel out the impact by offsetting.

SPRING

The spring equinox on or around March 20 marks a milestone in the forest calendar. From this day until the fall equinox—around September 22—the hours of daylight will be longer than the night. Temperatures will start to rise, and the first signs of new growth will appear. Colorful woodland flowers, such as bluebells and primroses, will bloom, making use of the bright light streaming through the bare tree canopy before the leaves shoot out of their buds. Hibernating animals stir, birdsong resounds, young are born, and the forest becomes a busy, noisy place again.

Spring is a great time to explore while using your camera and binoculars. There are so many daily changes to notice and, in early spring, so much light coming through the canopy before all the leaves are out and while ground-layer plants have not yet grown tall. As the season progresses, the quality of the light on the forest floor changes. Young, bright green leaves grow and thicken, forming a dense cover that can block as much of 95 percent of the light that hits the treetops. Thick foliage deadens sounds from outside the woods, adding to the sense of envelopment by nature. By the beginning of summer, the shade can make it noticeably cooler in the woods than out in the fields, and within a forest there will be numerous microclimates created as dappled sunlight filters through the branches.

A slow, early-morning stroll or time spent sitting quietly can expose you to the magical sounds of the forest awakening, such as nocturnal animals returning after a night of feeding, deer browsing in the crepuscular light, and fox cubs playing and barking. This really is a time that can lift the spirits and fill you with awe and wonder at nature's relentless cycles.

THE GREENING OF THE OAK

Spring is the season of awakening, growth, and reproduction for all deciduous trees, including the oak, which we will follow through the pages of this chapter. The structure of the bare branches that has defined the tree for the past four months will gradually be hidden, as the small brown buds burst open to reveal small, delicate, light-green leaves. These will grow quickly and stiffen to maximize food production from the energy of the sun. On a mature parkland oak tree, there may be as many as 700,000 leaves, which will eventually have a surface area of more than 7,500 square feet (700 square meters)—bigger than three tennis courts.

Like the cells of all green plants, cells in oak leaves contain the pigment chlorophyll, held in small structures called chloroplasts. Chlorophyll captures solar energy to power the chemical reaction of photosynthesis, which converts carbon dioxide and water into glucose and oxygen. The oak's growth requires huge volumes of water, and at its peak the tree will be pumping gallons of water every hour from its roots to its leaves. Water moves through the tree via small tubes, called xylem vessels, in the cambium (see page 119). These vessels are most active in the middle of the day, and on some thin-barked deciduous trees, such as beech and sycamore, you can—using a stethoscope—listen to the water moving.

Oaks are monoecious, meaning that each tree produces both male and female flowers. The male flowers, or catkins, emerge first and distribute their pollen on the wind to reach the female flowers of other oaks. This results in pollination, fertilization, and the formation of a tiny acorn, which contains the genetic code for the next oak generation.

Images clockwise from top left: an oak tree in leaf, bees in a tree hollow, wild garlic, a red deer after shedding its antlers, a sparrow singing, a bat flying

INSECT ACTIVITY

Spring is a good time to pay attention to insects, an often neglected but endlessly fascinating group of creatures that are vital to the woodland ecosystem—and to us. It's estimated that there are around 10 quintillion individual insects alive at any one time on our planet. Each has its own specialized niche, and some have evolved extremely odd feeding habits and reproductive behaviors. Insects don't necessarily follow a seasonal life cycle—in fact, there are all sorts of strange and varied ways that they develop from eggs to adults. Some cicadas, for instance, take seventeen years to metamorphose; others, like the mayfly, live just a few weeks, with the adult stage lasting less than a day—just long enough for the ephemeral creature to lay its eggs.

It's in spring that many insects come into their own as pollinators and show how crucial they are to sustaining so much of life. Many woodland owners keep bees for their honey and will be checking hives in March to make sure the colony still has enough reserves left from the previous fall. In a cold year, the keepers might feed the bees to see them through until they can feed on the nectar of the earliest spring flowers. The vital role that bees play in pollinating flowering plants is well known, but there are also hundreds of species of wasps, flies, beetles, moths, and butterflies that do a similar job.

The glades, rides, and edges of the forest hum in spring with the noise of myriad insects and flicker with the erratic movement of butterflies that have emerged from hibernation or overwintered as eggs, caterpillars, or pupae. Some species of woodland butterflies have definite annual cycles. For example, the distinctively shaped comma (*Polygonia c-album*), common across Europe, North Africa, and much of Asia, hibernates over winter as an adult while camouflaged as a dead leaf in hollow trees and log piles, before emerging on warm spring days to lay its eggs on stinging nettles.

MOTH ATTACK

*The explosion of spring greenery in the forest is extremely attractive to many insects, including the winter moth (*Operophtera brumata*), which lays its eggs on leaf buds in the early winter. Native to much of the world, the moth is also a highly destructive, invasive species in North America. The eggs hatch as the leaves start to grow, and a single caterpillar can eat up to 27,000 times its own body weight before dropping to the ground to pupate in June. The oak tree, however, has an ingenious way of defending itself against such attacks— it detects chemicals in the insect's saliva and produces wound hormones in response. These hormones travel around the tree in its sap, prompting all leaves to manufacture chemicals called tannins and phenolics, which make the leaves too bitter for the caterpillars to eat.*

The moment for a butterfly species to lay its eggs varies from early summer through until late fall. Once hatched, a larva can grow at a phenomenal rate to two hundred times the size of its egg within a few weeks. Pupation times within a chrysalis vary hugely depending on climate—from tropical species that emerge in a few weeks to some subarctic butterflies that take two years to metamorphose.

WAKE-UP CALL FOR BATS

For many woodland mammals, after a winter of limited food and having used up lots of energy just keeping warm, spring comes as a welcome relief. It's also a time to feed and give birth. Having hibernated in a torpid state since late in the previous year, bats will start to emerge and feed, making sure they gain more energy from food than they lose in flight. They will make short reconnaissance missions, then return to the roost to communicate to others whether conditions are warm enough to conserve sufficient energy, not too windy, and favorable for seeking out insects. If the weather is especially cold, bats may return to a torpid state until temperatures rise. In spring, night flights increase in length and frequency until a bat has regained weight and replenished its energy stores and, if female, is ready to give birth, which happens once a year. For such small creatures, bats lead relatively long lives, and you might find six different generations of bats in a single, exclusively female, maternity roost or nursery colony.

There are at least 1,400 different bat species, accounting for a quarter of all the world's mammal species—and there are still new variants to discover. Global bat numbers, however, are falling rapidly, with half of the North American species in decline due to a disease called white-nose syndrome. As the name suggests, the disease—first detected in 2006—is identified by a white fungus that develops on a bat's nose, usually during hibernation. If you visit a bat roost in the forest, try to cause as little disturbance as possible—and before visiting anywhere else that bats might live, get advice on how to decontaminate your clothing and equipment.

GRACEFUL FOREST BROWSER

Of all the larger woodland animals, the deer is the one you're most likely to have a direct encounter with; and on a springtime walk you might even find a freshly cast antler, if you're lucky. It's at this time of year when antlers, the most recognizable symbol of the deer, are shed to be regrown ready for the next rut—or mating display—in the fall (see page 27). Not to be confused with horns, which are permanent and made of the same stuff as fingernails, deer antlers are renewed each year from living bone. They are exclusively a male accessory, with the sole exception of reindeer, where females can also grow these spectacular appendages to signify social hierarchy, defend against predators, and forage in the snow for lichens to eat. The males of most species of deer also use their antlers as status symbols and to fight other males for the right to mate with breeding females. Not all deer have antlers; some, such as the Chinese water deer, have protruding tusks. Deer are all herbivores, so these tusks are not for hunting or catching prey but used instead to show dominance as males contest with each other for breeding females.

From the massive bull moose, standing more than 6.5 feet (2 meters) at the shoulder, to the highly endangered Indonesian "mouse deer," or chevrotain, which stands only around 12 inches (30 centimeters) tall—not much bigger than a rabbit—there's huge diversity among deer species. This diverseness also extends to how deer behave across the seasons. A year in the life of a deer can involve solitude, family life, and roaming in a herd—whichever helps most with finding food, keeping warm or cool, and raising the next generation.

FLOWER POWER

Plants need light to grow, and the annual herbaceous plants that emerge from the forest floor must take advantage of the short window when there are no leaves on the trees to block the light, but temperatures are warm enough to encourage growth. The timing of flowering is critical as there must also be the right insects active to pollinate the flowers. If an early frost killed off blooms or pollinators were late to emerge, then the plant couldn't reproduce. That's why many plants employ the strategy of flowering sporadically over a longer period to maximize the opportunities for success.

It's easy enough to spot dramatic changes in woodland flora, such as when wild garlic season has passed and it's time for bluebells to come through. It takes a little more effort to notice the subtler changes and the smaller, less dramatic plants. Picking a particular spot to come back to is a good way to train your eye and learn about a more limited range of plants in greater detail. If you can establish a permanent survey area in the woods, you'll see for yourself how one spot changes from season to season and from year to year.

1. Hammer four posts into the ground to mark the corners of a 7 foot (2 meter) square (**A**).
2. Paint the top of the posts white (**B**) to make the area easy to find and to keep anyone from walking into or through it.
3. Set up a fifth post outside the square (**C**) as a base for your camera, so that on each visit you capture an image of the same area from the same perspective and can compare all your photos across the year.

Bring your notebook, identification guides, and camera, and spend some time immersed in this small area, detailing every organism that you can find. Keeping a diary of the changes in this square over a year will teach you a huge amount about your chosen woods, your local woodland flora and fauna, and the seasonal changes that you can expect in years to come.

Identifying flowering plants can be tricky. Flicking through a guide for a picture that looks the same might work sometimes, but ideally you should learn to use the key that will appear at the beginning of

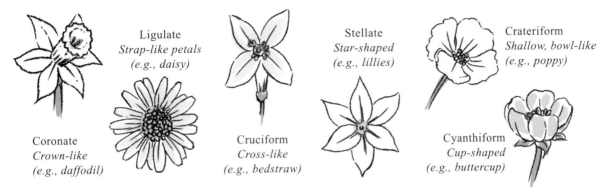

Ligulate
Strap-like petals
(e.g., daisy)

Stellate
Star-shaped
(e.g., lillies)

Crateriform
Shallow, bowl-like
(e.g., poppy)

Coronate
Crown-like
(e.g., daffodil)

Cruciform
Cross-like
(e.g., bedstraw)

Cyanthiform
Cup-shaped
(e.g., buttercup)

any serious plant identification book. Using a tool known as a "dichotomous key," this will ask questions about the plant and give two possible answers for each question; as you work your way through the questions, the options will narrow until you have the definitive identification. You may need a hand lens to magnify details on the plant, and you'll probably need to learn some specialist vocabulary to differentiate between shapes and parts of the plants.

Descriptive words for a few flower shapes can be seen above, but there are also many terms for leaf shapes and variations in other parts of flowering plants. These can help you communicate accurately about what you see and, crucially, arrive at the correct identification of what you have found.

BIRDS—SINGING, MATING, AND NESTING

You know that it's really spring when the early-morning birdsong—the dawn chorus—is loud enough to wake you a good hour before sunrise. Much like the trigger for the trees coming into leaf in the forest, lengthening daylight hours prompt male birds to start vocalizing to defend territories and to attract a mate. Why are birds so loud early in the morning? Well, singing draws attention, so perhaps it's good to do it in low light to avoid the attention of predators. Also, finding food in the dark is a challenge, so singing early is an efficient way of using the day.

If a male is loud and clear—and in luck—he'll attract a potential mate. This will likely involve a courtship ritual, which can be elaborate and prolonged, especially in birds that pair for life. Some bird pairs will sing duets, but in many species it's only the male that exercises the vocal cords in song. Colorful plumage is often used to attract attention and signify good genes, along with the striking of poses that show off feathers to best effect. The most spectacular mating rituals involve choreographed movements or dances—something like tests that the male must pass faultlessly if he's going to be considered to have good breeding potential. As many other creatures do, humans included, birds also woo their mates with food, proximity, body language, and well-decorated homes.

Nest designs are distinctive to each species and tailored to their size, habits, and need to avoid predators. The variety of nesting sites and designs is enormous. Some, such as large random-looking piles of sticks high in trees, are obvious, while others might be hidden in hedges, holes, and hollows. Although the only tools birds have are their beaks and feet, in a few short days they can build intricate structures made of grass, moss, mud, spiders' webs, twigs, and even human garbage, ready for mating and egg laying.

For birds that rear only one brood of chicks each year, there's less of a rush, and the mating season can last into the summer. For others, such as the blackbird, which might raise three broods of chicks in a season, there's no time to lose if the later chicks are to get enough food before they fledge and become independent a mere three weeks after hatching.

SUMMER

The busiest time of year in the forest, summer produces an abundance of food and materials for vegetation, insects, mammals, and human foragers alike. Maximum energy flows in as the sun's rays power the whole woodland ecosystem. Peak production of biomass happens when the greatest amount of sunlight hits the canopy, its green leafy material providing the food for the herbivorous insects and mammals that form the next stage in the forest's complex food chain.

Despite the full summer sun beating down on the treetops, it can be quite dark on the forest floor; where the canopy is at its most dense, as little as 5 percent of the available sunlight will hit the ground. This leads to a woodland microclimate and cooler soil temperatures in shaded areas, which limit what can grow in the ground layer and understory. In woodland of mixed age and species, however, the canopy isn't uniformly thick, and witnessing the pattern of dappled light and shade in full sunlight on a still, hot summer's day is one of the most joyous woodland encounters.

It's also a great time of year to experience the forest at night—maybe to sleep out under the stars in a tree house or hammock, go on a bat walk, or listen out for the calls of owl chicks as they summon their parents back from the hunt. On a damp, warm day, breathe in the distinctive smell of the forest after the rain has stopped. That smell is called petrichor, and it happens when oils secreted by plants in dry weather, along with compounds given off by soil microorganisms, are released into the air by light rain hitting the ground. As you breathe in the scents, you're literally catching the aroma of forest rain.

The sounds of human activity are often muted at this time of year, as much of the heavy forestry work winds down to avoid disturbing nesting birds and other animals. You might want to get busy with a few projects or work on your camp in preparation for the winter. It's a good time to process firewood, splitting and stacking timber so that it dries and becomes much lighter to move later in the year.

WOOD AND FOREST IN FULL BLOOM

By midsummer, our oak tree is photosynthesizing at full capacity, providing food for its own growth as well as countless individual insects from hundreds of different species. Mites, beetles, weevils, spiders, caterpillars, crickets, wasps, moths, and flies form complex food chains within the canopy of a single tree. Herbivores eat the leaves, seeds, and flowers and in turn become food for carnivorous insects and birds. Many of the insects have fascinating habits and life cycles, from the long-nosed, deep-drilling acorn weevil to the numerous types of tiny, non-stinging gall wasps. These wasps lay their eggs in the female flowers of the oak, inducing a tumorous growth called a gall, which grows instead of an acorn. The egg hatches inside this hard growth, where the grub, protected by the tough gall exterior, feasts on the rich food source before pupating and emerging through a tiny hole.

There are many different species of gall wasp, each producing a unique shape of gall, although the best known in this small corner of the insect world is the oak marble gall wasp (*Andricus kollari*), which produces what are sometimes known as "oak apples." This tiny creature has had a huge impact on human history in a most unexpected way. The husks of the galls that fall from the trees can be ground up and used as the main ingredient in the colorfast, indelible black ink that fueled the written word in medieval Europe and beyond, until dye-based inks took over in the twentieth century.

Images clockwise from top left: "oak apples," willow herb flowering after a forest fire, a bald eagle and chicks, a white-tailed deer and fawn, European bison

---

MAKING INK

Concocting your own gall ink is quite straightforward and connects you with both the oak woodland where you collect the galls and the scribes of old who used the selfsame writing material. Galls will fall from the trees from late summer, and with a little practice, it becomes easy to spot these anomalously spherical brown objects on the forest floor. Check that all galls have an exit hole (*fig 1*)—so you know the wasp has left home—and dry them until they can be ground to a powder in a mortar and pestle (*fig 2*). Mix the gall powder with a little water, and leave in a sealed mason jar for a week or two—or speed up the process by boiling the mixture for half an hour, then letting it stand to cool. Once strained (*fig 3*), the liquid makes an appealing brown ink wash. To turn it black, you need to add an iron solution made by leaving some rusty metal (nails or steel wool) in vinegar for a couple of weeks. This will react with the tannin in the gall mixture, turning it jet black in an instant. The final step is to add a small amount of dissolved gum arabic—a by-product of the acacia tree—as a binder and to help the ink flow smoothly.

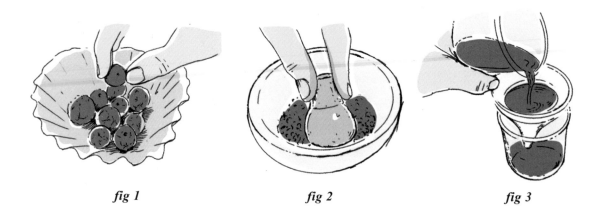

fig 1   *fig 2*   *fig 3*

WILDFIRES AND FOREST ECOLOGY

Climate change and ever-denser global populations make wildfires an increasing threat to people and property. They are, however, natural events crucial to the survival of some species. Lightning strikes in particularly dry summers are the most likely cause of forest fires, which with just a light breeze and plenty of combustible material on the ground in the form of leaf litter and fallen tree limbs can take hold and spread quickly, reducing thousands of acres of forest to ash and charred stumps. How can such destruction possibly be a good thing? Pyrophytes (plants resistant to fire), such as the San Diego wild cabbage (*Caulanthus heterophyllus*), actually require the chemical signals from smoke and charred ground to initiate germination. The lodgepole pine (*Pinus contorta*) needs the high temperatures found in the canopy in a forest fire to melt the hard resin sealing its cones and allow seeds to fall. Many tree species have adaptations to fire, such as thick insulating bark or the ability to produce new shoots from roots that have been protected under the soil. Ash from burned trees becomes a potent fertilizer for new growth, and diversity flourishes with the huge increase in light as the undamaged seed supply in the soil starts to germinate after the first rains. The process of succession then causes variation of species over time until the conditions are created for the original high forest to be reestablished. Modern forest management recognizes the need for periodic small or controlled fires in certain areas to burn up excess fuel on the ground, which can benefit the ecosystem and limit the overall risk of catastrophic wildfires. If there's a fire warning in your area, or you think that conditions are dry and dangerous, don't be tempted to light campfires or even use a camp stove.

ANIMAL PARENTS AND THEIR YOUNG

Deer. For deer, summer is a time to eat and put on as much weight as possible. They do this to meet the immediate needs of growing new antler tissue and producing milk for this season's young, and also to prepare for winter survival. All deer are herbivores that ruminate, or chew, the cud before passing food through their four stomachs. This highly efficient digestive system also allows deer to obtain most of their water from the vegetation they eat, which means that many of them can go for long periods without drinking. They will graze on grasses and lichens close to the ground and browse on the shoots and young leaves of many trees. When trees are in full leaf, you can often see that the branches of species on the edge of a meadow all grow at the same height above the ground. This browse line shows how high the deer in the area can strain their necks to eat the succulent young growth and is a helpful clue to the fauna you might look for on a woodland walk.

With rising temperatures, deer no longer need their dense winter coat of highly insulating hollow hairs and shed it in favor of shorter hair for the warm summer. Coat color can also vary to give better camouflage. Fawns or baby roe and fallow deer are born with spotted backs, so they can hide in long grass or scrub, where they are fed periodically by their mothers. This enables the fawns to save energy and put on weight more quickly, as well as remaining out of sight of predators. After three or four months, they wean and develop their adult coat.

For many deer species, late summer means that antlers are fully grown and no longer need the covering of velvet that kept the growing bone supplied with oxygen. As the velvet dies, it's rubbed off aggressively on young trees and thrashed against vegetation, with strands often left hanging from the exposed bone of the new antlers. For a short time, the antlers are bone-white, until stained by the tannin that's absorbed during the thrashing process.

Bats. In summer, bats are also busy, eating their own body weight in insects every night. Even tiny pipistrelle bats can eat up to two thousand midges in an evening, helping them to produce milk for their single pup for the next few weeks until they can fly and catch their own prey. The exoskeletons of the insects give bat droppings a peculiar quality. Although they can be mistaken for mouse droppings, bat droppings will crumble to dust if crushed rather than just squash. Once the bat young are fully independent, the females in the maternity roosts will disperse to find new roosts where they can mate.

Birds. For newly hatched birds, time is of the essence. From a very early age, they must get ready to deal with the cold, hunger, and predators. Some ground-nesting birds, especially waterfowl, emerge from the egg with highly insulating downy feathers and will swim once their oil glands develop after a few weeks, while many songbirds will be blind, naked, and totally reliant on their parents for longer. In the bird world, parents employ different strategies to ensure the best start in life for their young. The vast majority of birds have both parents involved in chick rearing, with males providing food for mother and chicks and the female guarding and keeping their young warm. Less than 10 percent of bird species form single-parent families, with mothers, in this case, being by far the most common carer of the young.

LOYAL NESTER

The bald eagle (*Haliaeetus leucocephalus*), the national bird of the United States, maintains a monogamous relationship with a single partner throughout its breeding life. Even though the eagles are independent during the winter months, in summer they will return to the same partner and nest to breed, mostly in the tallest forest trees, close to large bodies of water. The birds then take an equal share of responsibility in raising their young, including teaching them how to fly. When a young bald eagle is ready to leave the nest, its wingspan will already be approaching 6 feet (1.8 meters), so nests have to be truly huge. A pair of eagles in Florida in the 1960s built the largest nest ever recorded at 9.5 feet (2.9 meters) wide and 20 feet (6 meters) deep and weighing in at more than 2 tons.

TEEMING LIFE IN DEADWOOD

There's an old saying, "It takes an oak tree three hundred years to grow, three hundred years to live, and three hundred years to die." But even as the tree decays, it carries on as a vital habitat, supporting hundreds of other organisms for at least another hundred years. In the UK, 20 percent of woodland species rely on deadwood, and the amount of it in a forest is an excellent indicator of the overall health of a forest ecosystem anywhere in the world. Deadwood can be dead standing trees, fallen trees that have been left to rot, or stumps from felled or windblown trees. Whatever form deadwood takes in a forest, its presence can create a timeless, otherworldly atmosphere.

Lichens, fungi, and invertebrates all play a part in decomposing deadwood, and many of them provide habitats or food supplies for other animals in the food chain, such as woodpeckers. Mosses and even saplings can grow on the remains of a fallen tree, taking advantage of the nutrients released as it decays. The relationships between the organisms that decompose deadwood are complex. Some birds may depend for food on wood-boring insects, which are in turn reliant on fungi to break down solid wood before they can burrow into it. As the cellulose and lignin, which form the wood, are broken down, nutrients return to the soil to nourish the next generation of trees to grow where their ancestors fell.

DEADWOOD AND BARK BEETLES

Containing remnants of the huge primeval forest that blanketed northeastern Europe until well into the last millennium, Białowieża Forest is a biodiversity hot spot that covers an area of more than 540 square miles (1,400 square kilometers), straddling the Poland–Belarus border. Renowned for its unmatched numbers of wild European bison—the continent's largest land mammal—and hundreds of bird species, Białowieża is also remarkable for its particularly high proportion of deadwood—up to 50 percent of all the wood in the forest. From fungi to invertebrates and the rodents and birds that feed on them, it's estimated that as much as half the 12,000 recorded species directly depend on dead trees. Most of the forest, which lies outside the protected areas, has been commercially logged for decades, and recent political battles have raged between those who want to increase logging and proponents of conservation and sustainable forestry. Ironically, at the center of the controversy is an animal—a small beetle that can kill trees and create new deadwood habitats. The spruce bark beetle burrows under tree bark to lay its eggs, which when hatched eat the cambium layer of the tree (see page 119) and can potentially kill it. An infestation of these beetles in the Białowieża area has led to an official policy of increased logging to control the pest. Many ecologists claim that this is unnecessary and that replacing cleared areas of forest with single-species plantations will do little to restore the multilayered, mixed-aged, species-rich blend of trees that makes Białowieża such a rare and unique primeval woodland survivor. Will the infested trees be felled to save the forest, or will the forest recover from the beetle as it might from a forest fire? Only time and prolonged legal battles will tell.

FOREST SPELLS AND CURSES

It would be difficult to think of the denizens of the forest—such as elves, fairies, nymphs, goblins, dryads, and witches—without considering the spells, curses, and enchantments that are known to be their modus operandi. Every species of magical being has its own way of helping—or perhaps more often, hindering—the local human population; so gaining knowledge of their ways, as well as a few good counter-spells and remedies, is a wise precaution.

Universal in folklore, a spell is a form of words said to have magic powers over a person or thing at which it's directed. In the fairy tale "The Frog Prince," a bewitched frog has been under the spell of a wicked fairy for many years, only for it to be broken when a young princess befriends him in the woods and allows him to spend the night on her pillow—after which he reverts to a handsome prince. Incantations are a kind of melodic spell, such as the Wicked Queen's needy plea to the Magic Mirror in "Snow White": "Magic mirror on the wall, who is the fairest one of all?"

Enchantments are spells that create an illusion to deceive people, but as well as those of a detrimental nature, they may often have a positive objective, such as the good Fairy Godmother's enchantment that turns a tattered dress into a ball gown and a pumpkin into a coach to carry Cinderella through the woods to the ball. Of a more sinister connotation, curses are uttered to inflict punishment or harm in no uncertain terms on someone or something, usually stemming from the displeasure, outrage, or caprice of a fairy being.

OFFERINGS OF APPEASEMENT

There are said to be a number of ways to prevent spells and curses by appeasing magical beings with offerings, although these are specific to the species of being you have to deal with. Setting out pails of fresh milk, cream, and butter may pacify the local fairy population, and it's said that some fear the sound of bells—which are easy enough to bring along on camping trips.

Generally, it's a wise move to ask permission of wood and water nymphs, elves, fairies, and leprechauns before hunting and fishing in their territory. In fact, asking permission to do anything uncertain will mitigate unknown harms and prevent the unleashing of a fairy's wrath by accident.

POWERFUL PROTECTION

There are a number of protective measures you can take against recalcitrant beings who refuse to be placated otherwise. A small branch of the rowan tree, placed on your pillow at night or carried in a pocket, is said to provide protection against witches' spells, as witches have a dread of the tree's mystical properties. Those who find themselves lost on a forest path, perhaps walking around in circles for hours, may be under the enchantment of a mischievous fairy—here, invoking your ancestors to provide assistance can help break the spell.

In the folklore of the Dayak—an indigenous group of Borneo—the goblins of the forests have the unfortunate habit of stealing human souls, but not allowing the human in question to become aware of it. As a precautionary measure, when leaving the forest, a person should assume that their soul has been taken and simply ask for its return. And how do you escape if you've been cursed to live in a fairy underworld by the Queen of the Fairies? If you're like Tam Lin of the Scottish Borders, you enlist the help of your true love on Halloween to break the spell. In the legendary folk ballad "Tam Lin," Janet must pull Tam Lin off a white horse to the forest floor and ignore the succession of fearsome beasts that her love turns into, thus breaking the enchantment and returning him to the safety of human company.

FALL

Fall can be a season of drama and ostentation. All our senses are activated, as we hear the bellows of rutting deer echoing through the woods, admire changing leaf colors in outbursts worthy of a fireworks display, collect fruits and nuts to cook or store, inhale the mushroomy scents of the wood after October rains, and watch misty mornings give way to crisp, clear days.

It's also a time of preparation for the challenges and hardships of the months ahead. Shortening hours of daylight concentrate activity, imbuing everything with a sense of urgency. Looking up through the falling leaves, you can see birds migrating south in their familiar V-shaped formations. Animals are stocking up on food for the winter months when sustenance will be hard to find. Squirrels and jays stash acorns away in larders to be raided—and sometimes forgotten about. Bats and bears build up their fat reserves before they retreat to winter roosts and dens to hibernate.

With cooler temperatures and moisture in the soil, mushrooms start to appear, and foragers search, baskets in hand and eyes to the ground, for fungal treasure to take home and cook. After the first frost, tree planting season begins. Tree nurseries lift their stock of saplings from nursery beds ready to be planted out before the soil is frozen or sodden. Once birds have left their nests, foresters can begin their felling work, and those who rely on wood to heat their homes stack log piles close by and split kindling ready for the chillier winter days.

A PIG'S RIGHT TO ROAM

The abundance of tree seeds on the forest floor in fall gives rise to the ancient tradition of pannage—allowing pigs to roam freely through the woods to feast on protein-rich food, which also gives their meat a distinctive flavor. The practice was established in the New Forest in the south of England as a commoners' right by William the Conqueror in 1079 and is kept alive today by New Forest Commoners, who for sixty days can let their pigs forage for acorns and beechnuts. Although pannage was once common across much of Europe, including Germanic areas, where it was known as Eichelmast, or "acorn fruit," concerns about diseases being transmitted between wild boar and domestic pigs limit this once widespread tradition. The situation is even more serious in the United States, where millions of feral pigs—the ancestors of domestic animals first introduced by European colonizers in the sixteenth century and wild boar imported for hunting in the nineteenth century—cause billions of dollars of damage each year.

ROARING TIME

The clashing of antlers and bellowing of stags are defining sounds of many woodland walks in fall. At this time of year, during the so-called rutting season, the forest is a place to move with caution. You really don't want to get in the way of a hormonal stag that might see you or your pet dog as a big enough threat to want to attack. To be roared at and charged by a quarter-ton deer is an adrenaline rush best avoided. With planning, care, and a little fieldcraft, however, you can witness the mating behavior of deer from a safe distance. Leave dogs at home, and use binoculars from at least 160 feet (50 meters) away rather than getting too close to the action.

From early October to mid-November, many species, including elk and white-tailed, fallow, and red deer, display similar behavior, depending on climate and habitat. Males will have put on weight in the preceding months to prepare for the meal-free two weeks or so where they are busy herding females into a harem and fending off the advances of other males. In some species, particularly the fallow deer, males form a large group called a "lek," where they gather to compete in mating displays.

The rut—a word that goes back to the Latin *rugire*, meaning "to roar"—begins when shorter daylight hours trigger fertility and sexual receptivity in females and a huge increase in testosterone in the males, which in turn generates aggressive behavior and posturing. Activity may center around a wallow, where males roll in mud, urine, and semen to make themselves—believe it or not—more attractive. They may also thrash their antlers around to collect vegetation on their heads to appear bigger and will roar to attract females and scare off rivals. If the roaring on its own isn't enough, then two males will walk side by side to take the measure of each other. If neither animal backs down, it may lead to a full-blown antler fight. Early in the season, these fights might be relatively unaggressive and more ritualized—later, however, they can become deadly serious.

DEER CONTROL

In North America, deer face a number of predators, including wolves, coyote, and cougars. It's a different story in the UK, where deer have no natural predators, leaving herds to often grow unchecked. Overpopulation of deer can have negative consequences for the herd as well as for new woodland generation. Old, weak, and diseased deer that might otherwise be killed by other animals survive, allowing pathogens and genetic problems to proliferate. Bark shredding for food and fraying to rub the summer velvet off new antlers can severely damage young trees and hinder natural woodland regeneration. For these reasons, in the absence of wolves and other predators, stalkers control deer numbers by selectively shooting individuals to promote healthy, sustainable herds.

MULTIGENERATIONAL BUTTERLY MIGRATION

One of the most curious migration stories takes place in the fall air as monarch butterflies undertake their annual migration to central Mexico from as far north as Newfoundland in Canada. A "super" butterfly generation hatches from eggs laid on milkweed in the northern summer feeding grounds. These monarchs are larger than the generations born earlier in the year and are unable to breed. They fly all the way to Mexico, where they hibernate over the winter. The butterflies navigate using the position of the sun and an inbuilt daily clock in their antennae that tells them how far left or right of the sun to fly to keep the correct bearing. When the monarchs wake and become active in the spring, sudden hormonal changes enable them to briefly breed before they die. It then takes five generations of ordinary monarch butterflies, each laying their eggs on milkweed after they have completed their leg of the journey, to conclude the northward journey. This incredible migration pattern—an evolutionary mystery—has probably been happening uninterrupted for millions of years.

THE GREATEST TREK ON EARTH

In 2000, the world's largest herd of wild reindeer, the Taimyr of central Siberia, numbered around one million animals. Today, that figure has roughly halved and continues to decline as climate change takes a massive toll on Arctic regions. In a cycle that has continued since the end of the last ice age, around 10,000 years ago, every spring the reindeer undertake an annual migration of more than 600 miles (970 kilometers) to the lush grass of their summer calving grounds near the coast of the Kara Sea in northern Siberia. In fall, they return inland to the high-plateau boreal forest known as taiga. The reindeer must time the journey to the Kara Sea to perfection, crossing wide frozen rivers before they thaw and fill with snow meltwater. Calves born in spring then have to grow strong enough to swim the rivers on the fall leg of the journey, or they will perish. The wild reindeer's future is also intertwined with that of Arctic peoples. After the end of the Soviet era, the Siberian fishing industry collapsed, and now uncontrolled poaching for food is seriously threatening the survival of the Taimyr species. Changes in the timing of snowmelts, plus food scarcity, increasing mosquito populations, summer droughts, and high fall river levels, continue to play havoc with the migration, diminishing herd sizes as young reindeer die during the journey. This pattern is repeating across the whole arctic and subarctic regions, affecting wild and domesticated Scandinavian and Canadian herds in similar ways. As the reindeer suffer, so do the livelihoods of indigenous peoples and the integrity of the northern ecosystems of which they are a vital part.

GOLDEN FAREWELL OF LEAVES

Anyone living outside of the tropics is familiar with the annual deciduous forest cycle of green buds bursting into life in spring, casting deep shade in summer, and then—after an often spectacular color show—shedding yellow, orange, and brown leaves in late fall to leave winter trees bare-limbed. As the days shorten and the growing season comes to an end, our oak tree starts to undergo a process of transformation to help it survive through the coming harsher months. In the leaves, light-sensitive receptors called phytochromes react to changes in the amount of red light in the spectrum, which, like a chemical clock, activates hormonal changes in the tree to prepare it for winter. Pigments and nutrients in the leaves are broken down and reabsorbed into the tree to store over winter in an act of self-cannibalization. Then, to preserve moisture and energy in the tree, the leaves fall to the ground and are decomposed by fungi and invertebrates, adding additional nutrients to the forest soil.

Images clockwise from top left: a male deer in rutting season, honey fungus, monarch butterflies, New Forest pigs, fall leaves

LEAF CHROMATOGRAPHY

You can separate the different pigments in a leaf in a relatively simple home chromatography experiment.

1. *Cut a leaf into small pieces, and put them in a mortar and pestle. Add a few drops of water and some drops of isopropyl alcohol (sold as rubbing alcohol) as a solvent. Crush the mixture into a paste.*

2. *Transfer the paste to a mason jar, with just enough solvent to cover it. Put a lid on the jar, and warm it in a bowl of warm (not hot) water for about half an hour.*

3. *Cut a 0.75 inch (2 centimeter) wide strip of chromatography paper, if you can get it; otherwise, coffee filter paper makes a good substitute. Wrap the top of the piece of paper around the middle of a pen or pencil, and suspend the paper in the jar so that the bottom is in the liquid.*

4. *Wait for an hour. The different pigments in the leaf will be drawn up into the paper and separate into different stripes. You should see at least two shades of green—chlorophyll a and b—plus some yellow and orange, which are xanthophylls and carotene pigments. Try the experiment with different tree species to discover the surprising variety of pigments in leaves that might simply look green.*

SEEDS AND SURVIVAL

Many tree species have an effective strategy for reproduction to ensure all their seed cannot possibly be eaten by the birds and mammals that love the high-energy food. Trees produce variable amounts of seed each year—sometimes very little at all, which can limit the food supply and therefore the reproduction of seed-dependent creatures. Approximately every four or five years, in a so-called "mast year," there will be such an abundance of seed dropped that the animals that would eat it could never manage to consume it all. This ensures that at least some of the seed germinates and grows, carrying the species on for another generation.

Acorns—the fruit of the oak—are dispersed by jays and squirrels, who bury them in larders for a food supply over winter. Luckily for our oak, the animals don't necessarily relocate all of them, allowing germination of at least a few. The most effective dispersal mechanism for oaks in the past five centuries has been humans, who have planted millions of the trees to make use of their strong, durable timber. In France, high-quality oak for veneers is grown by planting acorns densely so that saplings form a thicket. Trees are regularly thinned until, after around sixty years, the straightest stems with fewest branches are selected to grow to maturity.

FUNGI EXPLOSION

The forest underfoot is alive with fungi all year round, but it's only with cooler, wetter weather that they come to reproduce and push their fruiting bodies above the soil. We know them as mushrooms or toadstools, and they exist to spread their spores in the wind and colonize new places. Spores are a little bit like seeds and can play an important part in the complex task of accurately identifying fungi. If you're interested in learning more, and especially if you want to eat mushrooms, then study the topic and search carefully—mistakes can be deadly. Don't rely on common names for mushrooms. In fact, many mycologists (people who study fungi) will only use scientific names and may not even know the local names. Don't rely simply on photos or drawings in an identification book. Use a wide combination of clues, such as habitat, associations with other species, color changes when cut, and timing of fruiting.

If you want to learn more about the color and patterns of spores, you can make spore prints and study them under a microscope—or just enjoy as pieces of mushroom art.

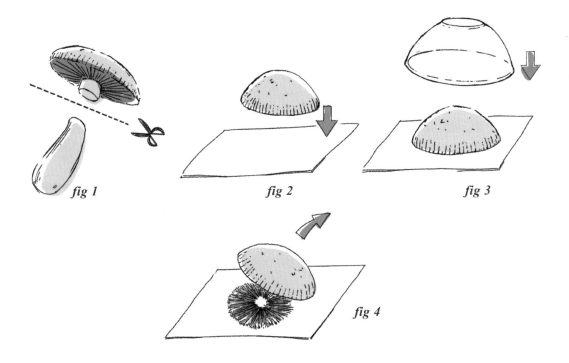

fig 1   *fig 2*   *fig 3*   *fig 4*

1. Pick a mature mushroom with a reasonably flat open cap and remove the stem (*fig 1*). Place the cap spore-side down on a clean piece of paper or card (*fig 2*). You might need to try different colors of paper to be able to distinguish different colors of spores.
2. Cover the paper and mushroom with a glass bowl to stop any disturbance to the print (*fig 3*). Leave for six to ten hours.
3. Remove the bowl and mushroom to see what you have (*fig 4*). Some prints can be extremely detailed and make attractive artworks. If you want to keep a particularly good one, stick it to the paper with fixative spray from an art supplier.

MUSHROOM MAGIC

*The most iconic mushroom of the fall woodland must surely be the red-capped, white-flecked fly agaric (*Amanita muscaria*). Its big impact on popular culture includes providing the inspiration for the homes of the Smurfs cartoon characters, the size-changing "super mushrooms" in the Mario videogames, and the dancing mushrooms in the Disney movie* Fantasia. *Some anthropologists even link fly agaric to the Christmas stories of flying reindeer. Apparently, Siberian reindeer liked to eat the snow where mushroom-ingesting shamans had urinated, so the animals could get a dose of some reality-altering chemicals. Legend has it that the most common psychotropic effects from eating fly agaric are sensations of flying and changing size. It makes for a good story, but it should be stressed that fly agaric isn't at all like other psychedelic mushrooms. It's unpredictable and has disturbing—even fatal—physical side effects. The mushroom should be treated as highly poisonous and avoided along with all the other amanita fungi.*

THE WOOD WIDE WEB

Human understanding of the interconnections between organisms in the forest has made great advances in recent years, and we now know that the huge mat of plant roots and fungal threads (known as hyphae) within the soil acts as a giant, interspecies communication network. It might sound somewhat mystical or far-fetched to imagine that trees can communicate with each other, but a large body of research on the topic now exists, with a catchy term the "wood wide web" popularized by scientist Dr. Suzanne Simard in 1997 in the journal *Nature*.

It's hard to conceive of these subterranean relationships without using terms that relate to how we humans communicate with each other, such as "talk," "speak," and "converse." It aids our understanding but doesn't mean that trees can feel or think in the ways that animals might do. The manner in which trees and fungi "help" each other is essentially an efficient system of interrelationships that has evolved over millions of years and persists because it aids the survival and reproduction of the species involved. That, in iself, is awe-inspiring.

At a microscopic level, the fungal hyphae are able to access nitrogen, phosphorous, and even water, and provide these to the trees in exchange for sugars that help the fungi grow and extend their network. The power of the wood wide web, however, extends far beyond a simple exchange of resources. Impacts on the whole ecosystem occur because the trees can communicate with each other and share vital information as well as influencing which beneficial fungi thrive and survive.

A plant's "choice" of which fungi to exchange nutrients with and which to defend against will influence the makeup of the fungal species available to other plants in the area. A healthy tree may be able to produce excess carbon, which can be made available to associated fungi, allowing them to extend their reach and therefore provide essential nutrients to other individual trees of the same species. When a tree is first infected by a fungus, it produces a disease response that improves its immunity to other pests and diseases.

The wood wide web also acts as an early-warning system to counter threats such as diseases and hungry herbivores. A tree when attacked will produce wound hormones. These chemical signals can be carried by the fungi and received by healthy trees hundreds of feet away. This advance notice of a local threat allows the trees to produce defensive chemicals in advance and lessen the effect of the threat.

Unsurprisingly, the biggest danger to the whole wood wide web comes from human activity. Plowing or digging forest soil, compaction from intensive forestry, and the use of construction materials that alter soil chemistry all have a serious negative effect on plant–fungi interactions, reducing their resilience and the health of the ecosystem. As you explore and enjoy being among the trees, consider the hidden world beneath your feet, where roots, microbes, and fungi create the conditions for the forest to thrive.

WINTER

It might be harder to motivate yourself to get outside in winter when workdays eat up the hours of daylight and weekends spent in a cozy house seem particularly appealing. Even though, just as in Narnia, it can feel like it's always winter but never Christmas, there are still many things to experience in a winter forest; and the daylight—although limited—can work wonders on your mood. You might catch the smell of campfire woodsmoke emanating from an old coat hanging by the door at home, tempting you back to your woodland camp. Maybe the early morning sun glints from the hoarfrost on the window. Whatever motivates you to get out, it's worth making that effort to experience the unique atmosphere of the winter woodland.

The forest at this time of year can feel pretty monochrome, almost eerily gray, with just occasional flashes of color as you catch sight of a robin, fox, or rowan berries out of the corner of your eye. You might hear chain saws buzzing as foresters fell trees empty of birds and drag their logs to the roadside. Sounds seem clearer and louder on a frosty morning as airwaves reflect and bounce off frozen ground, while on snowy days they are absorbed, and a quiet calm descends on the woods.

While all may seem still above ground, under the earth, where temperatures are more stable, many animals that you might think are hibernating are simply unseen, becoming active on the surface in the hours of darkness. Badgers will forage for food throughout the winter but may become torpid in long, cold periods. They will mate at any time of year, although they can delay the implantation of fertilized eggs until the turning of the year. Cubs are born six or seven weeks later and remain underground for the next two months before venturing out of the sett—the badger home—to feed in the spring.

In the woods, the contrast between coniferous and deciduous trees is at its most stark when needles remain but leaves have fallen. This is the time to look up through the canopy of a deciduous forest and see the birds' and squirrels' nests and clumps of mistletoe that have been hidden through the other seasons. The extent of vertical ivy growth becomes obvious, and birds can be spotted feeding on its dark, black berries. There really is much to experience in this cold, quiet time, and when you get to know the woods well in winter, you'll appreciate even more the profound change and awakening of spring.

DEER AND WOLVES

Winter is a good time to view herds of all kinds of deer as they congregate among the trees at lower altitudes. Roe deer, found throughout Europe and the Middle East, are unique among deer species. Just as female badgers do, female roe deer delay implantation of the eggs that were fertilized in the summer (earlier than other deer) to keep their offspring from being born in winter. They will often have two or three young, who will stay with their mother until just before she gives birth to her next brood. Male roe deer are extremely territorial and will aggressively defend their patch. In common with the white-tailed deer in North America, they tend not to roam in herds but remain as small family groups with males staying on their own.

Deer are ungulates, meaning that they walk on two toes. It's easy to see this when you're out tracking as these toes, or hooves, leave pairs of slots in damp ground or snow. Reindeer, also known as caribou, have a slack tendon just above their hooves, which makes a clicking sound when they walk as the tendon rubs

Images clockwise from top left: a bare oak tree, a little owl in a tree hollow, forest wolves in Canada, a Eurasian woodcock, mistletoe, deer in winter woodland

against bone. It's thought that this allows reindeer to locate the rest of the herd in the whiteout conditions of the boreal forests and tundra in winter snowstorms. It's a strange experience to be among a herd of feeding reindeer as they click all around you, seemingly oblivious to all but their next mouthful of food. Try never to disturb or frighten them as food is scarce and their survival depends on conserving as much energy as possible.

WINTER BIRD SPECTACULARS

While the fall may have witnessed the departure of many migratory birds to warmer climes, winter sees the arrival of visitors from arctic and cold continental climates, attracted by warmer temperatures and more abundant food. Some species will stay for the winter, while others are just passing through on their way farther south. Many of these are wetland birds attracted to mudflats, estuaries, and lakes to settle and feed over the winter. A few, like the woodcock, make their home among the trees.

Woodcock are unusual birds. They are technically waders but live and nest on the ground in young woodlands in upland areas. With eyes set wide on its head, a woodcock has a broad field of vision and uses its long prehensile beak to poke around in the earth for worms and other invertebrates. The Eurasian woodcock (*Scolopax rusticola*) is a close relative of the American woodcock (*Scolopax minor*), which is native to the eastern half of North America, where it's sometimes also known as a bogsucker, hokumpoke, or timberdoodle. Nearly a million woodcock cross the North Sea from northern Europe and Russia to the east coast of the UK every winter. Even though there are so many of the birds, they can be hard to spot, with their brown speckled plumage providing perfect camouflage against the leaf litter. Perhaps it's their reclusive nature that has given rise to the many stories and legends that surround the woodcock. Traditionally, the birds arrive on a "woodcock moon"—a full moon in November, often coinciding with the arrival of flocks of goldcrests, which were once believed to hitch a ride on the backs of woodcock as they crossed the sea. Legend also had it that the woodcock flew to the moon when they left on their spring migration. Researchers now think that there may be a peak in migration around a full moon, but that good visibility and advantageous wind speed and direction are likely to be much more important in the timing of the arrival of this enigmatic bird.

NATURE'S WOODY SURVIVORS

With all its leaves fallen to decay on the ground, our oak tree enters a near-dormant state to conserve energy and survive through the winter. The year's final season will bring many challenges, not least subzero temperatures and storm-force winds. To see it through to the spring, the oak must be strongly anchored in the ground and well insulated from the cold. Millions of years of evolution have equipped the tree with adaptations to deal with these pressures. The tree withdraws some water from under the bark, which concentrates sugars there, lowering the freezing point to stop cells from rupturing in extreme cold. The thick bark also insulates the cambium (see page 119) as well as protecting it from burrowing invertebrates, pests, and diseases.

It takes a great deal of force to blow a tree down, with shallow-rooted trees more vulnerable than those species with a wide and deep root network. A tree's roots seek out moisture and nutrients in the soil and are extremely adaptable. If they reach an area of high soil fertility, they will produce a dense network of fine, branching, ephemeral roots, which will extract all they can and then die off when they are no longer needed. The first root that emerges from the acorn as it germinates may go on to be a deep taproot that burrows straight down to anchor the tree into the earth.

Fungal attack may eventually lead to the hollowing out of a tree trunk, even to the point where you can stand inside the tree and look up to the sky. This isn't necessarily harmful to the tree. Short trees, especially those that have been pollarded (essentially coppiced above browse height), can afford to lose up to 70 percent of the core of their trunk before their structural integrity is undermined in any way. Most ancient oaks will have been hollowed out to some extent—and yet still they stand.

THE RETURN OF THE WOLVES

Yellowstone National Park in the United States covers an area of almost 3,500 square miles (9,000 square kilometres), mostly in Wyoming but also in parts of Montana and Idaho. It was designated a national park—one of the world's first—in 1872 to prevent commercial exploitation by big business and colonists seeking their fortunes. The vast region—around 80 percent of it forest—had already been populated seasonally by a wide number of indigenous peoples who followed the migrations of animals, such as the bighorn sheep and bison. In the early twentieth century, a policy of predator control led to the almost total elimination of the park's wolves, coyotes, and mountain lions, with a significant impact also on bear populations. The main prey of these top carnivores were deer, and without predators their numbers exploded. The elk (Cervus canadensis), also known as wapiti and a close relative of the red deer (Cervus elaphus), formed large herds, leading to extensive overgrazing with negative impacts cascading through the ecosystem. In 1995, the first wolves were reintroduced to Yellowstone from Canada. This innovative species reestablishment project was closely monitored and researched and is widely viewed as a success in ecological land management. As well as hunting elk and reducing herd numbers, wolf packs have forced the elk to move around more, dispersing their grazing and resulting in the recovery of willow and aspen trees, stabilization of riverbanks, and increased beaver and moose populations. Humans existed in this landscape alongside large carnivores and herbivores in the past, so with vision, insight, and understanding they should be able to do so again well into the future.

Spending time in the woods, exploring, camping, cooking, and making things, is generally pretty low-risk. Our human ancestors hunted, foraged, and lived on the land for most of the last 300,000 years—and they weren't just surviving. The fact that we're here today is a testament to how well they succeeded. Nowadays, our survival as a species means being able to differentiate between what we would like to have and what we actually need; between what will consume finite resources quickly or enable sustainable lifestyles; and between what will allow other living things to survive and flourish and what factors might force them into extinction.

Clearly, it's best to avoid survival situations in the first place, but if you're up for outdoor adventures, a little knowledge of what to do "just in case" will do no harm. The unexpected can happen, so think ahead and have several plans ready in advance. Check that you've packed everything you need, including a few items that will make life easier if you get into trouble. The basics should help you to start a fire, boil water, and put a roof over your head. Finally, let someone know where you're going and when you plan to be back. On a longer trip, try to have a system of check-ins with home and an action plan to be followed if you go incommunicado.

Let's imagine that you do suddenly realize that you're in trouble in the wild, with no immediate help at hand. You might be tired and hungry. You'll very likely feel stressed, and under such conditions hastily made decisions are unlikely to be the best ones. It's time to—S.T.O.P.
S: Stop, breathe, and try to calm down.
T: Think about your priorities, and remember what you've learned about survival.
O: Observe what's around you—the landscape and potential useful resources.
P: Plan what you'll do first, but don't leave it too late to act.

Read on to grasp the survival priorities, including making a fire, finding natural shelter, and getting clean drinking water. You'll also learn how to signal for help and administer first aid, in addition to mastering the skills and knowledge that will help you to thrive as well as survive.

2

SURVIVAL SKILLS

ESSENTIAL
TOOLS

What you take with you on your outdoor adventures will depend first and foremost on your attitude to life and the outdoors. Do you want to travel light with the minimum necessary and use your knowledge and ingenuity to improvise? Or do you want to be as comfortable and well prepared as possible for any situation?

Maybe you want to feel an affinity with the people who walked the land in distant times and confine your equipment to the things they would have used. Or you might be happier taking advantage of the technological innovations in textiles and performance clothing that allow you to stay warm and dry in all weathers. There are no prizes for being cold and wet in the pursuit of minimalism, but you can be encumbered by having too much stuff or paralyzed by thinking you don't have the right gear.

WHAT'S REALLY ESSENTIAL?

Humans are a little like magpies, collecting shiny things for their nests—and the outdoor equipment industry knows this. How you choose to equip yourself will have an impact on the types of experiences you have. Investing too much time and money in gadgets can put a barrier between you and the natural world, as well as having an impact on the environment far away from the forests that you explore.

You could argue that, like your ancient forebears, all you need are knowledge of the land and its plants and animals, along with the practical skills to meet your needs from them. However, not many will want to go fully Neolithic, so some more modern inventions, such as metal knives and saws, basic medicines and waterproofs, will be useful.

THINKING AHEAD

It's a remote possibility, but on an outdoor adventure the choice of equipment and meticulous preparation could mean the difference between life and death. You're unlikely to be ascending any Himalayan peaks, but it still pays to be prepared. Essential tools for survival means thinking about what you really need to survive, rather than what would be nice to have for the sake of comfort. Head out to the forest with a fire starter, cooking pot, and a water filter, and you'll be all set to forage some herbs and make a hot drink on the fire. Add a knife and pruning saw, and you can make pretty much anything you need, including many of the projects later in this book. Some items like the tarpaulin and water filter bag can be made cheaply at home if you have some fabric skills and access to a sewing machine. There's no need to spend a fortune, although cheap tools don't always last and will need to be replaced. Take only what you think you really need and can comfortably carry—and above all, keep it simple.

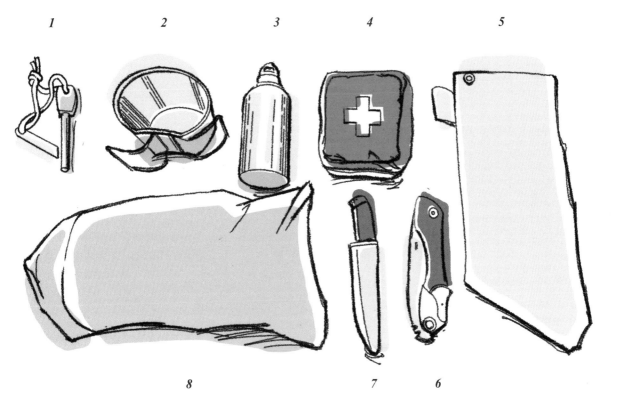

1. Fire starter—also matches
2. Dual-purpose drinking mug and cooking pot
3. Water bottle
4. Basic first aid kit
5. Water filter bag
6. Pruning saw
7. Knife
8. Lightweight waterproof tarpaulin

FINDING
NATURAL SHELTER

You've just realized that you're not going to make it back before nightfall. Maybe you got lost or forgot about the time. Whatever the reason, you're going to be out all night—what will you do? Wandering around in the dark might make things worse and could even be a little frightening. You remember all those great forest huts made of sticks and leaves that you've seen in pictures, but it would take too much time and energy to build one. It's time to look for the best shelter that your surroundings can offer.

STAYING DRY AND WARM

When night falls, the best thing to do is to stay put until morning—but you must keep dry and warm. This isn't just about feeling comfortable. Lose too much heat from your body, and you could get hypothermia (see page 59), which can happen in all kinds of climates and weather conditions, especially if you haven't eaten enough.

» *Keeping dry* is priority number one. Wet clothing or skin will cool your body temperature quickly, so finding shelter so that you stay out of the rain is vital. In the woods, sticking close to the trunks of thick conifers and evergreen broad-leaved trees such as holly might provide some shelter because the leaves and needles intercept the rain. Standing behind large tree trunks, walls, and boulders may give some brief relief in driving rain.

» *Staying warm* is all about insulation—keeping warm air and materials close to your body and not letting heat escape into the ground or atmosphere. To insulate the easiest way, think like a hedgehog, and bury yourself in as big a pile of dry leaves as possible. Save energy by minimizing any physical work.

SHELTER FROM THE SUN
Overexposure to strong sunshine can lead to heatstroke, dehydration, or sunburn (see page 59). Cover as much skin as you can, move slowly, and if possible, find nearby shade. You can create some shade by digging a shallow hole. Cover it if you can with a light scarf or tarpaulin.

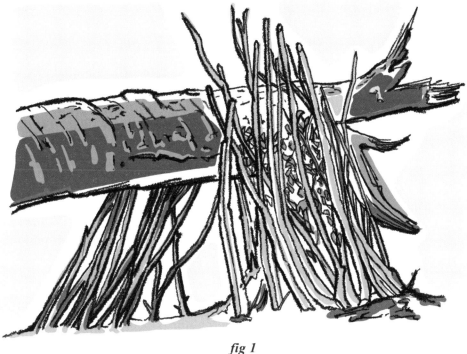

fig 1

FINDING SHELTER

Temporary shelter is all about using what's around you. This could be a naturally sheltered feature or something you can create quickly from materials that are close to hand and require little or no tools. Alternatively, you can combine what you might have in your backpack with what nature provides.

» A cave or large rock overhang could be the dream shelter. But before you get too comfortable in your new subterranean home, there are a few things to remember. Such places aren't just attractive temporary shelters for humans—all kinds of other animals like them, too. Carefully check out caves for signs of habitation, especially if bears or poisonous snakes or insects are known in the area. Look for signs of instability in the rocks above, such as large cracks or recently fallen debris. A fire might provide comfort and warmth, but in a cave or overhang it could also crack the rock above.

» If there's no obvious natural shelter, use what's close to hand—and improvise. A fallen tree might make a good frame to lean sticks against to make a lean-to shelter (*fig 1*). This can then be waterproofed with leaf litter, bark, or lots of green leafy material. But don't be tempted to shelter in the large hole created by the lifting of the fallen tree's roots. In heavy rain, the pit could fill with water and become uninhabitable, or the tree could spring back upright and crush anything under the root plate.

» Best of all, be prepared for the need to shelter by carrying a lightweight tarpaulin or an emergency shelter, sometimes known as a "bivy bag." Either of these can live at the bottom of your backpack in case of emergency.

BUILDING
AND STARTING A FIRE

A campfire is a powerful thing—community is forged, moods lighten, morale is boosted, conversations flow, and silence is comfortable. Humans today seem just as drawn to the campfire as their ancestors were, for comfort and entertainment as well as the necessities of heat, light, and cooking. This connection with the past and basic human needs is deep and vital—and as good a reason as any to become proficient at lighting and managing a campfire.

» Make sure you have permission to light a fire, and respect any local fire bans. Think about the purpose of your fire—is it a focal point for a social event, a means to cook food, or a place to dry your wet gear? This will help you decide what fuel to burn and how big the fire should be.

» Choose a good place to light the fire. Avoid sites near the base of trees or bare rocks—to minimize scorch marks—or peaty soils with high organic content that can smolder and burn underground for months. Keep the fire upwind of tents and buildings.

» Have a supply of clean water nearby to rapidly extinguish the fire or cool potential burns. Tie back long hair and loose clothing.

» There are many different fire styles, or "lays," for different purposes. For now, though, it's best to keep it simple; and to maximize your chances of success, spend time preparing your fireplace and collecting the right fuel.

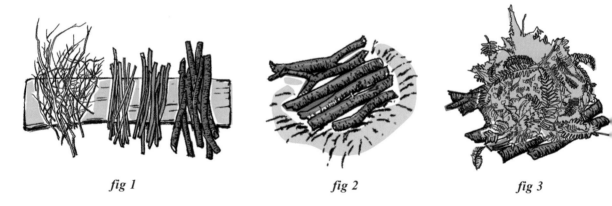

fig 1   *fig 2*   *fig 3*

1. Clear any combustible material like dead leaves or pine needles from around the site to make sure the fire doesn't spread. Collect natural tinder, such as birch bark or bracken, or just use absorbent cotton balls or rounds and scrunched-up newspaper.

2. Collect an armful of different-size kindling. Sort two handfuls of the thinnest twigs—thinner than matchsticks and ideally at least 12 inches (30 centimeters) long. Arrange the rest into piles of pencil-thick and finger-thick twigs (*fig 1*).

3. Make a base or raft of thumb-thick sticks (*fig 2*). Lay your tinder on top of the base (*fig 3*). This will keep it off damp ground and allow air to flow under the fire. Lay the bundles of thinnest twigs on either side of the fire base, ready to pick up as soon as the tinder ignites.

BASIC PRINCIPLES OF FIRE MAKING

Think about these simple principles each time you light and tend a fire. They will help you adapt to different situations:

» *Heat rises—so the heat needs to be underneath the things you want to catch fire.*
» *Fire needs heat, fuel, and oxygen. Take one away, and the fire goes out.*
» *Twigs catch fire more easily than logs—sort your fuel into sizes and add the smallest first.*
» *Wet wood makes lots of smoke and not a lot of heat. Find dry fuel.*

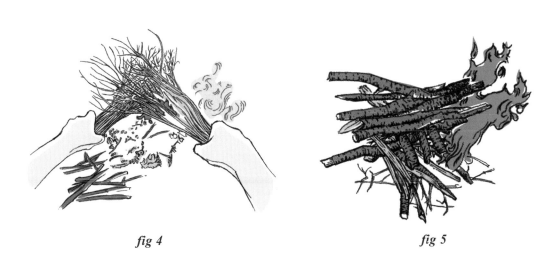

fig 4   *fig 5*

4. Using a match, a lighter, or a fire starter, set fire to the tinder (*fig 3*).
5. Pick up the two bundles of thinnest twigs, and hold them in a cross shape, low over the burning tinder without squashing it (*fig 4*). You should start to hear crackling as the tinder catches.
6. Gently lay down the bottommost bundle of burning twigs, and move the top bundle so that it's over as much flame as possible. When it catches, gently set it down on top of the first bundle.
7. Place your pencil-thick twigs one by one on top of the burning twigs in a crisscross pattern to create a core of embers (*fig 5*). The fire is still delicate at this stage, so be gentle.
8. Add the finger-thick twigs in a tepee shape over the core to create a stable fire. Now you can relax a little and gradually add larger-diameter wood that will burn for longer.

Stop adding fuel some time before you need to leave, and fold any unburned ends of wood into the fire, so that you are left with mainly ash. Add water to the ash to make sure that everything, including the ground underneath, is cold to the touch. Either bag the cold, wet ash or distribute it in undergrowth, making sure that you leave no trace of your fire site behind.

FINDING AND
FILTERING WATER

In theory, a person can survive three days without drinking any water. However, a serious lack of water—dehydration—rapidly affects decision-making and energy levels, so it's essential to keep hydrated. That doesn't mean you can just dip a mug in the nearest pond to quench your thirst. Drinking untreated water carries significant risks to health from pollutants such as pesticides, heavy metals, bacteria, viruses, and parasites from human and animal waste. You can reduce all potential problems by treating any water that you consume. In an emergency, you might have to balance the risks of dehydration against the risks of drinking unfiltered water from untrusted water sources—but it's better to avoid that in the first place!

WATER COLLECTION AND SAFETY

When exerting energy in outdoor activities such as hiking or climbing, you lose water through sweating and exhaling, and might need to drink 2.5 or 3.5 quarts (3 or 4 liters) of water a day. That's a lot to carry, especially if you're out for a few days, so try and plan where you're likely to find drinkable water.

» No matter how desperate things get, don't ever drink seawater! It will dehydrate you.
» Avoid eating snow—it takes a large volume to provide any worthwhile rehydration, and in the attempt you'll lower the body's core temperature, putting you at greater risk of hypothermia (see page 59). Melting snow first is a much better idea.
» As the saying goes, "We all live downstream," and what the land is used for upstream will affect how drinkable flowing water is in a stream or river. Intensive agriculture or upland grazing make contamination more likely. Avoid drinking where toxic plants, such as water dropwort (*Oenanthe crocata*) or water hemlock (*Cicuta* species), grow nearby.
» Be wary of small lakes and ponds. They may be stagnant and carry waterborne diseases.
» Rainwater will be as clean as the material that you collect it in. Hang out a clean tarpaulin, coat, or even a plastic bag at a gentle angle, and peg down halfway along one side to make a valley. Place a pot under the valley to collect the runoff (*fig 1*).

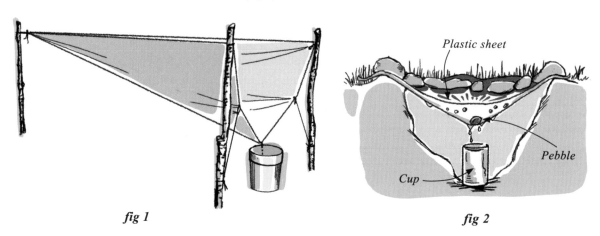

Plastic sheet

Pebble

Cup

fig 1   *fig 2*

» You can collect atmospheric moisture using a solar still (*fig 2*). First, dig a hole and place a cup in it. Rest a sheet of plastic over the top of the hole, weigh down the edges, and place a large pebble in the center to make a depression. Sunlight will cause small drips of condensation to form and collect in the cup. But don't expect too much—it's a slow process and produces only small amounts of water.

» On boggy ground, you can dig a hole and let it fill with water. The contents may be murky and so should be filtered and purified before drinking (see below).

» The sap of certain trees, such as birch (*Betula* species) and maple (*Acer* species), is clean, clear, and tasty to drink. In early spring, it can be collected by cutting a branch and hanging a collecting vessel over the pruning cut on the tree. Only do this in an emergency since it can harm the tree.

Water filter bag

PURIFYING WATER

There are two steps of ensuring the safety of the water you collect—filtration and sterilization.

» *Filtration.* This can be as basic as straining water through a T-shirt or an improvised filter of moss layers, gravel, and sand in a container with a hole in the bottom. Alternatively, carry something designed for the job, such as a water filter bag or a ceramic or activated charcoal water filter. Some of these products claim to remove virtually all harmful chemicals and pathogens and eliminate the need for sterilization by heat or chemicals.

» *Sterilization.* Once you've strained your water, you need to sterilize it. If you're able to start a fire (see pages 44–5) and have a pan, bring the water to the boiling point. Keep it there for a minute. Virtually all harmful pathogens should be killed in that time. The easiest option is to use chemical sterilizer tablets. It's a good idea to keep a strip of these in a backpack pocket, just in case. Always follow the package instructions.

MAKING STRING

If you're in the wild and need to hold stuff together, you'll have to manage without glue, cement, nails, screws, and nuts and bolts—modern essentials that we all take for granted. But you can make your own cord or string using forest resources, a skill vitally important for nonindustrial societies across the globe and throughout the ages. At one time, natural fibers were used for pretty much every holding job—lashing poles together for shelter, sewing skins to make clothes, knotting nets to catch fish and animals. Initially frustrating, string-making is really satisfying when you get the hang of it—and it's something you'll be glad you learned.

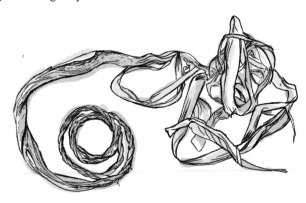

QUICK CORD CHOICES

Makeshift cord, or withy, can be made by twisting a sapling, willow branch, or part of a multistemmed tree, such as hazel. The stem should be less than 0.75 inches (2 centimeters) in diameter—grab it near the ground with both hands, then twist it like you're wringing out a cloth. This separates the fibers lengthwise without breaking them. Keep twisting as the branch kinks until you have a long length of separated fibers, and then cut them off from the base.

Thin, shallow tree roots are another fast cord option. Excavate them from the trunk outward, then cut and use as they are to bind poles together, or split them lengthwise with your fingers to make finer lengths for sewing or weaving.

THE ART OF STRING

Many fibrous natural materials can be twined to make string. Exactly what you use depends on the time of year and the species available. The inner bark of some trees, such as lime (*Tilia* species), sweet chestnut (*Castanea sativa*), and western red cedar (*Thuja plicata*), along with the fibers of many plants, including iris, hemp, flax, nettle, sedges, willow herbs, and yucca, make excellent cordage. Once you've mastered the basics and can spot a plant with long fibers, then you can experiment and see what works where you are.

1. Harvest your plants and separate the fibers (*fig 1*). Some fibers, such as those in flax and lime bark, need to be soaked in water before they will separate. Once separated, dry the fibers in the wind and sun.
2. Dampen the fibers—this might seem odd after drying them, but it makes the fibers temporarily more pliable and easier to work with.

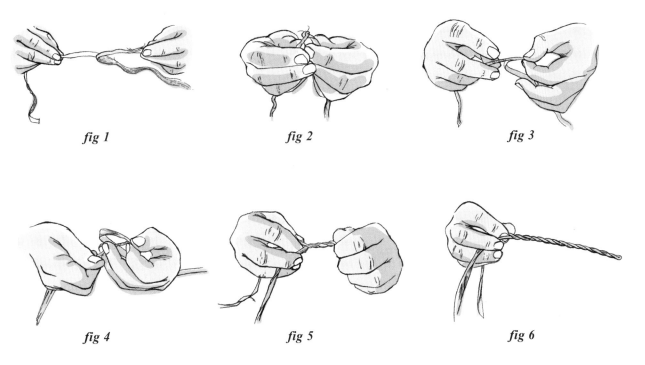

fig 1   fig 2   fig 3

fig 4   fig 5   fig 6

3. Choose a long strand, and start twisting it almost halfway along the length until it kinks (*fig 2*).
4. Hold the kink in your nondominant hand—this will be one end of the string (*fig 3*).
5. Twist one of the strands either toward or away from you—whichever feels most natural. It doesn't matter which way, but once you've started, all twisting must be done in the same way. Stop just before the strand wants to kink, and clamp it with two fingers (*fig 4*).
6. Do the same twisting actions with the other strand.
7. Clamp both twisted strands with your dominant hand to keep them from unwinding. Let go with the other hand. The tension should wind both strands together to make a short piece of two-ply string (*fig 5*).
8. Pinch where the two strands now meet, and repeat from step 5 as many times as necessary until you have the length of string you need (*fig 6*).

Eventually, this process becomes automatic, and it's a relaxing thing to do while chatting by the fire. With time and patience, you could even twist enough to make a bag or a net. Rope is similar to string but is made of bundles of strings or yarn plied together to make a stronger, stiffer type of cord that will tie bulkier knots. See pages 148–9 for instructions on tying individual knots.

READING CLOUDS
AND WEATHER SIGNS

The weather plays a big part in the enjoyment of being outdoors. When it's calm, all is well. But sudden storms and high winds can cause discomfort and even danger. Reading weather signs so that you're alert to imminent changes is a good skill to learn. You're then ready to get your waterproofs out before the rain hits or know when it's time to get back indoors as a storm approaches. You can learn much about the weather just by being aware of what's happening when you're out and about—taking note of how the wind is behaving and the recurring patterns of clouds.

WATCHING THE WIND

Wind is simply air moving from one place to another—from high to low pressure areas in the atmosphere. It might bring warm, wet air from a tropical ocean; cold, wet air from a polar sea; or hot or cold dry air from the continental interior, depending on the season. What is the dominant or prevailing wind direction in your area—what kind of weather does that usually bring? A change in wind direction will at least tell you what type of air to expect, its temperatures, and its moisture content. It can also help you understand the weather associated with low-pressure systems and the passing of weather fronts.

LOOKING AT CLOUDS

Pay particular attention to how high the clouds are. Rainy and windy, low-pressure or cyclonic weather is associated with a pattern of decreasing cloud height and increasing rainfall, then a dry spell with warmer temperatures, followed by heavy showers and cooler temperatures. Put simply, a wedge of

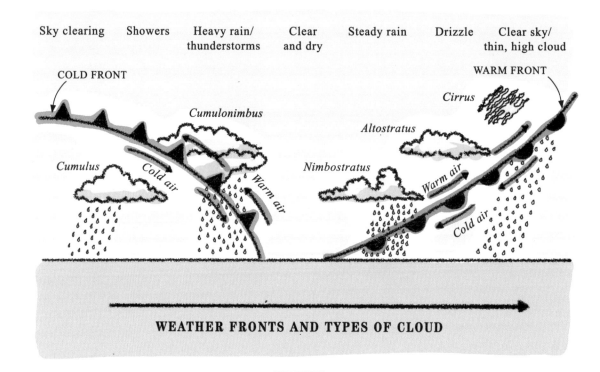

WEATHER FRONTS AND TYPES OF CLOUD

Mammatus clouds *Shelf clouds*

warm air is pinched by cold air on either side as the low-pressure system moves across the land. In midlatitudes between 35 and 65 degrees, in both north and south hemispheres, the system flows from west to east. The clues to what might happen next are in the height of the clouds and changes in the air temperature. Clouds form along the boundaries or "fronts" between these air masses. As a warm front passes, the first clouds to appear in a clear sky will be high and wispy cirrus clouds. Within a few hours, these will be followed by midaltitude altostratus clouds and then thicker low-level rain-bearing nimbostratus clouds. As this rain passes, the air temperature will increase for awhile before the arrival of the cold front with its heavy, persistent rain and possibility of thunderstorms.

» After a period of very hot weather, look for tall, anvil-shaped cumulonimbus clouds that are likely to bring heavy rain, hail, or even thunder and lightning.

» Shelf clouds and wall clouds are associated with big storm systems, and although they might look similar—they both hang down below the main mass of cloud—they are quite different. The shelf cloud is usually at the leading edge of the storm and extends across the length of the main mass of clouds. As the clouds pass overhead, the weather will get windier and colder before rain falls a few minutes later. A wall cloud also hangs below a storm but is more isolated and may rotate—storm chasers look for persistent wall clouds that have increasing rotation because that's where tornadoes are most likely to form.

» Also watch for mammatus clouds, suspended underneath large storm clouds. They are named from the Latin word *mamma*, meaning "breast" or "udder," but they look more like bubbles or cotton balls. Mammatus clouds are associated with storms but don't necessarily indicate that anything as serious as a tornado will form. However, it's best to take shelter quickly after you spot these clouds—just take a photo first!

MYTHICAL FOREST BEINGS

Murmurings of elusive beings lurking in woodlands circulate across the globe. Corporeal or ethereal, this compelling cadre of forest personalities—whose presence may be felt but rarely seen—include enchanted humans and benevolent guardians of wildlife, hybrid humans, and misunderstood creatures of the dark, verdant woods.

Irish legend tells of the hunter-warrior Fionn Mac Cumhail, or Finn MacCool, who lived in the forest and ate the Salmon of Knowledge, bringing him great importance and a band of followers called the Fianna. While out hunting, he met his wife, Sadbh, who first appeared as a deer under the enchantment of a Druid but reverted back to a beautiful woman. The story goes that Fionn built the Giant's Causeway stone formation in County Antrim as part of a bridge to Scotland, where he traveled to fight the giant Benandonner.

The Green Man is a sylvan spirit that symbolizes the yearly rebirth of springtime. Appearing as a disembodied face with vegetation growing out of his mouth, and sometimes nose and ears, he's found in many cultures, infrequently appearing as the Green Woman. Although deemed a pagan fertility symbol, the Green Man is found in the carvings, roof bosses, and imagery of churches and cathedrals in Western Europe and Britain, in a blending of paganism and Christianity. It was not until 1939, however, that Englishwoman Lady Julia Raglan first coined the term "Green Man" in reference to these evocative images.

OLD WORLD WONDERS

Scandinavian folklore offers many intriguing forest characters. The troll-like Huldra is a beautiful and flirtatious young woman who sports the long tail of a cow—which she's canny enough to hide when encountering humans. Huldra resides by woodland streams and rivers. Said to be a child of Adam and Eve, she was quickly hidden by her mother when God came to visit—as Eve had not yet suitably bathed her—and so Huldra was banished to remain hidden from human society, a lost soul who yearns for company in her wild solitude.

A water spirit named the Fossegrimmen appears as a handsome young man who sits naked beneath a waterfall, playing his violin. All the music of nature comes from him, including the wind rustling through the trees and the water tinkling through streams. It's said that if a music student comes to him with an offering of food (he's partial to a chunk of meat), Fossegrimmen will drag the student's fingers along the strings until they bleed, after which they will play with a magical vivacity.

FEVERISH TALES

Sasquatch, or Bigfoot, originates from Native American mythology of the Pacific Northwest, and sightings are fairly common. The apelike giant is said to be covered with black or brown fur, walk upright, and possess a rank smell as he bounds through the woods, occasionally disrupting settlements and campsites, and sometimes leaving huge footprints. Some conjecture that Sasquatch is the "missing link" between apes and humans, but researchers have attempted to prove this in vain.

From Australian Aboriginal lore comes Kinie Ger, half human and half quoll (a catlike marsupial), and possessed of crazy, gnashing teeth. Its human legs propel it to chase unsuspecting people and animals, dispatching them without mercy using a spear. The Porotai of Māori mythology is a being made of half flesh and half stone, with two faces. It's invisible to humans; when a person thinks they are tripping over a stone, it may be a Porotai that has taken a dislike to them. The Manaia is another Māori hybird being, but with a more protective nature. With its bird head and male human body, the Manaia acts as an envoy between humans and the souls of their dead loved ones, passing messages between this world and the spirit realm.

SENDING SIGNALS

Today, most people rely on handheld devices for navigation and to call for help. But a dropped phone or dead battery could leave you with only your own initiative to fall back on. It's good to have a plan B for when you might get into trouble and modern technology lets you down. Some basic pieces of equipment will do the trick. With luck, you'll never need that rescue plan—but it pays to be prepared.

If you're lost or need medical help quickly in a remote location—and you're not carrying a personal locator beacon—you'll need to create signs that look human-made and can't be mistaken for a natural event. The more of these methods you use at once, the higher the likelihood that someone will spot at least one of them and get the help you need.

FLASHLIGHTS AND MIRRORS

If an airborne search has been launched, there are many ways you can signal to the plane or helicopter. Use a flashlight or a reflective surface to create flashes of light that can travel a long distance. Make your pattern of flashes regular—the alpine distress signal, for example, is six flashes in a minute, followed by a minute break and then another six flashes. The same signal pattern also applies to using a whistle or shouting to attract the attention of rescuers. A widely recognized distress signal is the Morse code SOS— an unbroken pattern of dot, dot, dot, dash, dash, dash, dot, dot, dot.

FLYING THE FLAG

Flags have the advantage of maintaining a constant sign that people are present. They can be placed all the way around an area to send a message in numerous directions. Plant flags on highly visible places, such as trails or headlands, especially in groups or patterns that are clearly designed to stand out from the natural surroundings. Even better, write messages on your flags, using charcoal or mud if you don't have a pen.

SPELLING IT OUT

Using messages written on the ground to signal to aircraft is effective, although collecting the materials and laying them out can burn up a lot of energy. Make sure the sign contrasts with the ground—for example, use dark vegetation on light sand or white stones on dark soil. Keep it simple—SOS or HELP will get the message across—and add an arrow pointing toward your camp location.

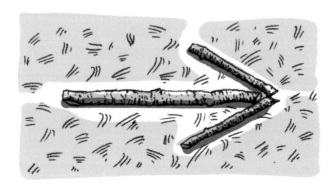

fig 1   fig 2

HOW TO MAKE A SIGNAL FIRE

From the earliest human civilizations, signal fires were used to send simple messages quickly across long distances. They remain one of the best ways to attract attention and get help in an emergency.

1. Find a clear, wide open space or an exposed hilltop to build your signal fire. It should be near enough to your camp that you can get to it quickly if you hear or see potential rescuers. You also don't want a signal fire to burn out of control and devastate a wilderness area.

2. Gather three poles around 6.5 feet (2 meters) long, combustible material to start a good hot fire, and fuel, such as green leaves and branches, which will create lots of billowing, white smoke (*fig 1*). Plastics, rubber, and petrochemicals will make acrid black smoke, so use them only in a real emergency.

3. Build a tripod from poles around—they can be roughly lashed together with vines, withies (flexible twigs), or branches—see "Making String" on pages 48–9 (*fig 2*).

4. Prepare a fire with dry tinder, kindling, and fuel wood in the base of the tripod (*fig 3*). If possible, cover the fire material to keep it dry and ready to be lit when needed.

5. Lean your smoke-making signal fuel on the tripod over the unlit fire to keep the starter fire underneath dry and ready to light at any time (*fig 4*). Leave a small gap around the base for airflow and to allow room to light the fire. Keep extra fuel well away from the main fire, so that you can add it in a controlled way without it all catching at once.

6. When you spot a potential rescuer, light the fire and keep it burning (*fig 5*).

At nighttime, flames will make a better beacon than smoke. If you can create a pattern of three fires in a triangle, this is unlikely to be mistaken for anything other than a distress beacon.

fig 3   fig 4   fig 5

WHERE TO CAMP?

Nomadic humans never had to apply for camping permits or pay to stay at a campsite. The situation now is very different and varies hugely from country to country. Check what's allowed locally, and pay attention to accepted etiquette and indigenous custom—and the law.

WILD CAMPING

Flat ground is a priority for a good night's sleep—but not always easy to find. Riverbanks, especially the inside of a bend, might have a flat area to camp on, but watch out for boggy ground, biting insects, and flash flooding during the night. Camping on a dry riverbed is a bad idea—conditions may be dry overhead, but rain far away can fill a river and soon wash you and your tent away. Check for—and avoid—other hazards like rockfalls, dead or hanging tree branches, and animal tracks and burrows. Although exposed to wind, high camp spots can offer fantastic views and feelings of awe and wonder—as well as fewer insects.

THE JOY OF HAMMOCKS

Perhaps the ultimate in lightweight wild camping is to sleep in a hammock (see page 204). It allows you to camp on steep hills and uneven or rocky ground, while a tarp pitched above makes an adjustable roof to keep you dry and sheltered from the wind. In hot weather, a hammock is cool and airy with none of the stuffiness of a warm tent. In cold weather, you need good insulation under your body to avoid heat loss. Pitch your hammock between two sturdy trees at about chest height. Lying in a hammock at a diagonal with the material high at one side of your head and lower at the other means that you can lie flat.

EVERYMAN'S RIGHTS—THE FREEDOM TO ROAM

Camping and hiking in North America's vast national parks are widely acceptable, but you may need a permit to camp. Check ahead with the US National Park Service or Parks Canada. In Scandinavia, Scotland, and other northern and central European countries, the right to walk, camp, and forage freely across country are culturally and legally enshrined. Roaming rules vary from country to country, but generally travel should be on foot and camping done out of sight of dwellings and away from the road.

DRESSING
FOR THE FOREST

There's no need to go shopping for expensive gear just to go out in the woods. You should consider, though, how you dress for each situation. Think about what you're going to be doing, the weather conditions, the kind of terrain, the necessity for any shelter, and protection from fire. If you're intending to get away from the crowds, it's better to forget what you look like and just consider the practicalities.

» *Warmth.* Outdoor clothes need to keep you warm (or cool) enough when you're sitting still and when you're moving. Lots of thin layers will insulate you well and allow you to regulate your temperature by shedding or adding clothing. Cold hands and feet can be uncomfortable or painful, but it's the core of your body that needs to be kept at the right temperature to avoid hypothermia (see page 59).

» *Waterproofness.* Clothing material should resist the rain but also let moisture out of your body to keep it from being soaked in condensation.

» *Quick drying.* If you're using a lot of energy and therefore sweating to keep cool, the material next to your skin should wick moisture away to keep you comfortable. You want outer layers that will dry out quickly by the fire—putting on cold, wet clothes in the morning is horrible!

» *Fire retardant.* If you're spending time by the fire, you need a waterproof that doesn't melt when hit by sparks and ash flakes. Tightly woven natural fibers tend to be more fire-resistant and will smolder rather than melt.

» *Toughness.* When you're moving through dense vegetation, your clothing should protect your skin from scratches and be strong enough to resist thorns and scratching branches.

» *Ease of movement.* If you're climbing or moving quickly, it's important to have clothing that helps movement rather than restricts it.

» *Sun protection.* In high summer in the forest, most harmful sunlight is intercepted by the canopy of trees, but a hat—preferably one that protects ears as well as head—is still recommended.

» *Covering up.* Unless it's uncomfortably hot, keeping arms and legs covered offers some protection from scratches, bites, and stings.

» *Footwear.* The choice depends on weather conditions and the activity you're undertaking. Some people like to go barefoot in the woods, but for any heavy work, or if you're using an ax, put on sturdy boots—with reinforced toe caps to be extra sure.

» *Natural fibers.* Clothing made from natural fibers may lack some of the waterproofness and breathability of fabrics that derive from petrochemicals, but it has many advantages—not least from an environmental perspective. Good-quality merino wool clothing, including base layers, is flame-resistant, warm, and comfortable, and it can be worn for longer before washing than clothing made from artificial fibers. Cotton canvas is tough and can be waxed for improved water resistance. Military surplus clothing is a cost-effective solution for outdoor wear—as long as you don't mind the camouflage look!

NIGHTTIME SAFETY

In folk culture, such as fairy tales, the woods and the dark are full of negative associations. Nighttime away from the lights and sounds of buildings and roads can, indeed, be an unnerving experience, but with repeated exposure, walking in the dark can become liberating.

There might be times when it makes most sense to keep moving in the dark. In hot climates, for example, you'll use less energy and need less water when traveling in the cool of the night. Sometimes, nighttime journeying is unavoidable—perhaps, if you have to get up early to reach the beginning of a climb or high ridge walk, or if you're tracking nocturnal animals.

MASTERING THE WOODS AT NIGHT

» Practice using your night vision instead of artificial light. Flashlights and head flashlights illuminate a narrow area of ground, making the rest of the scene seem much darker. This is fine if you need to do something close up like find clean socks in your backpack but not if you're walking around and have to remain aware of the wider surroundings.

» Pace out and memorize the route from the campfire to your sleeping place. Leaving the light of the fire and walking through the trees to a tent or hammock spot without a flashlight is a liberating feeling.

» If you're in the mountains or an area with cliffs and steep slopes, stay alert, move slowly, and stick to the most obvious paths.

» Plan your nighttime outdoor adventures around the time when the moon is at its fullest for maximum natural light.

» Keep the woodcraft to daylight hours—you're much more likely to have an accident with a sharp tool if you're tired or straining to see.

NIGHT VISION

Many nocturnal animals have special adaptations to allow them to feed at night. Bats use echolocation—bouncing sounds off objects in their path—and owls have elongated eyes that maximize the light-collecting area of their cornea. Humans have much better night vision than you might think. In daylight, cone-shaped cells in our eyes allow us to pick out sharp detail and color. At night, rod-shaped cells take over as they are more sensitive to contrast and movement, especially in our peripheral vision. The cells become flooded by a protein called rhodopsin, which converts light into electrical signals. Bright light destroys rhodopsin, so just a glance at your phone will seriously diminish your night vision for at least half an hour. If you need light—a flashlight to read a map, for example—hold one eye closed until you turn the light off to preserve the night vision in the other eye.

DEALING WITH EXTREME
HEAT AND COLD

As the Scouts say, "Be prepared." Think about where you're going and what you might do in unexpectedly extreme conditions. Heat and cold can adversely affect the core temperature of the body where our vital organs are located, and on exposed skin or extremities. That could mean hypothermia and frostbite in cold weather, heatstroke under hot conditions, and dehydration in both. A good rule of thumb in unfamiliar conditions is to watch what the locals do—and copy it.

HYPOTHERMIA
It only takes a drop of 3.6 degrees Fahrenheit (2 degrees Celsius) in the core organs to induce potentially fatal hypothermia. This can happen in wet, windy, or cold weather—and be aggravated by lack of food, strenuous exercise, and low morale. Typical hypothermia symptoms in order of onset are:
» shivering, slurred speech, "out of character" or irrational behavior
» poor judgement, drowsiness, uncontrollable shivering, and no interest in staying warm
» collapse, hallucinations, slow, shallow breathing, and weak pulse
» drifting in and out of consciousness and no longer shivering—danger signs that a person's temperature has dropped below 90 to 91 degrees Fahrenheit (32 to 33 degrees Celsius).

If anyone shows these signs, wrap them up to conserve heat—for example, share body heat under an emergency blanket or sleeping bag—and feed them chocolate or another high-energy food. Don't rub the person to warm them or offer any alcohol, caffeine, or tobacco.

FROSTBITE
This can affect fingers, toes, ears, nose, and lips when exposed to extreme cold. Frostnip is the first stage, as blood vessels constrict to keep heat in the core, and will be felt as cold, numb skin with pins and needles. If this continues, it becomes frostbite, where the fluid in skin and muscle starts to freeze. Either condition requires medical attention. Deeper tissue freezing is very serious and can lead to tissue death and amputation. As with hypothermia, warm frostnipped skin with indirect heat not rubbing.

DEHYDRATION
A body that loses more water than it takes on becomes dehydrated, which can happen in hot or cold weather. Dehydration—best indicated by dark urine rather than thirst—can cause loss of strength and stamina, headaches and dizziness, and bad decision-making. Always hydrate at the beginning of the day, and keep drinking water throughout. Sweating can cause excessive water loss in hot weather but also in the cold, due to extra layers. You also lose moisture through exhaling into cold air.

HEATSTROKE
When the internal body temperature rises above 105 degrees Fahrenheit (40.6 degrees Celsius), heatstroke happens. Someone with external heatstroke will probably have stopped sweating and be disorientated, whereas someone who has overexerted in hot weather will likely still be sweating. Cool the person as quickly as possible in cool water or a stream of moist, cool air.

FOREST FIRST AID
AND NATURAL REMEDIES

You're whittling by the campfire as the sun sets, when you lose concentration for a second and take a slice out of your thumb. A long way from help, you need to stop the bleeding and treat the wound until you can get to a hospital or clinic. Could you manage in this situation? Accidents can happen, so it makes sense to know how to deal with the most likely and most life-threatening. If all else fails, nature has some remedies of its own—but proceed with caution.

GETTING TO KNOW FIRST AID

The aims of first aid are to preserve life, prevent worsening, and to promote recovery until expert medical help arrives. It's not about curing anyone or playing paramedic, nurse, or doctor. A first aid kit should be a permanent resident of your outdoor bag, but you need to know how to use it. Whatever you plan on doing, a couple of hours of training to cover bleeding and cardiopulmonary resuscitation (CPR) is never wasted. For forest situations, outdoor training is much more effective than sitting in a conference room watching presentations and practicing on a flat, carpeted floor. Your confidence will be massively boosted by a day or two of realistic scenarios like carrying out CPR on a muddy riverbank under a holly tree. First aid qualifications should be renewed at least once every three years, but the more frequent the updates are, the better. Invest in a wilderness or mountain medicine course if you're likely to be away from immediate medical help for a prolonged period.

WHAT SHOULD BE IN YOUR FIRST AID KIT?

This depends on where you're going and what you intend to do, but dealing with burns and wounds is top of the list for the projects in this book. Keep your first aid kit in a bright-colored waterproof bag in an easy-to-access place.

- » *Medical gloves*
- » *Resuscitation face shield with valve*
- » *Foil or thermal blanket*
- » *Sterile cleaning wipes*
- » *Assorted nonfabric bandages*
- » *Nonadhesive dressings*
- » *Micropore tape and zinc oxide tape*
- » *Conforming bandages*
- » *Small roll of plastic wrap*
- » *Sterile wound dressings*
- » *Vial of eyewash*
- » *Painkillers for personal use*
- » *Sachets of rehydration treatment*
- » *Glucose tablets*
- » *Tick-removal tool*

DOCTOR NATURE

Natural remedies should be approached with extreme caution—you really need to know what you're doing if you intend to use foraged plant material to treat anyone. A misidentification could kill instead of cure, so seek training from a qualified medical herbalist before trying any of these folk remedies. Here are a few well-known plants that can be foraged and used externally for on-the-spot first aid.

» Yarrow is said to stop bleeding and was carried into battle by Roman soldiers.
» Usnea or "beard" lichens can be used on wounds as they contain a natural antibiotic—usnic acid. They should never be ingested.
» Sphagnum moss earned its medicinal stripes in World War I, where it was dried and used to dress wounds. It's antiseptic and absorbent and is worth getting to know on high boggy ground.
» Douglas fir sap has antimicrobial properties and can be used to seal small cuts and prevent infection. Balsam fir is unrelated but has similar properties.

NATURE'S OWN BANDAGE

Birch polypore is a bracket fungus found only on birch trees. Around 4 to 8 inches (10 to 20 centimeters) across, it varies from white to a milky coffee color, with white pores underneath and a strong mushroomy smell. The thin layer on the polypore's underside can be used to make breathable, antiseptic, adhesive "bandages" to cover small cuts.

1. Remove a ripe, good-sized polypore from a birch tree (*fig 1*).
2. Lightly score a rectangular shape into the underside of the fungus using a small knife (*fig 2*).
3. Gently peel the cut rectangle away from the base (*fig 3*).
4. Apply the "bandage" to the wound (*fig 4*).

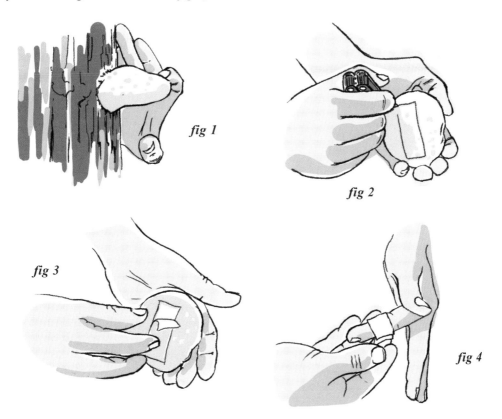

fig 1

fig 2

fig 3

fig 4

BEATING THE BUGS!

Every animal has its niche and function in the ecosystem, but some are hard to love when they want to feast on your blood or skin. Prevention is the best cure, so make sure you take precautions if you're entering major bug territory—and if you do get bitten, act quickly to minimize any potential further complications.

PREVENTING BITES

There are plenty of things you can do to continue outdoors in more bug-frequented areas without too much irritation.

» Wear a fine mesh head net with a tight neck worn over a wide-brimmed hat to keep flying, biting insects like blackflies, midges, sand flies, and mosquitoes from coming into contact with exposed skin. In mosquito-prone areas, use a sleeping net.

» Keep equipment in your backpack or tent to keep a biting insect from hitching a ride.

» Make life harder for mites and ticks by covering up and tucking pants into socks.

» Use an insect repellent—one that works against a wide variety of species. Popular off-the-shelf products are often based on the chemical DEET (N,N-diethyl-m-toluamide), which in strong concentrations may harm humans and the wider environment. Citronella alternatives are often kinder but less effective.

There are also a variety of DIY options:

» Pineapple weed (*Matricaria discoidea*) likes to grow on compacted ground and is found all around the world. If crushed up and rubbed on clothes and skin, it can deter flying insects.

» A traditional Nordic recipe can be made by mixing beeswax, pennyroyal oil, and birch oil. The resulting paste may darken the skin and make you smell like an old barbecue left out in the rain—but it does work!

» A more unhealthy way to avoid being bitten is to sit downwind of a smoky fire—particularly if you burn things like the heads of reed mace (*Typha latifolia*), cedar bark (*Thuja plicata*), or crumbly rotten wood. If you're sleeping in a natural shelter, you can smoke it out like this to encourage invertebrate inhabitants to move elsewhere awhile.

DEALING WITH TICKS

Ticks are arachnids—closely related to spiders—with at least 900 species worldwide, occurring in most habitats. Tick bites don't hurt—you probably won't notice until you see the tick attached to your body—but they do carry the risk of severe disease. In different parts of the world, ticks can transmit diseases such as Lyme disease, tick-borne encephalitis, babesiosis (Texas fever), and Rocky Mountain spotted fever. Effective vaccines for tick-borne encephalitis are available.

Some people never seem to get bitten, and others are veritable tick magnets. If you're bitten by a tick, it's important to remove it properly as soon as possible to minimize the risk of disease transmission. There are many myths about tick removal, such as burning and smothering, which are ill-advised and can irritate the tick, making infection more likely. Only follow the removal methods advised by medical professionals, such as the following instructions.

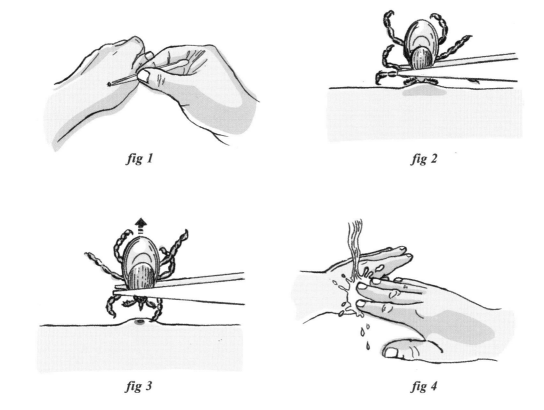

fig 1

fig 2

fig 3

fig 4

1. Use a clean tick-removal tool (available online) or very fine tweezers (***fig 1***). Avoid squeezing or crushing the tick.
2. Grasp the tick as close to your skin as you can (***fig 2***).
3. Slowly pull upward (***fig 3***). If you're using a tick tool, twist as you pull. It doesn't matter which direction you twist.
4. Either keep the tick in a sealed pot for analysis, or dispose of it in the toilet. Don't squeeze a tick to kill it as you might spread infected blood.
5. Wash your hands well.
6. Clean the bite with an antiseptic or soap and water (***fig 4***).
7. Draw a circle around the bite mark in marker pen, so that you can keep an eye on any target-like rash that may develop there later.
8. If you develop a rash or feel unwell after a bite, speak to your doctor.

Check online for local maps showing where there are high incidences of any tick-borne diseases, but don't let worries about ticks deter you from spending time in the woods. If you take preventative measures and do thorough daily checks for ticks, that will help keep you safe and healthy.

TREE CLIMBING

If you can't see the wood for the trees, then climbing a tree could gain you a vantage point and a different perspective on the world. You might need to climb to see farther—to look for signs of water, perhaps—to keep your scent off the ground to watch wildlife, to escape from danger, to relax, or just for the simple physical challenge. You might have seen arborists climbing with ropes, harnesses, and all types of technical gear to access and work on every part of a tree. Doing this requires training and expertise. Recreational tree climbing without equipment can still require great skill and is by definition risky. But like most things, risk can be managed—so, read on.

If you're going to climb, then spend some time looking for the right kind of tree. It should be strong and healthy enough for all the branches to take your weight and not a home to birds that might be disturbed. Also look for any delicate epiphytes emerging from the bark that might be damaged as you climb. These are plants that grow on other plants, using them for support but independently sourcing their own water and nutrients.

GOOD CLIMBING TECHNIQUE

Remember, it's not a competition. Take climbing slowly, if you can, to build your confidence. There's no need to push yourself to go as high as possible; just enjoy being wherever you get to.

» Use big branches as holds—they should be as thick as your wrist or bigger (**A**).
» Hold branches as near to the trunk as you can (**B**).
» Don't use dead branches as holds.
» Try to keep three physical points of contact on the tree at all times.
» Make sure you can climb back down— you'll know this only with experience, so start low and climb down, then go a little higher.
» Watch out for insect nests, especially wasps and bees—if you spot one in your tree, it's time to retreat (**C**).
» Check that the ground that you'll drop onto is clear (**D**).

THE SECRETS OF THE OLD-GROWTH GIANTS

*Along a wide strip of land beside the sea from central California northward to southern Oregon in the United States lies the home of the gigantic coast redwood (*Sequoia sempervirens*). One such tree, nicknamed "Hyperion," is, according to Guinness World Records, the tallest tree on the planet at nearly 384 feet (117 metres). Its age is estimated at between 600 and 800 years old, although the oldest living specimens of the species could be more than 2,000 years old. These trees may be the tallest, but they aren't the largest by mass, an accolade that goes to their close relative the giant sequoia (*Sequoiadendron giganteum*), which can have a diameter of up to 40 feet (12 metres) at its base.*

The locations of the tallest trees are often kept secret as the ecosystem in their canopies is unique, fragile, and prone to damage. Recreational tall tree climbing is banned in national parks to protect these trees and the many species of plant and animals that depend on them. Scientists trained in advanced tree-climbing techniques are allowed to explore the forest world far above the ground. Their research is especially important as around 95 percent of the unique forest habitat of the coastal redwood forests has been lost due to felling in the nineteenth and twentieth centuries, including more than 30 percent of the giant sequoia.

Food prepared and eaten outdoors, alone or in company, is an entirely different experience from eating in a restaurant or at home. For some reason, everything tastes better, and children especially will try foods around the fire that they would turn their noses up at otherwise. Chefs know that it's not just taste, texture, and presentation that affect how we enjoy food but also the ambience in which it's eaten. It would be difficult to beat the atmosphere of an evening spent among friends around a crackling fire with a meal prepared in the wild and cooked over glowing embers.

In this chapter, you'll learn about foraging for wild plant foods, including important tips on what not to pick, let alone eat. Whether you prefer a plant-based diet or are happy to kill animals and eat their meat, there's something here to start your journey into exploration of the huge array of wild foods that you'll never see in the grocery store. Discover common plants that yield useful leaves, flowers, roots, seeds, and fruits. Learn how to prepare fish and fowl for the table, and dip into recipes that will get you started on a variety of cooking techniques ideal for the campfire.

Collecting your own wild food presents a golden opportunity to recognize the complex webs of life, to notice what eats what, and appreciate how easy our lives today are made by farmers, grocers, bakers, and butchers. Foraging in forest, field, and river gives us some rare moments to consider our relationship with food, agriculture, and "nature." You might even find yourself in the presence of another animal that sees you as potential prey. Hearing the howl of the wolf pack or seeing the tracks of a bear are sobering reminders that we're not really the top predator in the food chain.

3

FOOD AND THE FOREST

ESSENTIAL
TOOLS

To go out and about and collect your own food requires little essential equipment. It's perfectly possible to just indulge in ambulant consumption—simple, carefree browsing and grazing on what you find as you wander. When it comes to mealtimes, you'll want a tool or two to prepare what you've collected and something to cook it in. But that's pretty much it. You'll start to wonder what a fully equipped kitchen is really for.

FINDING THE FOOD

To forage for a meal or for food to preserve and store, you'll need some form of container that will let mushrooms, fruit, and flowers breathe and ideally keep them separate. Collecting in plastic bags can squash foods or make them sweat, wilt, or discolor, so use woven baskets or cloth bags to carry your hoard. A shoulder bag or waist pouch is also handy, as it leaves both hands free for collecting.

Always take your trusty knife (see page 41) for cutting back brambles, slicing mushrooms, and harvesting woody stems. Special mushroom collecting knives have a curved blade as well as a small brush built into the handle for cleaning off soil and pine needles as you go. It's also useful to have a pruning saw (see page 41) and first aid kit (see page 60) in your bag, just in case.

As you learn to identify the wild foods where you live, it becomes important to take along at least one reliable plant identification guidebook and maybe a wild food book that highlights any harmful look-alike plants or fungi. Don't rely on phone apps—batteries die and signals get lost—although they can be a useful cross-reference if you want to consult another source to confirm an identification.

Dutch oven

Aluminum cook set

It's often better to forage in dry weather, when the food you collect is most likely to be in good condition and store more easily when dry. You still need to be prepared, however, for all conditions, so be sure to take along waterproof clothing, a map of the area, and a headlamp flashlight if there's any possibility of being out after dark.

It might seem surprising, but the humble umbrella is one of the most useful pieces of foraging equipment. Use the curved handle to reach up and pull down bending branches, so you can collect fruit that would normally be out of reach. Turn an open umbrella upside down to catch ripe crab apples as you gently shake a branch, or simply use it to keep you and your basket dry in that unexpected rain shower.

COOKING THE FOOD

What equipment you use for cooking in the forest depends on how many people you expect to feed. At a minimum, it's good to have a metal mug with folding handles, which can also double as a cooking pot. If you're carrying all your equipment, a lightweight aluminum or more expensive titanium cook set will suffice. If there are a few helpers and your destination is not too distant, then a solid cast-iron skillet and Dutch oven are a pleasure to use. Improvisation is often the order of the day—a stick tripod can be made to hang pans over the fire, or a simple rack from an old oven can be rested on logs as a campfire stove.

Mushroom knife

Metal cup

Foraging bag

FORAGING FOR FOOD

Searching for food in the wild—or foraging—is perhaps the easiest and most vital link to our ancestral, pre-agricultural, and subsistence farming roots. By noticing what's in season, how animals, fish, and birds migrate, and where food is most varied and abundant, you can begin to understand where nomadic people in the past might have chosen to live as they followed the best sources of available food. Foraging can also better acquaint us with the behavior of the animals—apart from ourselves—that move through woods and forests.

THE MODERN FORAGER

Finding and collecting wild food is having a resurgence in popularity, not only as a way to eat cheaply and healthily, but also to fulfill an increasing desire for a direct connection to the natural world. The range of what's available will vary through the seasons as plants grow, flower, and produce seeds, with spring to late fall the most bountiful time to forage. As well as a way of getting good food for free, the outdoor search for culinary delights provides easy exercise and the chance to explore.

With increasing pressure on the world's remaining wild places, it's important to forage responsibly and learn not just about the edible and useful plants around us but how they fit into the broader plant communities and ecosystems. This involves being observant, asking questions about why certain things grow in certain places, and researching the ecology of your own bioregion.

TIPS FOR LEARNING

» Keep a wild food diary—whenever you're out for a walk, make a note of any edibles that you find, including their location and whether they're in flower. You can plot this on a homemade woodland map—see pages 184–5.

» Keep it simple—learn about the obvious and common plants in your neighborhood; immerse yourself in knowledge about one seasonal plant at a time; use multiple sources of information and absorb any stories or interesting facts about what you forage; find out if there are any dangerous look-alikes; then actually pick, process, and eat your woodland bounty.

FORAGING ETIQUETTE

» Only pick what's common and plentiful, leaving plenty behind to go to seed or spore, and for other animals to eat.

» Foraging should never put at risk the plant or its community by excessive or untimely harvesting.

» Keep it legal—check the national and local rules about picking on public land, or ask permission if you're on private land. Harvesting for personal use is often allowed, but it's likely that a license will be needed if you pick or collect for commercial gain.

» Be aware that there may be different rules on digging for roots and tubers compared with picking parts of plants above ground.

» Picking in protected areas or nature reserves is bad practice, even if not technically prohibited.

STAYING SAFE

Every year, there are news reports of people ending up in the hospital from accidentally eating toxic plants or mushrooms they have picked or had cooked for them. With plants, this often involves species from the Apiaceae (previously called Umbelliferae) family, which includes harmless carrots, parsnips, fennel, dill, and parsley as well as harmful hemlock. Dangerous species can often look very similar to their innocuous family members, so if you're in any doubt, don't touch, let alone eat.

» It's essential to be 100 percent sure that you've correctly identified any wild food before you eat it or offer it to others. There's a wealth of good free food growing in the wild but also plenty of plants that could make you sick—or worse.

» Use multiple sources for identification, cross-check information, and learn from local experts.

» Make sure that the areas you pick from haven't been sprayed with pesticides or herbicides—be particularly careful on field boundaries.

» Don't pick from the roadside, where vehicle fumes could have contaminated any food.

» On path edges, try to pick above the height that dogs urinate.

» Wearing gloves and long sleeves means that you can avoid skin irritation from certain plants.

» When foraging on the coast, check the state of the tides, so that you don't get cut off from dry land.

» When collecting shellfish, check the water quality. Watch especially for algal blooms, which can contaminate filter feeders such as mussels and oysters and cause serious poisoning. Also, only harvest wild shellfish in months with an "R" in the name (in other words, avoid the warm summer months).

» Don't gorge on wild foods that are new to you. Taste a little first, then wait awhile just in case you have an undiagnosed allergy.

WILD FOOD MENU

To get you started, here's a selection of a few easy-to-identify fruits, nuts, seeds, greens, roots, flowers, and fungi with a wide global distribution. Even though they are common—some would say, boring—plants, they all have much to recommend them in terms of taste as well as food value.

» *Stinging nettle* (*Urtica dioca*). You need to pick it with care, but the nettle makes a tasty green to add to soups and stews. The young tips are best harvested early in the growing season. Later in the year, once the nettles have flowered, the time has passed for eating leaves as they start to produce cystoliths (deposits of calcium carbonate), which can impair kidney function. The seeds, however, are good to collect and eat, and they store well for sprinkling on your breakfast cereal throughout the winter.

» *Elder* (*Sambucus nigra*). This woody shrub is a real wonder, with its magical, midsummer display of fragrant flowers, which can be harvested to make the tastiest cordial—or even champagne. Only the flowers and berries are edible, so don't eat the leaves or chew the bark. Some people report sensitivity to elderberry fruit, and it's recommended that you cook the berries before adding to a jam or compote. Oh, and don't forget to ask the elder witches for permission before harvesting.

» *Hazelnuts.* A fine source of protein, hazelnuts (or filberts) can be eaten as they are, or they can be roasted and used to make a nut butter, flour, pesto, or nut loaf. Harvesting can be difficult, since the nuts are also highly appealing to squirrels, who will eat them while still green. If you find a good source, you can pick the nuts green and lay them out in trays in a warm, dark place until ripe and good to eat. Use a nutcracker or a stone to open the nuts; don't be tempted to crack the shells with your teeth.

» *Mint* (*Mentha* species). The abundant aromatic plant, which grows wild in wet or damp soils, adds a sweet, clean, refreshing flavor to many foods and makes great infusions. There are many different species of mint, which can make exact identification tricky. All have a distinct minty smell, but make sure you use at least a couple of other identifying characteristics as well.

» *Burdock* (*Arctium lappa*). Native to much of Europe and Asia, burdock also grows widely in North America. Its starchy, stringy root can be baked whole in the embers of a fire, peeled and chopped into chunks in a stew, or sliced finely to add to a stir fry. Harvesting the long root involves quite a lot of digging, traditionally with a digging stick. Just cut a sturdy straight stick about 24 to 32 inches (60 to 80 centimeters) long, carve one end to a wedge—with one side steeper than the other—and harden over a fire. Kneeling beside a burdock plant, dig a hole next to the stem using a jabbing motion, and work toward where you think the root should be. Expose as much of the root as you can before levering it gently upward from below. Pulling the root is likely to break it. Burdock is a biennial plant—seek it out in late fall, and find plants at the end of their first growing season, which won't have a stalk or the characteristic burrs. These plants will have stored lots of energy in their root to enable the plant to flower the following year—or to be ready for us to eat.

» *Fat hen* (*Chenopodium album* or *Chenopodium berlandieri*). Known by a variety of names, including goosefoot and lamb's-quarter, this vigorous, fast-growing plant is viewed mostly as a weed. To prehistoric people across the northern hemisphere, however, it was an important food, not just foraged but deliberately cultivated for its leaves—to use as a potherb—and seeds, which could be ground into a flour. The plant's close relative quinoa (*Chenopodium quinoa*) was cultivated in South America for its seed and is now a familiar sight on the shelves of whole food stores.

» *Chicken of the woods* (*Laetiporus sulphureus*). This is a very distinctive mushroom that grows on hardwood trees in cool temperate forests. Its bright yellow, wrinkled, overlapping shelves, partway up the trunk, make the fungus relatively easy to identify. It's best cooked in stews and casseroles and is chicken-like more in texture than taste. The fungal food is widely eaten and served in restaurants, but sometimes people have mild allergic reactions. As always, test a small portion first.

» *Blackberry and raspberry* (*Rubus* species). The plants from which these fruits grow are known as brambles, briars, and caneberries, depending on your location. They are widespread, with lots of variation. When you have eaten your fill of the fresh fruit—in season from mid or late summer through to the first frosts—it's time to make all the jam or jelly you can.

SUPER-SIMPLE BLACKBERRY JAM

Once you have foraged a load of blackberries, you could eat them all at once or prolong the pleasure with this easy jam recipe. You will need 2.2 pounds (1 kilogram) blackberries, 30 ounces (850 grams) gelling or jam sugar (with pectin), and the juice of a lemon.

1. In a big glass or ceramic bowl, lay the fruit and sugar in alternate layers, cover, and let sit overnight. This helps the sugar dissolve and will reduce cooking time.
2. Put all the fruit and sugar into a jam pan or heavy, wide-based saucepan, and add the lemon juice.
3. Cook on low heat until the sugar is completely dissolved, then boil for five minutes. To check if the jam has reached a setting point of 220 degrees Fahrenheit (105 degrees Celsius), use a candy thermometer, or put a drop of the hot mixture onto a cold plate and see if it forms a skin that wrinkles when prodded. If the jam isn't ready yet, just keep cooking and check every three minutes.
4. When ready, skim any scum off the top of the pan, let it sit for ten minutes, then pour into warm, sterilized jars.

This jam will keep for at least six months, but you're likely to want to eat it all well before that.

FOREST FISHING

Unless you were initiated as a young person into the dark arts of angling, with its bewildering array of equipment, lore, and specialisms, then it can be pretty hard to grasp the basics. As an adult beginner, there's only one way to go—get out and try it. These few improvised techniques are for catching food when you're desperate and have no other options. They may or may not be legal where you live—before you try anything, check out and follow any local regulations (see "Fishing and the law" below).

» *Handline fishing.* Just pack some fishing line and a selection of hooks. Tie your hook onto the line, attaching a small pebble about 6 inches (15 centimeters) below the hook to act as a weight. Wind the line around your water bottle or a tin can, and cast the baited hook into the river, stream, or pond, using an underarm throw. Keep gentle tension on the line, so you can strike when you feel a fish take the bait.
» *Rounding up.* You can channel fish through a narrow entrance into a shallow pool by making traps, dams, and weirs from sticks or rocks. Once caught in the pool, the fish can be pulled out of the water.
» *Trout tickling or noodling.* This involves finding the spots under overhanging banks where fish can hide and take refuge. The idea is to move really slowly and get your hands underneath the fish's belly, where you can let it get used to the touch before increasing your grip and tossing it out onto the bank.

Making your own hooks from thorns and line from natural cordage (see pages 48–9) is a worthwhile experiment, but you really need to learn about fish habits and behavior to achieve success. You may not catch anything at all, but if you look at each trip as a learning opportunity, then every experience will at least spark your curiosity and lead to questions asked and answers found.

FISHING AND THE LAW

Angling is almost always restricted in some way by national or local legislation. Rules about what species and size of fish can be caught, as well as specific restrictions on methods of catching them, exist for welfare reasons as well as to prevent overfishing and maintain an element of fairness in an activity that many people enjoy. Different regulations may apply to saltwater and freshwater environments. Check to see if you need a landowner's permission, a rod license, or specific equipment to catch particular fish before you head out with your pole and line.

PREPARING FISH

Maybe you've struck it lucky and caught a fish by your own hand. Or perhaps you've bought a whole fresh fish from a store or right off the boat. Either way, you'll need to prepare the creature before cooking it. This is an extremely tactile process, and where to make a cut can be judged by feel as much as by any rules.

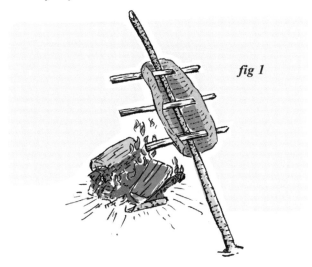

fig 1

1. Scrape the fish from tail to head with the back of a knife on both sides to remove the scales. Watch for any sharp dorsal fin bones as you scrape, then rinse the fish under running water.
2. Make a shallow cut with a sharp knife into the cavity, along the belly of the fish from the vent—usually just in front of the fin closest to the tail—to the base of the skull, under the gills.
3. Remove all the internal organs with one hand. They should come away fairly easily without much mess. Run a thumb down the spine inside the cavity, and if needed, make a quick cut with the knife to remove the final parts.
4. Rinse out the cavity with running water.
5. To remove the head, make a diagonal cut behind each of the head fins, then twist off. To remove the tail, cut through the tail vertebrae, taking care not to waste any of the flesh. Save the head and tail to make a stock for soup.

At this stage, you can simply bake your fish directly on the fire, wrapped in paper, clay, or even seaweed. Another great way to cook a whole fish on the fire is to ponasse it—spread open and grilled on a framework of sticks over the fire (*fig 1*). First, remove the backbone from the gutted, headed, and tailed fish by placing the cavity downward on a board and pressing firmly all along the backbone with the heel of your hand. Turn the fish over, and use both hands to carefully work the spine away from the flesh. Cut some long skewers of fresh wood, then thread them through the width of the fish to spread it out in one flat piece. Make a split in a 3 foot (1.5 metre) long thumb-thick stick a little longer than the length of the fish. Push the fish into the split, and bind the top of the split to hold it all together. Lean the stick over the campfire—one end in the ground, the other supported at an angle of about 45 degrees—until the fish is cooked through.

TRAPPING GAME

Although wild animals have been killed for food since the earliest human days, the practice of catching them can elicit strong emotions. Whatever your ethical position, the physics of traps, the woodcraft involved in making them, and the fieldcraft needed to snare intended prey can make a fascinating study. However, you should only trap an animal if you genuinely need to eat it.

THE DEADFALL TRAP

There are any number of deadfall traps, from the Paiute—named after a Native American tribe—to the Siberian deadfall and split-stick trap, which can snare anything from bears to mice. A deadfall trap uses bait to lure an animal and the weight of a falling stone slab, rock, or heavy log to kill it. The example below of a figure-four deadfall trap requires some practice to make and experimentation to test and vary the sensitivity, but it's ultimately a satisfying achievement when you get it to work.

WHAT YOU WILL NEED
» *two straight sticks, each 8 inches (20 centimeters) long and 0.6 inches (1.5 centimeters) thick*
» *one thinner stick, 0.3 to 0.4 inches (0.8 to 1 centimeter) diameter and about 12 inches (30 centimeters) long—ideally dead and stiff rather than green and flexible*
» *a big flat rock or split piece of heavy hardwood*
» *knife*
» *saw*

1. Whittle one end of one of the thicker sticks to a wedge such as a screwdriver tip. This will be the upright "post" stick (**A**).
2. About 2.5 inches (6 centimeters) from the end of the other thick stick, carve a notch to engage with the top of the post stick. Carve the other end to a wedge. This will be the angled stick (**B**) that holds the heavy rock or log.
3. About 2.5 inches (6 centimeters) from the thicker end of the thinnest (bait) stick (**C**), carve a notch to engage with the wedge at the wedged end of the angled stick.
4. Hold the trap together to figure out where to carve the trigger notch (**D**) on the bait stick. Carve this notch at 90 degrees to the notch at the bait stick end. You need to be quite precise with these angles, or the trap won't hold together when you try and set it.
5. Square off a section of the post stick to catch the trigger notch on the bait stick, and then set the trap with a heavy flat stone or log balancing against the angled stick to keep it in place (**E**). Watch your fingers! It's a good idea to place another rock under the edge of the trap rock to keep it from hitting the ground and squashing your fingers while you're working on it.

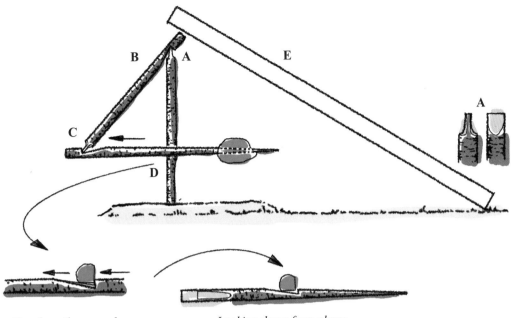

Looking from the ground up   *Looking down from above*

If everything is balanced, you can test the trap by gently nudging the end of the bait stick with a long twig. Place an overripe banana under the rock to see the effect. It should fall at the slightest nudge. If not, you might need to tweak it a little for greater sensitivity. If the rock is too heavy, it can lock the trap together really tightly, in which case, try a slightly lighter rock. In theory, the rock should be around five times the weight of the creature you intend to trap. Scale the rest of the trap to size for different prey.

You'll need to study animal movements and habits to position your trap with the right bait in the right place to be successful. Placing obstacles to funnel the animal into the trap, making it approach from the trigger-sensitive side only, should improve your chances of success. In reality, you might need to make and set a dozen deadfalls at once in different places to actually trap one animal.

IS IT LEGAL TO TRAP OR SNARE?

It depends on where you are. In the United States, the law varies from state to state. In the UK, The Wildlife and Countryside Act and the Wild Mammals (Protection) Act effectively prohibit the use of improvised traps, although some designs of snares are permitted. Other countries require licenses stipulating approved methods. It's not always easy to find a definitive answer to whether homemade traps or snares are allowed by law, so start from the assumption that they aren't until you get authoritative advice to the contrary. Practice on private land, and keep all pets and children well out of the way, so they cannot get injured by accident.

TREE LORE

Trees have always been intimately connected with humans. Their presence provides shelter, food, medicine, and beauty. It's easy to identify with trees and their natural cycles, and—with many of them outliving humans—assign to them meaning and intelligence. This has generated a wealth of legend and lore that has grown up around types of trees and even single specimens.

Dating from the twelfth century, Queen Elizabeth's Oak in Greenwich Park, London, UK, is renowned for the part it played in the childhood of Elizabeth I (1533–1603), at a time when the parkland made up the grounds of the Palace of Placentia, birthplace of her father, King Henry VIII (1491–1547). The young Elizabeth is said to have picnicked under the oak's branches and perhaps in its hollow, and Henry may have danced around it with her mother, Anne Boleyn. Although the tree died in the nineteenth century and was blown over in 1991, it remains as a monument—and a habitat for insects and fungi.

Another legendary English tree is the almost 1,000-year-old Major Oak, located in Sherwood Forest, Nottinghamshire. In this tree, Robin Hood (possibly a real man in the thirteenth century) and his troupe of "merry men" supposedly hid in the forest, planning their philanthropic adventures to take from the rich and give to the poor.

Near Kadiri in southern India, the branches of a spectacular banyan tree (a type of fig) called the Thimmamma Marrimanu covers an area of 5 acres (2 hectares). Legend has it that in 1434 a grief-stricken woman named Thimmamma threw herself on her husband's funeral pyre—considered an act of devotion at the time—and the tree sprang from the ashes. It's said that childless couples who pray beneath its canopy will have a child the next year.

NATIVE SPECIES

In many Native American cultures, birch is an important tree, used in making canoes, maps, boxes, and houses. In Ojibwe (Chippewa) folklore, the birch tree is a sacred gift from Wenabozho, a benevolent cultural hero: It cannot be struck by lightning, so provides good shelter in storms, and the dead are wrapped in its bark for burial.

Cedar is especially sacred to Native peoples who use it, employed in sweat lodge ceremonies and other rituals, where it's connected with prayers, healing, protection against illness, and dreams. The Lakota Sioux believe that burning flat cedar purifies a space and removes adverse influences, ushering in more positive spirits.

TREE HUMANIZATION

Due in part to their extreme longevity, trees are imbued with souls in many cultures; in some, people also believe that the souls of their ancestors reside in trees. Australian Aborigine groups believe that humans pass through many incarnations before they are reborn as their own ancestors, and during the interim state, their spirit may lodge in certain trees. Native Papuans hang strips of red or white cloth among the tree branches—always in multiples of seven—where they believe their ancestors' spirits live. Since ancient times, the Chinese have planted pine and cypress trees on graves—this is believed to strengthen the deceased souls in the afterlife.

In the mythology of some cultures, trees can feel pain and also be subject to curses—the same as humans. A Nubian legend from North Africa tells of a warrior who looked at a colossal tree with the evil eye; afterward, the tree crashed down and died. In Irish folklore, if a person confides their dream to a tree, its leaves will wither and fall: This is because dreams were believed to come from the devil. Some trees are thought to be evil themselves while still subject to veneration. In the old forests of Roman Catholic Europe, crucifixes were hung from tree branches considered infested by demons, although the very act of placing holy symbols on them symbolized their inherent worth.

PLUCKING A BIRD

From quails to turkeys, pigeons to pheasants, and ducks to geese, there are plenty of wild birds that will provide a good campfire meal. If you're unable to hunt wildfowl or other birds yourself, you can often source birds from a game dealer or ask—very nicely—someone who shoots if they might get some for you. We're not in the supermarket here, where birds are presented "oven-ready." You'll have to deal with feathers, bone, and all the rest—but the reward is taste on a completely different level.

KEEPING IT BASIC

When there's an abundance of pheasants from winter shoots, it's rarely worth plucking a whole bird. Once a bird has hung long enough to suit your taste, just cut through the skin—with feathers still on—down the breastbone, and fillet the breast meat from either side of the bone. To remove the legs, cut off the feet and lower leg with bone-notched kitchen scissors (or pruning sheers), then work your fingers behind the knee and pull away from the skin. Cut through the flesh at the top of the thigh until you can see the joint in the leg bones, which you can then pull free. Cut off any yellow fat, wash the meat, and then cook as desired.

THE FULL PREPARATION

If presentation matters and you want to serve that perfect roast pheasant, then you'll need to pluck the feathers out without tearing the skin. Work standing over a trash can—feathers flying everywhere can make quite a mess.

1. Begin with the long tail feathers, and pull each one out straight, away from the bird. Do these one at a time, then repeat for the long feathers on each wing.
3. Start on the middle of the bird's back, pulling feathers out a few at a time, with short, sharp tugs, toward the neck—against the grain.
4. Turn the bird over, and work on the breast. Hold the skin down with one hand to keep it tight, and pull a few feathers at a time from the tail, toward the head. Don't rush things by plucking too many feathers at once since it's easy to tear the skin.
5. Pluck the legs next. Make sure that the area around the knees is plucked well before you cut off the meatless feet and lower legs.
6. Pluck the wings, and then remove the end of each wing at the first joint by cutting through the skin, bending the bones back, and then snipping the tendons.
7. Find the crop full of grain at the base of the neck, and gently pull it toward the head before cutting through the neck, close to the breasts.
8. To remove the innards, make a small cut at the rear end of the bird, so you can reach inside with two fingers under the bottom of the breasts and scoop out all the internal organs. You may want to keep the heart and liver for pâté or stock.

Once the innards and head have been removed, slow simmer any discarded remains of the carcass with onion, garlic, and herbs to make a fantastic stock. Any uneaten scraps should be buried a good distance from the camp.

SMOKING AND CURING

Long before freezers and vacuum packing arrived on the scene, smoking and curing were important ways to keep food from going bad and to ensure supplies for hard times. Bacteria that spoil food thrive in moisture and heat, particularly in the warmer months, when you can't easily control temperature. Salting, drying, and smoking, however, create conditions that arrest spoilage, prevent food poisoning, and add delicious and intriguing layers of food flavors.

THE MAGIC OF SMOKE

A perfect introduction to the culinary tradition of food smoking is to create your own campfire smoker—see pages 154–5. But first, it's a good idea to grasp some of the principles of smoking, so you can either follow a recipe or learn to improvise.

» Most meat, fish, cheese, and vegetables can be smoked to add flavor and extend shelf life. Different types of wood—such as chips from hickory, apple, oak, or beech—provide distinctive tastes and smells. Woodsmoke deposited on the surface of foods also contains chemicals that increase acidity and stop the growth of harmful microbes.

» The process of smoking over a campfire is pretty simple, involving just a constant supply of smoke over the meat or other food, at a temperature of at least 122 degrees Fahrenheit (50 degrees Celsius)—and ideally, not more than 194 degrees Fahrenheit (90 degrees Celsius). That will dry and slowly cook the food. Cold smoking at lower temperatures of 68 to 86 degrees Fahrenheit (20 to 30 degrees Celsius) only affects the surface of the food, which will then still need to be cooked.

» Smoking food is a sensory and instinctive process that rewards practice. Be patient and don't rush things. If you're familiar with the store-bought product, then wait until your own smoked food looks and feels similar. Try and cut thin slices of meat to maximize its surface area and make it easier to check that the food is thoroughly cooked.

WORTH ITS SALT

Curing involves the introduction of salt to food, either as a liquid brine, a dry rub, or an added ingredient in cured sausage recipes, for example. Salt helps to dehydrate meat or fish, allowing the food to keep for a long time. It can take 55 pounds (25 kilograms) of salt to dry-cure a whole leg of pork in a saltbox, whereas something like salami or pepperoni requires a smaller, more precise measure—perhaps around 2.5 percent of salt by weight of the food.

CAMPFIRE COOKING

Whether you're lighting a quick fire in a survival situation (see pages 44–5) or building a fireplace for your fixed camp (see pages 152–3), it's highly likely that you're going to use it to cook up a tasty hot meal. Managing the fire to provide the heat needed for the duration of cooking is a challenge that also comes with opportunities to add flavor to your food that you'll never get on a gas or electric stove in your home kitchen.

» For hot flames to boil a pot of water or to maintain the heat for frying, keep a good supply of medium-sized kindling to hand, so you can keep feeding the fire to maintain the same flame size for as long as you need.
» If baking, broiling, or roasting directly over the fire, avoid cooking over flames since they will either burn the outside of the food too quickly or cover it with an unpleasant layer of soot. A bed of hot, glowing embers is much better but requires a little advance planning. Burn lumps of dry, dense hardwood such as oak or beech until the flames die down, which will leave you with glowing coals—ideal for cooking.
» For longer baking, you'll need to resupply the fire with fresh coals. In this case, it helps to have a longer rectangular fire with new fuel added at one end and the cooking taking place over coals at the other. You can rake new hot coals to the cooking end to keep an even heat going—or scoop some up to put on the top of a closed pot or a Dutch oven—a heavy, lidded, cast-iron cooking pot (see pages 68–9)—to provide additional heat from above.
» Baking without utensils is really easy and a handy technique to practice. This works best on a well-established campfire that's been on the go for a few days and has a deep bed of fine, dry ash. Bury single items such as flatbreads or foraged roots in hot ash at the edge of the fire, and then place a few hot coals over them. Use a pair of tongs (see page 165) to remove the food when ready, then

KEEPING IT CLEAN
Food poisoning is a risk you really don't want to take, especially in remote areas, so make sure that food is prepared with clean hands and utensils on a clean surface, preferably off the ground. Find out how to make a fresh, clean cutting board on page 164. Several bacteria that cause intestinal upsets are commonly found in soil, so outdoors, there's no five-second rule, where you can pick up dropped food and eat it! If you're preparing high-risk foods, especially for others, make sure that they are cooked as thoroughly as you would cook them at home.

just blow the ash off and eat. Although it's instinctive to think of this as dirty, the ash has been sterilized at hundreds of degrees and is perfectly clean. Timings can be tricky, but with practice, the results can be stunning—with the added bonus of no dish washing.

» How hot is hot enough? There's no temperature gauge on a campfire, but luckily, the nerve endings in your skin will do a good enough job at approximating heat levels. Hold the back of your hand around 8 inches (20 centimeters) above the cooking area. If you can keep your hand there for five seconds, the temperature is approximately 300 degrees Fahrenheit (150 degrees Celsius); three seconds equates to roughly 400 degrees Fahrenheit (200 degrees Celsius); and if you can only manage one second, then the fire is really hot and probably more than 575 degrees Fahrenheit (300 degrees Celsius). To adjust the heat, just raise or lower the height of the pot or pan above the fire. Getting the temperature right is a knack that you'll acquire with experience.

» As you experiment with campfire cooking, you might want to hang pots from a tripod, place a long grill over the fire, use a pot stand or trivet, make a smoker, or just rest a Dutch oven on the embers. You could simply wrap food in aluminum foil and place it on the embers, but this is wasteful—even if the foil is recycled—especially when there are so many other fun and intriguing ways to cook on the fire.

PIT COOKING

The great impression of a pit-cooked meal, when the lids are removed and the feast is seen for the first time by the assembled company, makes this type of outdoor cooking a real hit for celebrations and special occasions. Pit-cooking traditions have existed for thousands of years on every continent where humans live, from the *tandir* or *tandoor* of the Middle East, central Asia, and India to the *imu* or *umu* of Polynesian island cultures and variations across North and South America, Europe, and Africa.

Pit cooking is basically a way of slowly baking or roasting—meat, fish, and also vegetables—in an oven that's preheated and insulated to allow food to cook using radiant heat from the sides of the pit rather than directly over hot embers. The method works well where the ground is fairly dry but not if the soil is deep and damp, since much of the heat is lost in drying out the earth. Alternative aboveground ovens include a dome of rocks or even a clay package placed on an open bed of hot coals. You should never try pit cooking in peat soils because the fire can slow-burn underground for months and cause wildfires.

MAKING A PIT OVEN

This will be a rewarding journey of discovery. Repeated testing will help you fine-tune the process for your location and your favorite recipes, but the general instructions below should help you make a start.

WHAT YOU WILL NEED

» *spade or shovel*
» *rocks, but not from a river or the sea: They may explode when heated (see page 153)*
» *dry wood for fuel*
» *firelighting materials*
» *big, nontoxic leaves—such as palm or burdock—parchment paper and newspaper, hessian sack, or clay to make packages*
» *patience . . .*

1. Dig a hole. It needs to be about 12 inches (30 centimeters) bigger—on all sides—than what you intend to cook. A hole around 3 feet (1 meter) square and 1.5 feet (0.5 meters) deep should be about right for a big family meal. Keep the soil from the hole—you'll need it again in step 6.
2. Line the hole with large rocks, stones, or bricks if available—or even a really large, broken up terracotta flowerpot. If you don't have these on hand, don't worry, just go ahead and see what happens.

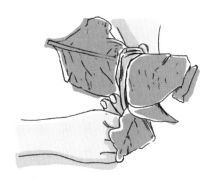

fig 1   fig 2

3. Use the instructions on pages 44–5 to light a decent-sized fire in the pit (*fig 1*). Keep feeding it, and let it burn for a few hours until the walls of the pit are hot and there's about 12 inches (30 centimeters) depth of really hot coals at the pit base.

4. Wrap your meat in parchment paper (scrunch it under running water to make it better conform to the shape of the packet), then wrap the packet in wet newspaper or large, thick, nontoxic leaves (*fig 2*). A joint of meat can also be wrapped in thick pastry dough to protect it from direct heat and preserve its moisture. You could wrap it in foil, but it's much more interesting and environmentally friendly to use alternatives.

5. Place the wrapped food packets on top of the hot embers. You could cover the coals first with some thumb-thick branches of wet wood, such as apple or hickory, to add a smoky flavor to the meal.

6. Cover the pit with branches, a wooden board, or aluminum sheet, then again with a wet blanket before covering with the soil from inside the hole. This will not only insulate the oven but reduce the oxygen supply and keep the meal from combusting.

7. Remove the layers over the pit, and carefully retrieve the food packets. Timing is a judgement call, since there are so many variables that can affect the heat in the oven. Try a time one-third longer than you would use in a conventional oven, and then check to make sure that everything is cooked thoroughly. A large joint of meat could slow-cook overnight and be ready for lunch the next day. Smaller portions may only take two or three hours. Finally, before eating, double-check that the food is thoroughly cooked—you don't want to give your companions food poisoning! Serve the feast to your guests, and enjoy.

A WOODLAND COOKBOOK

Cooking in the wild is a sensory adventure of taste, smell, and guesswork that's incomparable to making food in a home kitchen. The journey is endless, and as you encounter new recipes, you'll increasingly ask the question "How could I do this over the fire?" The only way to answer that is to gather the ingredients, light that fire, and try it.

These recipes make use of a mixture of foraged, homegrown, and store-bought ingredients. They are chosen for their interesting cooking methods and novelty, as well as for flavor.

BAKING BREADS

The classic damper or stick bread is just a twist of dough on the end of a stick, which is held over the fire until golden brown. Add sugar, cinnamon, honey, or jam to make an excellent snack or dessert. Bread can be baked in stone-lined pits (see pages 84–5), tin cans, or a Dutch oven (see opposite), in the ash of the fire or—as flatbread—directly on hot coals. But how about baking a loaf in a flowerpot?

Flowerpot loaf
1. Season (with several coats of vegetable oil) the inside of a clean, unglazed 5 to 6 inch (12 to 15 centimeter) diameter terra-cotta flowerpot and a clay drip tray big enough to cover the top.
2. Mix and knead your favorite bread dough.
3. Cover the hole in the base of the pot with a piece of broken flowerpot, then fill the flowerpot half full of dough and let it prove near the fire for twenty minutes.
4. Put the clay lid on, and set it in the embers of your fire. You can add a few coals on top of the lid to help provide even heat all around. Timing is by guesstimate and depends on the volume of the pot. Try the same time as you would choose to bake something in the oven, then check the bread. With practice, you'll get more and more accurate as you adjust timing and fuel supply to get the perfect results.

BROILING AND ROASTING

Small pieces work best. A whole chicken on a spit might look great, but the risk of getting sick from uncooked meat isn't worth the social media photo opportunity. A campfire feast is a special occasion, so it's worth splashing out on quality ingredients, such as a good cut of steak. Get a bed of coals really hot, place a clean grill over them, and cook the well-seasoned meat hot and fast, so that it's seared and smoky on the outside and tender and pink in the middle. Serve with a simple salad of foraged local greens.

SMOKING

To make the most of the smoky flavors that campfire cooking can produce, try this smoked eggplant and garlic Lebanese appetizer.

Baba ghanoush
1. Slice two eggplants in half lengthwise, and chop a bulb of garlic in half sideways, exposing the center of each clove.
2. Roast the garlic on a grill over a smoky fire, until the cloves have shriveled and charred slightly.
3. Set the eggplants flesh side down on the hot coals, until the flesh is soft and can be scooped out into a bowl.
4. Peel and mash the half garlic cloves with the back of a fork, and add to the eggplant flesh.
5. Add 2 tablespoons of good olive oil, and if you like the taste, 1 tablespoon of tahini. Season with salt and pepper, and enjoy with chunks of your flowerpot bread.

POT ROASTS

With its ridged lid to hold hot embers on top, a heavy cast-iron Dutch oven is ideal for pot roasting. Campfire baked beans are a one-pot meal that can either be made the old way with bacon and sausage, or without for a hearty vegan feast. This classic has a few basic ingredients that can then be added to and experimented with. Try using coffee as the liquid, adding chopped salami or chorizo, sweet potato, cilantro, and cumin seeds—or chilies, if you like it hot. The quantities given here are for a main meal for six hungry adults.

Bean feast
1. Heat some oil in the Dutch oven pot, and fry two chopped onions, a few cloves of chopped garlic, and about 1 pound (500 grams) of bacon cubes for a few minutes.
2. Add 2 tablespoons of dark sugar and 2 tablespoons of tomato paste to the pot. Stir and cook for another couple of minutes.
3. Add 2 pounds (1 kilogram) of soaked (or canned) cannellini, pinto, or kidney beans (a blend is good) and about 1 pound (500 grams) of chopped tomatoes. Add just enough water to cover.
4. Let the pot simmer until the beans are soft, or bake them by placing the Dutch oven on the embers, placing the heavy lid on top, and letting the beans bake without stirring or removing the lid for at least an hour. Add hot embers to the lid of the oven to create even heat for baking.

FOREST BEVERAGES

Y̧ou won't get a deep, rich, Italian espresso with a mighty caffeine kick in the wild, but woodland coffee substitutes can be comforting hot drinks on a winter's day by the fire. If tea is your favored tipple, then the woods are full of plant leaves and flowers that, steeped in boiling water, make refreshing and revitalizing brews. Sometimes called herbal infusions or tisanes, they are more commonly referred to as "teas," although their tastes and properties differ from the actual tea plant, *Camellia sinensis*. The teas below have been chosen for availability and flavor rather than specifically for their health benefits, of which there are many. They should generally be brewed with water at about 176 degrees Fahrenheit (80 degrees Celsius).

COFFEES

» *Dandelion root "coffee."* Pick at least fifteen long dandelion roots—but be prepared for some vigorous digging in heavy soils. Wash them and cut off all the thin, straggly pieces. Chop the roots into chunks as you would with a carrot, spread them out on a metal sheet, and roast slowly in the oven or over a campfire until well toasted but not charred. There's no need to grind the roots—just boil a couple of tablespoons of them in a mugful of water for ten minutes before straining into a cup.

» Another coffee substitute—though more of an acquired taste—can be made from acorns. They need to be boiled repeatedly first in several changes of water to reduce bitterness, before peeling, drying, grinding, or chopping and then gently roasting.

TEAS

» *Lime.* Not the citrus fruit but the whole flowers of the lime or linden tree (*Tilia* species), which can be collected in midsummer, dried slowly in a dark place, and then stored throughout the winter. Lime tea is said to be a mild sedative, so just brew between three and ten blossoms per cup.

» *Mint.* There are many different wild and garden mint varieties (*Mentha* species), which can all be harvested and used fresh or dried to make teas. Mints like damp ground, have square stems, opposite leaves, and an extremely distinctive smell.

» *Spruce, pine, or fir needles.* All conifers with needles have the potential to make really varied teas. Collect fresh green needles, and chop them into small pieces to brew. The needles can also make a cold infusion or sun tea—left in a glass in a sunny place to infuse rather than steep in hot water.

» *Nettle.* The saying "nettle tea makes you pee" refers to the slight diuretic properties of the common nettle (*Urtica dioca*), although this isn't really an issue with young leaves from the top of the plant collected in the spring. There are many good reasons to embrace drinking nettle tea, from its high levels of antioxidants to its ability to help alleviate seasonal allergies. Nettles should not be used during flowering or after the plant has flowered.

» *Pineapple weed.* A plant found around field entrances and path edges, pineapple weed (*Matricaria discoidea*) is related to chamomile and in some places is even known as "wild chamomile." It has yellow-green petalless flower heads, which have a distinctive pineapple smell when crushed. The flower heads are best brewed fresh but can also be dried and stored.

8 inches
(20 centimetres)

fig 1

HOW TO MAKE IVAN CHAI

This caffeine-free tea was once commonly drunk across Europe, produced in great quantities in the town of Koporye near St. Petersburg in Russia—hence the name "Ivan." The tea is made from the leaves of fireweed or rosebay willowherb or (*Chamaenerion angustifolium*), a tall annual plant with a purple spike of flowers and veined, willowlike leaves that spiral up the stalk. The plant is a ruderal, meaning that it likes to grow on disturbed ground, so look for it on the edges of fields, tracks, and land that has fallen into disuse. Collect the leaves before or during flowering but not once the plant sets seed.

1. Strip the leaves from the stalk from about 8 inches (20 centimeters) below the flower (*fig 1*). Pick through and discard any small stalks from side branches.
2. Wilt the leaves in a plastic bag in the sun for several hours.
3. Scrunch and roll small bunches of the wilted leaves between your palms until they turn dark and feel damp—and smell like cut grass. You can also do this by kneading the leaves in a basin.
4. Place the pile of scrunched leaves on a cutting board. Roughly chop the leaves, then put them in a ceramic or glass bowl.
5. Compress the leaves with a plate, cover with a damp dish towel, and allow to ferment at room temperature. The leaves are ready when they have a sweet, fruity smell with a hint of honey. This can take between 24 and 48 hours, depending on temperature.
6. Heat the leaves to stop fermentation. Lay them out in a thin layer on a sheet, and place in an oven at a low temperature for 1 to 2 hours or until they are dark and dry like tea leaves. Alternatively, dry the leaves on cardboard sheets in hot sunshine. When you're sure the leaves are totally dry, you can store them in airtight jars.
7. Brew some leaves in a teapot as you would with loose-leaf tea, and strain into cups for a reviving and—some say—energy-giving drink.

In the Grimm Brothers fairy tale "Hansel and Gretel," the first time the brother and sister of the title were abandoned deep in the woods by the woodcutter and his wife, they cleverly laid a trail of white pebbles to mark the way home. The next time, they were taken even deeper into the forest and left a useless scattering of breadcrumbs. If only Hansel and Gretel had known other ways to navigate in the woods, the cannibalistic witch-in-the-gingerbread-house episode could have been avoided! No one likes to get lost, so read on for help in finding your way through the forest, day or night, on or off course, with a map, or simply by looking at sun, stars, trees, and animal signs.

A navigator's tools can appear intimidating to the uninitiated. Charts, sextants, maps, and compasses all carry a certain mystique, but with the right skills—and following simple principles, tips, and clues—you can demystify the "dark arts" of navigation and grow in confidence as you get to know exactly where you are, where you're going, and the routes you need to follow.

Sometimes there's a good case for just leaving the map at home. If you have no particular agenda or place to be, it can be liberating to just meander and allow yourself to be drawn toward whatever attracts your attention. If the weather is clear, visibility is good, and you're in an area with few natural hazards, then drifting around the woods will give you a different perspective to when you're focused on a destination and finding it with navigational aids.

The confidence to wander is best built on the foundation of solid, well-practiced navigational skills and an ability to read the land as well as a map. Seeing not just what's there but also learning the stories of how the land came to be shaped by rivers, glaciers, volcanoes, wind, and rain will enrich your outdoor experience and your feeling of being part of—rather than apart from—nature.

4

NAVIGATION

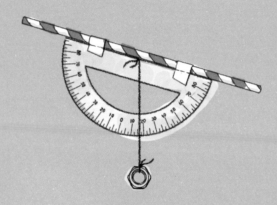

ESSENTIAL
EQUIPMENT

Most of us are likely to have some familiarity with maps and possibly a compass, but an increasing number of people would struggle to navigate without a smartphone or GPS. For that reason, digital devices are included here as essential tools, although the importance of learning to read a paper map can't be emphasized enough, especially if you're venturing any distance from roads and buildings or cell phone coverage.

Map reading isn't just an important skill for when your battery dies or there isn't a signal. Maps tell stories, they allow you to look ahead, see the landscape at a glance, and help you to make new plans when things change. They can be waterproof and written on, and they are easy for you and others to gather around and discuss routes. You can even sit on them. A map may be the best souvenir of a trip away from home, and you can lend it to friends to share the same trip with them. Maps on handheld devices can be used in a similar way, but they lack the permanence and security of a hard copy.

TRADITIONAL MAPS
There are many types of maps, showing different elements, such as weather, geology, political boundaries, and distribution of animal species. The type you need for navigation is a topographical map, which marks physical features, such as hills and rivers, as well as things like land use, buildings, tracks, and boundary markers. For a broad overview of an area, you can use a large-scale map (1:50,000 or 1:100,000 scale). This is more useful for trip planning than navigating on the ground. A 1:24,000 scale map (1 inch on paper equals 24,000 inches or 2,000 feet on the land) is detailed enough to take bearings from and allows you to navigate to small features. The style, scale, and units used will vary from country to country, but if you're used to reading maps, you should adjust easily to shaded contours or U.S. customary units to metric differences. You'll learn how to use your map to navigate on pages 94–5.

MAP APPS AND MORE
Digital maps on handheld devices are available free or on subscription. The OpenStreetMap project is free to use, open-source (free to modify), and community supported. Many cell phone apps use OpenStreetMap data, and maps can be downloaded to your device for offline use. They can also be customized and printed if you have access to a large-format printer at a print store or an office.

Navigation apps can give turn-by-turn directions and often voice guidance. Digital map editors allow you to add to and edit a map directly, and some can even overlay map data onto the view from your phone camera to augment reality with place names and spot heights. Not essential but nice to have are route-recording apps, which can plot where you've been, the time taken, and heights climbed and descended, and act as a memento of your trip, a training aid, or a way to share your particular journey with others.

There are even phone apps that show maps of the stars. Alternatively, a star map printed on a bandanna serves multiple functions and might just help you out one day when your phone isn't working.

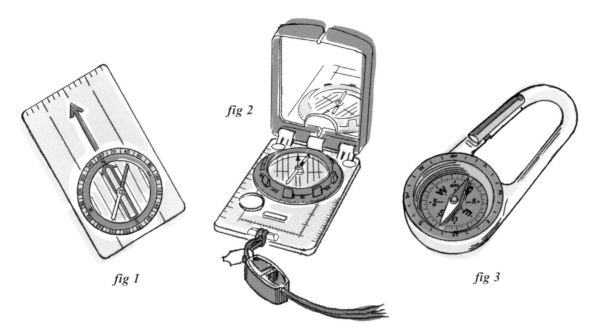

fig 2

fig 1

fig 3

COMPASSES

Aside from the GPS compass app on a phone or dedicated device, there are three main types of compass for outdoor activities on the land.

1. The most common is the baseplate, orienteering-style compass (*fig 1*). It has a rotating dial around the rim, which can be moved to align with map grids and take bearings to the nearest degree (see pages 96–7).
2. Sighting compasses have a lid with a little window and open at 90 degrees to the baseplate (*fig 2*). These are awkward to use properly but can be really accurate in skilled hands.
3. Small key fob or carabiner clip compasses show the cardinal directions and might be useful for a quick check of general direction (*fig 3*). Really cheap ones might not be all that accurate.

EXTRA EQUIPMENT

See-through waterproof cases with neck straps will keep your maps dry, but they can be bulky and cumbersome. The cheap and cheerful alternative is to use a large, clear ziplock freezer bag or buy waterproof maps coated in plastic or printed on material that doesn't rip or dissolve when wet.

Pace beads—a set of thirteen beads strung onto a cord—are a simple navigational aid that allow you to keep track of how many paces you've walked and estimate how far you've traveled. Each set of beads is divided by knots into two—nine beads to measure each 100 yards walked (roughly 100 paces) and four to measure each 1,000 yards. You can easily attach them to a map case or backpack strap to use.

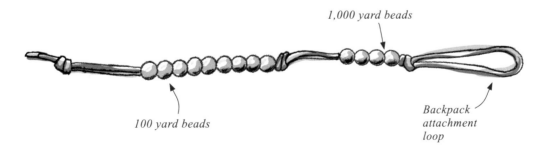

1,000 yard beads

100 yard beads

Backpack attachment loop

MAP READING

Successfully using a map to navigate when you're out and about is as much about reading the land as reading the map. Maps aren't an objective, value-free record of a landscape. Their content was chosen by mapmakers who put their preferences, aesthetic taste, and even political views into their documentation of topography. What's highlighted and—perhaps even more interestingly—what's omitted can reveal much about who made the map and why.

Try and see the big picture by putting a paper map on the floor and standing up to look at it. If you wear glasses, take them off or just squint your eyes, so that the map is out of focus. Don't get sucked into the details, but instead ask yourself what big patterns you can see. Is there a big, featureless blue section? Can you see patches of green or gray? The map's legend will tell you what land use each color represents, as well as the symbols that represent specific features. Only when you have got the overall picture of this landscape should you sit down, put your glasses back on, and take in some of the detail.

WHERE AM I?

Maps with a superimposed grid make it easy to pinpoint a location using a set of numbers or coordinates called a grid reference—in exactly the same way that you would plot a point on a graph. In a crisis, this feature might be vital for directing emergency services.

Can you find the spot where you're staying or plan to start a walk?
1. Locate the place on the map for which you want a grid reference.
2. Find the bottom left corner of the grid square containing the location (*fig 1*).
3. Look along the top or bottom of the map sheet to find the two-digit number for the vertical line that runs through this corner (here, 54). Make a note of it.
4. Do the same for the horizontal line that makes up the bottom of the square (here, 66), and write it after the first number.

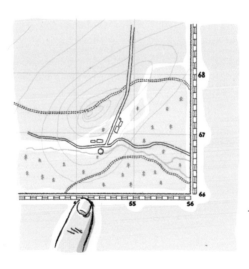

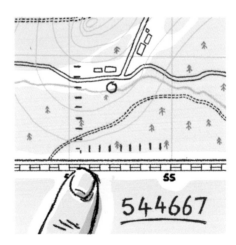

fig 1   fig 2

5. This four-figure number (here, 5466) uniquely describes that map square, and anyone else with the same map sheet will be able to find the square for which you've given the grid reference.
6. Depending on the scale of the map, the four-figure grid reference may well describe a whole mile square and won't be particularly useful for finding specific features. For much finer detail, you can subdivide each large square into 100 smaller squares and use the same principle of reading up and across to create a six-figure grid reference—here, 544667 (*fig 2*). Remember to start counting from the bottom left of the grid square that the feature is in. Use a series of six-figure grid references to describe a route in advance to let others know where you're planning to walk.

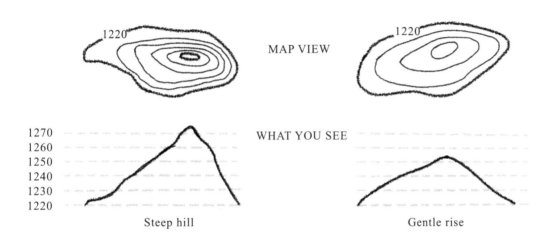

MAP VIEW

WHAT YOU SEE

1270
1260
1250
1240
1230
1220

Steep hill   Gentle rise

UPHILL OR DOWNHILL?

Conventions for showing height on maps vary from country to country, but the most common way of indicating the altitude and shape of the land is with contour lines. These thin lines are drawn on the map, joining points at the same height above sea level. There's usually a fixed height gap between contour lines. You'll find what this gap is in the map's legend. Shaded mountain maps are usually lit from the top left, or northwest, even though on most of our planet's surface this never happens.

» A hill or mountain will look like a nest of concentric lines. The closer the lines are together, the steeper the slope (see above). Take care not to confuse a hill with a pit or crater. To determine which, you need to look at the numbers on the contour lines or a spot height in the center of the feature. If the smaller circles have higher numbers than the larger circles, then you're looking at a hill not a hole.
» Ridges and valleys are more easily confused, but the clue to differentiating between them again involves looking at the actual height numbers on the contour lines.

All this may come naturally, or it may take practice. Using a map and compass when you don't actually need them will build confidence and help you relate the real world to how it looks on paper.

USING
A COMPASS

I f you can read a map, visibility is good, and you can see landscape features around you, then your compass will get very little use. In poor visibility or a featureless landscape, however, it's vital that you carry this small but ingenious piece of equipment and know how to use it.

ORIENTING OR "SETTING" YOUR MAP

If your map has grid lines, set your compass dial so that the printed arrow is parallel with the straight edge. Place the compass over the map, align the straight edge with a grid line, and rotate the map until the printed arrow and red compass needle meet. Your map is now oriented with the physical world. It's good to keep your map oriented north so you can refer to features in the landscape and see them in the right place on the map. If you're walking south, then the text on the map will be upside down, but the features will be in the right place relative to your viewpoint.

NAVIGATING TO A SPECIFIC PLACE

You won't often want to travel in exactly the direction of one of the compass cardinal points. For this reason, the compass dial is marked into 360 degrees, and you can use this feature to take a bearing from the map and then walk on that bearing, using the compass to accurately navigate to a specific location.

1. If you're at point A and want to walk to point B, first place your map on a flat, horizontal surface. As you look at the map, north should be at the top of the sheet.
2. Place the long straight edge of your compass on the map between A and B, with the printed arrow on the baseplate pointing in the direction that you want to travel from one to the other. Ignore the compass needle at this stage.
3. Turn the compass housing (the raised circular part), so that the lines within it are parallel to the north–south lines on the map below and the printed red arrow is pointing north (*fig 1*). Keep ignoring the needle.
4. Check the map legend to see how many degrees difference there are between grid north and magnetic north (*fig 2*). Turn the housing by the appropriate amount to add or subtract these to your bearing, depending on whether the variation is east or west.
5. Read off the number of degrees at the black index line on the compass housing (*fig 3*). This is your bearing.
6. Take the compass off the map, and turn it until the red end of the needle is over the printed red arrow inside the housing.
7. Look along the compass, and keeping the north needle steady over the printed red arrow, choose a landmark on that line to walk to (*fig 4*). Don't choose a sheep or cow as your landmark—it's a surefire way to get very lost! Keep the distance between landmarks short so you can continue checking the bearing and avoid veering off. It's better to walk to a landmark than try and keep looking at the compass as you walk, especially on rough, uneven ground.

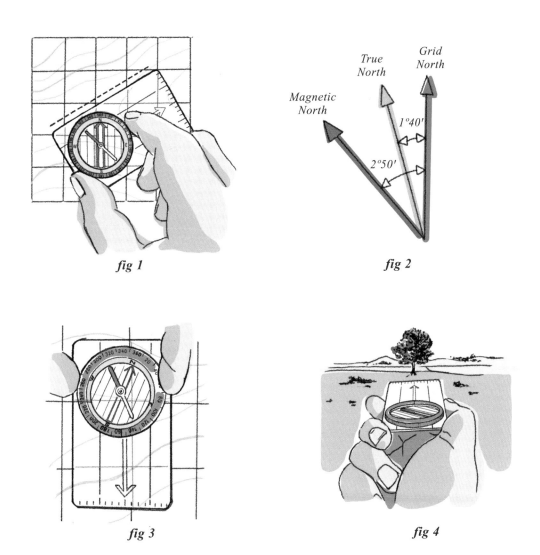

fig 1

fig 2

fig 3

fig 4

In foggy weather or on featureless terrain, stay in one place with the compass, and send a companion a short distance to act as the landmark. Signal to them to move left or right to stay on your line. Walk to them, and repeat the process. This is a laborious but safe way to stay on the right bearing and not get lost.

THINGS THAT YOU DON'T NEED TO KNOW BUT ARE QUITE INTERESTING

Compasses work on the basis that they have a needle that aligns north–south with Earth's magnetic field. Earth spins on an axis that's more or less fixed—in human timescales, at least. However, magnetic north and south are always on the move. The magnetic North Pole is currently in Canada, about 310 miles (500 kilometres) away from the true North Pole, and is estimated to be moving 6 to 25 miles (10 to 40 kilometres) per year. Every few hundred thousand years, Earth's polarity is reversed. This sounds catastrophic, but it would take a few thousand years to complete and wouldn't have too much impact apart from messing around with our compasses!

ORIENTEERING
SKILLS

Originating in Sweden at the end of the nineteenth century as a form of military training, orienteering is an international competitive sport that involves navigating between checkpoints, called controls, as quickly as possible using a map and compass. The combination of map reading, route planning, physical fitness, and experiencing varied terrain makes orienteering a sport with plenty of skills that can be transferred to personal adventures in the woods and beyond. Some forests have established permanent courses with downloadable maps that anyone can try out at any time. To get started in competitive events, it's a good idea to join an orienteering club and learn from experienced participants.

There are many techniques involved in using the map and compass to move quickly through the landscape. Finding the balance between fast motion and accurate navigation is the key to success. Setting the map (see page 96) is extremely important, so that you can relate the image on paper to the landscape directly in front of you. In essence, the map stays in the same orientation, and you move around it as you change direction.

SMART NAVIGATION
Success in orienteering isn't always about running as fast as you can along the most direct route between destination points, known as "controls." It's also about moving more efficiently over easier ground. Using some of the following techniques should reduce the chance of navigational mistakes.

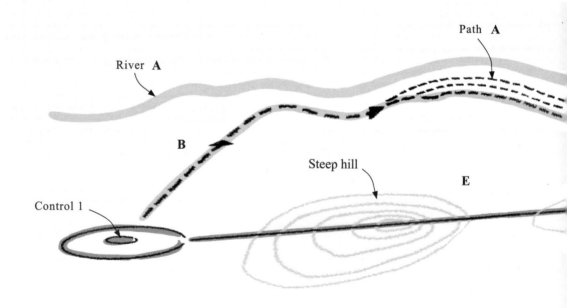

» When you're learning to navigate, following "handrails"—straight-line features that help you get from A to B, such as paths and rivers (**A**), but also fences, banks, and walls—can be very reassuring. Move off course (**B**) to follow one, and then leave the security of the handrail when you get close to the control (**C**).

» Watch for "catching" features—big, obvious things, such as a road, hedge, or church steeple—just beyond the control you want to get to (**D**). Reaching one will let you know that you've gone too far. You can then turn and navigate carefully for a short distance until you find the exact spot of the control.

» Deliberately navigating to one side or the other of the control, using handrails and catching features, is known as "aiming off." This technique is useful if you want to avoid difficult terrain, such as a series of steep hills (**E**), that lies between two controls.

» Judge distances by pacing. To do this, you need to have already figured out how many strides you take in covering 100 yards (91 meters) on flat ground. Measure out 100 yards (91 meters) on even, level ground, such as a sports field, and walk it, counting each time your leading foot touches the surface. This number will be your reference for how many steps you take on flat ground when actually navigating. You can then make adjustments for going uphill or downhill and for moving at different speeds.

» Rather than travel a long way on a single bearing (see pages 96–7), pick several clear features along the way to make shorter legs, each with its own bearing. Even if you have to zigzag a little, this can be quicker and more accurate than trying to stick to a straight-line bearing over a long distance.

» If your control is in a bland, featureless area, chose an "attack point"—an easily identifiable feature that's relatively close to your control, from which you can take an accurate bearing.

All these techniques can be applied to general navigation. They are good fun to practice and will hone your skills with map and compass.

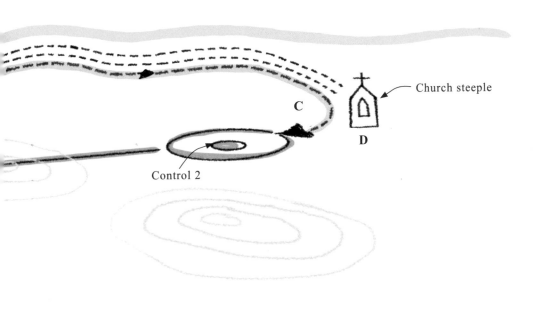

C

Church steeple

D

Control 2

CLUES IN THE TREES

Looking for natural patterns in trees and woodland and learning how to explain them will help you develop an awareness of the main factors that affect tree growth—sunlight, moisture, wind, slope, soils, and the grazing of herbivores. Of these, sunlight and weather conditions are particularly directional, and the way that they affect plant growth will provide plenty of clues as to which way you're facing.

WIND

Isolated woodlands have shorter trees on the side facing the prevailing wind. The windward trees will give those behind a little more shelter, and they'll become progressively taller the farther away they are from the wind. If you get the right kind of side-on angle, you'll see this clearly and, knowing the direction of the prevailing wind, be able to figure out which direction you're facing. The effect of the wind can also be seen in exposed individual trees, where the canopy grows in the direction the wind has blown it and sometimes looks like a breaking wave.

A tree's roots anchor it to the soil and keep it from getting blown over. The roots will grow in response to the forces acting upon them and are longest on the windward and leeward sides, making a kind of diamond shape around the tree, with the longest axis indicating the dominant wind direction. You can spot this in buttress roots at the base of the trunk.

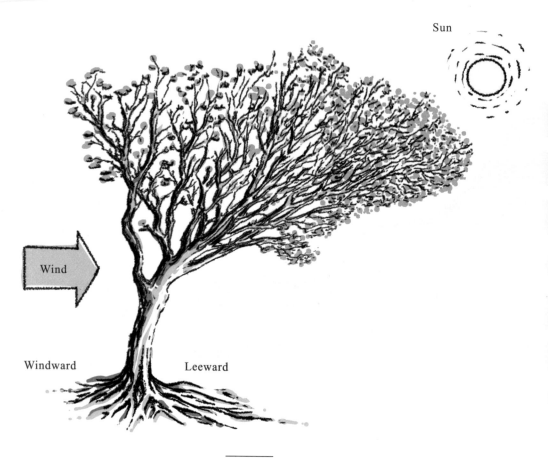

Sun

Wind

Windward   Leeward

Also, species of trees and other plants change in response to weather conditions. As you get closer to the sea, only salt- and wind-tolerant species thrive. When you climb a mountain, types of trees will change with the altitude and eventually give way to shorter species and shrubs, until you hit the timberline, where conditions are too harsh for any trees to grow.

SUN

The sun plays an important part in sculpting the shape of individual trees. The side facing the nearest pole will receive less sunlight overall and so produce less growth. On the sunnier side, a tree will maximize photosynthesis by optimizing growth of branches and leaves.

The degree of sunshine or shade can also affect the size of leaves on different sides of the tree. Leaves growing in the shade will be larger and thicker to make the best use of the limited available light. On the sunny side of the tree, smaller, thinner leaves photosynthesize more efficiently and also track the sun. This difference, especially if spotted across many trees, can be a good indicator of north and south.

MOISTURE

If you're looking for water to drink or a river to follow, a useful clue from a distance is to look for the purple haze of alder trees, which thrive, along with willow, on riverbanks and marshy floodplains. Find out which species in your area prefer damp or dry ground. This little bit of knowledge can help you choose your route and give advance warning of changes in the environment. Lack of moisture, however, can reduce the height that trees reach compared to the same species with adequate water.

GROWTH RINGS

Windblown or felled trees can reveal how they grew, if you know how to interpret their growth rings (see pages 120–1). Rings close together indicate a tree that grew slowly. If, on the other side of the valley, the same species has widely spaced rings, it may have grown more quickly because it received more sunlight. This can give an indication of which direction is north and which is south. For example, a north-facing slope in the northern hemisphere will receive a lot less light than the south-facing slope of a valley—a situation reversed in the southern hemisphere.

AIR QUALITY

Many trees—and other plants that grow on them—are badly affected by pollution. Industrial areas are usually sited on the outskirts of U.S. towns and cities, so that smoke and pollutants do not blow over residential areas and affect the inhabitants. Knowing a few indicator species that either do or don't grow in the presence of airborne pollutants can help with navigation. Lichens are especially useful for this. Some flat, crusting lichens, such as *Lecanora conizaeoides*, can be extremely tolerant of pollution, whereas other bushier species, such as *Usnea ceratina*, will only grow in extremely clean air. No lichen at all means the air quality is particularly bad. This can help you know if you're near a main road or upwind of a polluting industrial plant.

RED SKIES AND RECUMBENT COWS: WEATHER TRUTHS AND MYTHS

W eather is a subject of endless fascination in all corners of the globe. After all, it largely dictates the activities and shape of each day. Of the upmost importance for agricultural communities and members of the seafaring trade, weather has inspired a number of proverbs and myths throughout the ages. Some have a foundation in meteorological fact; others are pure fiction.

Using simple powers of observation, it may be possible to track and predict weather trends over time. Farmers, sailors, forestry guardians, and gardeners alike make it their stock-in-trade to keep one step ahead of weather fronts and storms. Studying the appearance of the sky, sun, and moon—as well as animal behavior and plant cycles—is a time-honored way to try to forecast approaching weather.

Proverbs vary according to location and with differing levels of accuracy. The ever-popular "Red sky at night, shepherd's [or sailor's] delight," for example, holds grains of truth, depending on which direction the weather system in your area comes from. If it comes in from the west, the saying is often true: A beautiful sunset means that the air is clear enough for the rays of the sun to reach you, hence a fine day is likely tomorrow. However, taking into account that events like volcanic eruptions and atmospheric pollution can change the color of the sky any time of day, this saying isn't always reliable.

CHILLY GAZING

It seems that the old adage "Cold night, stars bright" proves more accurate, as the high pressure that creates clear skies also brings colder temperatures at ground level, making it easier to see stars twinkling and planets gleaming on colder nights. But is it ever "too cold for snow"? This all depends on how far the thermometer drops. Water vapor is needed in the air for snowflakes to form; and while hot air holds a lot of vapor, the colder the air, the less vapor it holds. Therefore, in areas where the temperature drops to minus 40 degrees Celsius and Fahrenheit (the scales read the same at this point) or below, snowfall becomes unlikely as there's so little moisture in the air. In many parts of the world, such as northern North America, Russia, the Arctic, and Antarctica, it does indeed become too cold for snow.

"A ring around the sun or moon, means rain will come quite soon" is a somewhat accurate saying, in the sense that the halo effect around the moon or sun comes from light passing through ice crystals in the upper atmosphere. This can mean that a low pressure system is on the way, indicating an approaching storm.

PRESCIENT WILDLIFE

Animals feature in a quite a few forecasts. So, do cows really "lie down when it's about to rain"? While it's tempting to believe in bovine powers of weather divination, there is no scientific evidence to support this saying. Cows may recline because they feel like chewing their cud up close, or they may simply be relaxing. "When swallows fly high," on the other hand, is indeed likely to indicate dry weather. In dry conditions, warm thermal air rises, and insects get caught up in the thermals. And as insects provide food for swallows, the birds soar higher up into the sky—sometimes hundreds of yards—to snag a meal.

Finally, "Pine cones open when good weather is on the way" is firmly backed up by science. In drier conditions, pine cones open as the scales shrivel up. In higher humidity (damp and rain), pine cones return to their usual closed form.

READING WOODLAND

Exploring new woodland is like opening a surprise gift. The view from the outside offers an inkling of what might be contained within; anticipation builds—but what will you find inside? To read a woodland, you must decipher the clues that will tell its story. That means searching for and interpreting the signs in the woodland landscape and its relationship with plants, animals, and people. Then you can make sense of what you see now, what was here before, and what might happen in the future.

The oldest woodland, known as old-growth or "primary," has grown up with minimal human interference, although now only about one-third of the forest on Earth remains undisturbed. To recognize old-growth forest, look for trees of different ages and species growing together and dead trees left standing or fallen. The soil on the forest floor will be largely undisturbed, with plenty of tree litter, such as leaves, bark, and branches, providing vital materials and habitats for insects, birds, mammals, amphibians, and reptiles, and for plants and fungi.

Much of the world's woodland has been shaped by human activity over thousands of years. To understand how and why particular woodland was managed, you need to discover the economic activity that went on in the area in times past. Were timber products needed for agriculture, shipbuilding, mining, or charcoal burning? What type of wood was most valued; how often was it cut? A forest may have been an important hunting ground, in which case you may find banks and ditches that contained deer and boar to be hunted with hounds. Banks and ditches may also indicate a barrier that prevented grazing animals from entering woodland and damaging its trees.

Another way to spot woodland that has its roots deep in the past is to step back and take in the lay of the land. If woodland has an irregular edge, this could be caused by centuries of changes in

Plantation woodland

Primary ancient woodland

use and ownership of the surrounding land. Humans have long cleared forests to create land for cultivation, but some natural features acted as obstacles that allowed woodland to survive. Look for woodland that has steep slopes—too difficult to farm—or that follows a winding stream or river—too boggy or marshy for planting.

FARMED FORESTS

In some parts of the world, the saying "A wood that pays is a wood that stays" still holds true, and where there's sustainable forestry, the biodiversity that has evolved over millennia is maintained. In other places, old-growth forests are clear-cut for quick economic gain and may be replaced with plantations of fast-growing trees.

Plantations are basically farms where the crop takes decades to mature. It's much easier for a forester to calculate the density of a woodland and estimate the volume of timber if trees are planted in straight lines. Not all new planting conforms to this pattern, but if you can differentiate distinct lines of trees, then you're likely to be in a plantation. If the forest is composed of a single species and all the trees are a similar height and girth, then again, you're probably in a plantation.

RISING FROM THE ASHES

Nature's own clearance and replanting program can be found in the regrowth of a forest after a storm or fire. When the canopy of tall trees is removed, there's a huge increase in light levels at the forest floor. Seeds that are dormant in the soil can all start to grow at once and lead to a dense thicket of the same species and age. It's now a race—a competition to grow tall and capture as much sunlight as possible. The losers in the race will languish in the shade, unable to photosynthesize, and they will die. In this way, the woodland is thinned, and the successful trees will have more room to grow.

Signs of human activity   *Fire regrowth*

IDENTIFYING ANIMAL
TRACKS AND SIGNS

Getting to know your way around your area develops as you become familiar with routes, landmarks, vegetation patterns, and the shape of the land. But don't forget its nonhuman inhabitants—the tracks, trails, and signs they leave behind can give fascinating insights into animal behavior, as well as help you navigate.

Take a close look at the ground in a field, meadow, or forest—slight differences in the earth or plants may show you where an animal has passed. There might be an obvious well-used trail, worn by deer over many years, or you might even spot the change in tone of blades of grass brushed in one direction by the belly of a badger as it walked by in the night.

Animals tend not to waste energy, taking direct paths as they move, so tracking their well-worn routes can be an efficient way to navigate. Observe large patterns first, then obvious signs like droppings, and finally, small details such as individual footprints. Look for tracks on bare ground, muddy riverbanks, and fresh snow, and under fences—or you can even sieve some fine soil onto the ground to capture the tracks of animals using that path. Look for pads, toes, and claw marks in an individual print. The gap between prints shows the animal's stride and may indicate its size and speed.

ANIMAL SIGNS

» *How old is a track?* It could be useful—and reassuring—to know whether a large carnivore track by your camp is fresh or several weeks old. Make some marks or footprints yourself in different materials, from sandy soil to heavy clay, and observe over time how they change in different weather conditions. Tracks in fine, damp soil will have good definition when fresh but deteriorate rapidly in the rain.

» *Scratch marks or gnawed bark.* This can tell you which animals are active in the area. For example, deer have front teeth only in their lower jaw and will rip strips of bark upward on a tree trunk.

» *Feeding signs—nibbled nuts and cones.* You can identify which rodent nibbled a hazelnut by the pattern of tooth marks around the hole in the nut. Squirrels will crack a nut into two pieces, whereas mice will gnaw a round or ragged hole and leave tooth marks on the surface of the nut.

» *Scat or droppings.* A carnivorous animal may leave traces of a prey's hair or bone in its droppings. Herbivores will leave behind largely fibrous droppings. Particular shapes indicate a type or group of animals—deer droppings, for example, are often piles of pellets, pointed at one end with a concave depression at the other. Fox scat is pointed, twisted, and has an unmistakably offensive smell.

» *Nesting and resting signs.* This could be a nest of twigs high up in a tree, like a squirrel's drey, or a patch of bare earth, scraped free of leaves and twigs, where a deer might have curled up to sleep. Deer beds or "couches" are a good place to explore to find shed hairs.

WHOSE FOOTPRINT?

Feline or cat tracks typically have four toes on the front and back feet, while the pad has two lobes at the front and three at the back.

Canines, including foxes and wolves as well as the domestic dog, all share common characteristics in their tracks, such as four toes, possibly with claw marks. The pad behind the toes can have a vaguely triangular shape.

Mustelids are a group of animals that includes weasels, badgers, otters, martens, and mink. Their tracks show five toes, often with claw marks, but are highly varied, as the many mustelid species are adapted to very different habitats and behaviors.

Ungulates, such as deer, walk on two toes, which leave marks like two slots on soft ground. Sometimes the impression of two additional dew claws can be seen when the animal has gone through soft, deep mud.

Ursids, or bears, have five toes on their front and back feet, arranged in a line in front of a wide, narrow pad on the front feet and a much longer pad on the back feet. The biggest toe is on the outside of the foot. But most importantly—bear tracks are unmistakably big!

Rodents, from beavers to squirrels and field mice, are extremely diverse, but all will show four toes on the front foot and five on the rear. Habitat and feeding signs can be good clues to identification.

USING
YOUR SENSES

A t school, we learn that humans have five basic senses—but there are others. Knowing where you are and how to get to places you want to get to is crucial for human survival. We commonly call it our sense of direction, but it's only recently that psychologists and neuroscientists have found out how it actually works. In 2014, researchers at University College London won the Nobel Prize in Physiology for the discovery that the sense of direction is largely located in the entorhinal cortex at the base of the brain. So-called "place cells," grid cells, border cells, and head-direction cells appear to enable navigation.

Place cells are neurons that fire one by one as you move through a place and encounter various landmarks. Grid cells form a sort of hexagonal coordinate system that links the information and memory about each of the places together. This "grid" helps with dead reckoning—determining your position by estimating the direction and distance traveled—or figuring out your current location depending on where you've been. This ability isn't much use in urban environments, where visual cues govern navigation, but in woodland or at night it becomes much more important. Head-direction cells respond differently depending on which way you're facing and allow you to access the relevant grid of places in that direction. Finally, border cells represent navigational barriers relative to your current position. These might be the walls of a room, a cliff edge, or something like a river or dense thicket.

TRAINING YOUR SENSE OF DIRECTION

Many migratory animals, such as birds and turtles, have a sense called magnetoreception, which allows them to perceive and use Earth's magnetic field for navigation. There's no clear evidence that humans can do this—without the aid of a compass—but you can develop a better sense of direction, even if you think yours is terrible.

» Pay close attention to what's around you. As well as using visual clues and landmarks, notice smells, changes in temperature, and where shadows fall. It's like learning to read clouds and weather signs. Recognizing patterns will help you find your way and keep on a particular course.

» Rather than thinking about routes from A to B, try to form a mental map of an area, with landmarks as nodes and routes as the ways between them. In your local area, you can build that mental map by changing the routes you take between places.

To really make use of an accurate mental map, you need to develop awareness of where you're located and in which direction you're looking. When people give directions, they often use terms like "left," "right," and "straight ahead." But these are relative to the person doing the directing and don't help if someone turns around or starts a route facing the wrong direction. Using absolutes, such as north, south, east, and west, takes away the uncertainty and also allows you to talk about maps in a meaningful way. To try this out, you could carry a compass (see pages 96–7) and check it regularly, or just use the compass app on your phone if it has one. Remember, there's no "above" or "below" on a 2D map!

FOLLOW YOUR NOSE

Many animals perceive their world more through smell than sight. Although smell evokes powerful memories in humans, we sometimes neglect it when bombarded with other information. The smell-scape of woodland is often overlooked, but consciously paying attention to the odors that you encounter, where they originate, and how they mingle will give you a whole new world of insights into the place you're moving through. Make a point of sniffing as you move; hone in on particular fragrances; notice how plant smells merge and are more intense if you rub those plants. The bigger the picture you construct of your environment, the better you'll get to know it, the more you'll feel at home in it, and the better you'll find your way around it.

LOOKING TO THE SKIES
FOR DIRECTION

"The question then is how to get lost. Never to get lost is not to live; not to know how to get lost brings you to destruction, and somewhere in the terra incognita in between lies a life of discovery."
Rebecca Solnit, A Field Guide to Getting Lost

Getting lost can be a good thing if you know that it's temporary—you have a chance to explore without thinking where you're going next. With no map or compass, though, and no navigational clues in your immediate natural surroundings, you may start to feel disoriented. If so, stop, sit down, and breathe deeply—wandering aimlessly or rushing around trying to find the last landmark you remember is only going to make matters worse. The difference between panic and success could lie beyond our planet, in the celestial world, which provided the earliest means of human navigation.

fig 1   *fig 2*   *fig 3*

USING THE SUN
On a bright, sunny day, plant a stick in the ground, and look at the shadow it makes (*fig 1*). When the sun is at its highest point in the sky, the shadow of the stick will be aligned north–south. Whichever hemisphere you live in, the tip of the shadow will point toward the nearest pole. If you miss the sun's highest point, then track the tip of the shadow for at least an hour and place stones at the tip of the shadow every few minutes (*fig 2*). The stones will make a line that aligns roughly east–west (*fig 3*).

WRITTEN IN THE STARS

At night, you have the stars to help you to find direction. Around 4,500 stars can be seen with the naked eye—light permitting—and sailors, traders, and wanderers have been navigating by them for thousands of years. Throughout that time, stars have appeared to human sight as fixed points, even though their light has already traveled for millions of years when it reaches our retinas. Various human cultures have categorized and named groups of stars according to their own creation stories and religious beliefs, which make them easier to remember, find, and use as navigation reference points.

EYES TO THE NORTH

The classic northern hemisphere technique is to find the constellation Ursa Major, which is sometimes called the Big Dipper, the Great Bear, the Plough—or even the Saucepan. Find the side of the "dipper" opposite the handle, and draw an imaginary line between the two stars that form this shape. Extend the line higher in the sky and you will see a bright star, called Polaris or the North Star, which never varies far from true north.

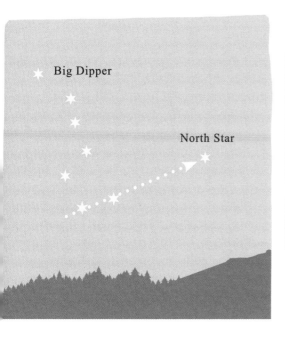

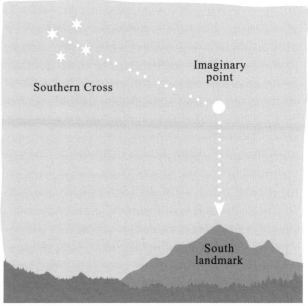

EYES TO THE SOUTH

In the southern hemisphere, you can find true south by using the Southern Cross—a compact, kite-shaped cluster of five bright stars. Looking at the cluster, imagine a line extending from the foot of the long axis of the cross. Estimate another four similar star clusters along this line, then drop a line to the horizon. This is roughly south.

FOLLOW THE HUNTER

Apart from Polaris, though, you can't just pick a star in the direction you want to travel and walk toward it, since Earth is spinning and the star will move from east to west. However, if you can see the horizon at sunset, look for the first rising star of Orion's Belt—the three stars that form the "belt" of the constellation Orion the Hunter. This star is called Mintaka, and it's the third star in Orion's Belt as you look from left to right. Wherever you are in the world, Mintaka always rises due east and sets due west. You'll then know where due west is and can bookmark it using a distant landmark.

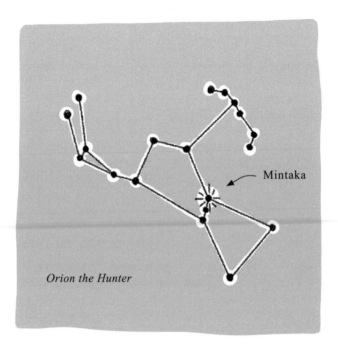

Mintaka

Orion the Hunter

USING EARTH'S MOVEMENT

For a simple and practical way to find your approximate direction at night, bang a stick into the ground so that the top is at eye height when you sit or crouch down. Then move forward about 3 feet (1 meter) and bang in another, taller stick. Sitting or crouching behind the shorter stick, line the tops of the two sticks up with a bright star, and watch how its relative position changes in about 20 minutes. Remember, the stars aren't actually moving, it's the earth that's spinning. If the star appears to move right, you're facing south. Conversely, if it seems to move left, you're looking north. If the star rises, you're looking east; if it descends, you're facing west.

LOOKING FOR LATITUDE

If you know the latitude of where you live, you can always walk north or south until you're on the same latitude, and then traverse that line until you arrive home—or close to home. If you're able to figure out the angle between your location on Earth and Polaris, you can calculate your latitude (how far north or south you are). The simplest way to do this at night is to face Polaris and extend your arm, making a fist that sits just above the horizon. Estimate how many fists there are between the horizon and the star, with each fist representing about 10 degrees. The number of degrees is roughly your latitude.

MAKING A CLINOMETER

A sextant—in the unlikely event you had one lying around—would give a more precise latitude, but you really only need a clinometer, a much simpler device that measures angles of slope. There are clinometer phone apps—or you can make one with a protractor, a drinking straw, and a piece of string.

You'll need:
» protractor or a piece of card with an arc marked out in degrees
» drinking straw or hollow plant stem
» length of thread or fine string
» weight (a washer or some paper clips) to tie to the end of the string

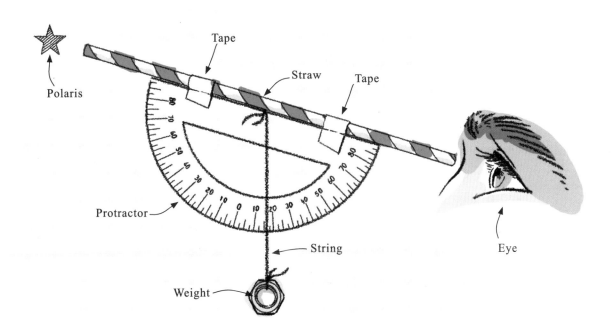

1. Glue, tape, or tie the straw onto the straight edge of the protractor.
2. Tie the weight onto one end of the string.
3. Tie the other end of the string onto the protractor, so that when the flat edge is horizontal, the string hangs at 90 degrees. Sometimes there's a hole in the middle of the flat edge of the protractor that you can thread the string through.
4. Raise the straw to your eye, and look through it at Polaris.
5. Pinch the hanging string against the curved edge of the protractor, so that you can take an accurate reading of the degrees.
6. Subtract your reading from 90 to find your latitude.

Crafts associated with woodlands, once vital to the relationship between humans and the land, are among the most endangered of all traditional occupations. These skills are the accumulated practical knowledge of managing and harvesting the raw materials growing in woodlands, processing them, and turning them into products that people need for everyday life and work. Efficiency and sustainability were always important aspects of traditional woodland crafts, but there was also a strong aesthetic element, showing that generations of people didn't just care about getting a job done but also took pride in how it looked.

The skills we talk about tend to be those used for woodland management in times past, when social groups were hunting and gathering or involved in labor-intensive agriculture before mechanization decimated the rural workforce. Often, these skills were inherently sustainable, using local resources that were needed year after year. Local habitats and wildlife benefit hugely from the harnessing of this type of resource management, but it requires localized, specialist knowledge, a tolerance of hard physical work in all weathers, and a market or need for the skill or product. Often, one or more of these things are in short supply, with a risk of traditional woodland crafts dying out. Thankfully, many of the skills in this chapter are kept alive by a small body of craftspeople, wildlife conservation organizations, and dedicated enthusiasts and hobbyists.

The following pages will help you tackle some of the traditional woodland and forest crafts. In the process, you'll find out much about how differently life in the past was led in your locality, maybe enabling you to track down and learn more from the specialists that are still out there. Besides developing your own practical skills, you'll also gain a greater awareness of how the ecology, economy, and society in your area are still inextricably linked. Even if you never lay a hedge or coppice a woodland, the techniques and principles you learn in working with the materials will apply to all manner of other tasks as you construct and create your own forest projects.

5

WOODLAND SKILLS

ESSENTIAL
EQUIPMENT

As well as the general-purpose knife, pruning saw, and first aid kit that will be regular fixtures on your outings to the woods (see pages 40–1), you'll need some additional tools if you want to expand your range of activities and practical projects. Many traditional woodland tools are specialized and therefore rare and expensive, but you can often safely use an alternative tool for the same job if you're not going to be doing it on a regular basis. Old axes crop up in yard sales and flea markets, and a local blacksmith or metalworker might be willing to make up a froe and wedges from pieces of scrap.

Don't worry about what is the "best" of each tool (especially axes). Start with what you can get hold of, and as your skill and understanding increase, you'll learn from experience what to look for when upgrading your tool collection. There are some instances, though, when buying cheap is a false economy. A cheap bow saw will be a miserable object to use, and it's worth investing in a supply of fresh blades to keep sawing pleasurable rather than painful.

THE WOODLAND TOOL KIT
» *Ax.* From felling trees to chopping firewood to carving spoons, an ax is an invaluable, multipurpose tool for a wide range of woodland crafts and activities. There's a huge variety of options for—and just as many opinions on—axes for general use. See pages 124–5 for more advice.
» *Wedges.* These very basic items are particularly useful for splitting large logs. A couple of wedges and a hefty mallet will bring this extremely satisfying task within your reach (see pages 128–9).
» *Billhook.* Developed for coppicing (see pages 138–9) and hedge laying (see pages 144–5), billhooks are highly collectible, and old ones can fetch quite high prices on auction sites. You may be lucky, however, at yard sales and pick up interesting traditional tools like this for reasonable prices. New, mass-produced billhooks lack the romance of a tool that has perhaps been the key to a skilled craftsperson's living for decades.
» *Froe.* A simple but highly effective tool, the froe has a long, thick-wedged blade and right-angled handle. It's hefty to carry around but immensely satisfying to use—once you have the knack—when it comes to cleaving wood (see page 129).
» *Bow saw.* Of all the tools, a bow saw is probably the most essential. Making just about anything from wood involves sawing, so a good quality 21-inch bow saw is worth the investment.
» *Pruning shears.* If you get into basketmaking (see pages 142–3), then you'll need pruning shears. Try and find a pair that can be completely disassembled for regular cleaning and sharpening.

1. *Billhook*
2. *Wedges*
3. *Pruning shears*
4. *Bow saw*
5. *Ax*
6. *Froe*

GETTING TO KNOW
GREEN WOOD

Many preindustrial societies had a strong tradition of working with green—untreated—wood, supplied in large quantities by the coppicing of woodland trees (see pages 138–9). Over the past century, the products of the coppice worker have been displaced by mass-produced metal and plastic, but the skills of green woodworking are kept alive by a small number of craftspeople and a growing band of hobbyists. In forest and woodland, green wood is the most natural material to hand and generally easier to work than hard, dry wood, which often requires a workshop with specialist equipment. This chapter reveals some of the techniques and tools that have developed over millennia to make the best use of the strengths and peculiarities of green wood.

IT'S ALL ABOUT MOISTURE

Green wood is freshly cut wood that hasn't had a chance to dry out—a process known as seasoning. As wood seasons, it becomes harder and lighter, possibly losing between a third and a half of its weight. Many woodworkers prefer the stability of seasoned wood, which keeps its shape over time, while green woodworkers take advantage of the particular properties of unseasoned wood, which can be softer than hardwood, put less wear on edged tools, and often split without sawing. Also, joints made with green wood have the ability to tighten as the wood dries and shrinks.

MEASURING WOOD WETNESS

Moisture content (MC) is calculated by weighing a piece of freshly felled green wood and then drying it completely in an oven before weighing it again. If the timber from a tree has a moisture content of 100 percent when green, this means that the piece in your hand is made up of equal parts dry wood and water. Believe it or not, the weight of water lost is sometimes more than the weight of the dried wood left behind, meaning that the MC can be greater than 100 percent—even up to 150 percent for a species like cottonwood. Ash has an MC of less than 50 percent and can, in theory, be used as firewood when green. However, it's always best to burn seasoned wood, especially in a woodstove, where tar residue can build up in chimneys, bringing the risk of a flue fire. The general rule of thumb for seasoning hardwood for burning is to allow one year of drying for every inch of diameter.

KNOWING THE WOOD

The key to working with green wood is understanding the material, how it grew, and what will happen to it as it dries out. Wood in the round—not cut into planks or beams—mainly dries from the sawed ends, where the rapid drying of the cut section can cause radial cracks to form. With luck, these won't extend far up the log, although some logs will have cracks that run parallel to the rings—known as "shake"— which means that the log can fall apart when split or milled. When green wood is split, worked, and shaped immediately, tensions in the log are reduced and the surface area for moisture loss increases. This leads to fewer splits and cracks—as long as subsequent drying is not done too quickly.

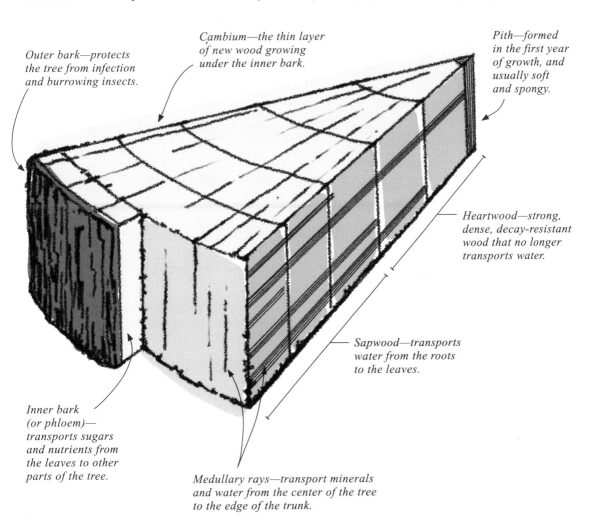

Outer bark—protects the tree from infection and burrowing insects.

Cambium—the thin layer of new wood growing under the inner bark.

Pith—formed in the first year of growth, and usually soft and spongy.

Heartwood—strong, dense, decay-resistant wood that no longer transports water.

Sapwood—transports water from the roots to the leaves.

Inner bark (or phloem)— transports sugars and nutrients from the leaves to other parts of the tree.

Medullary rays—transport minerals and water from the center of the tree to the edge of the trunk.

HOW OLD
IS THAT TREE?

The quickest way to be sure of the age of a standing tree is to cut it down and count the annual growth rings. However, that's not always practical—or desirable. Better to find a felled tree stump, which on its own can tell you a huge amount—not only about the age of the tree but also the conditions in which it grew and even significant life events, such as lightning strikes and droughts.

CLUES IN THE RINGS

Trees in climates with distinct seasons show their different rates of annual growth as growth rings. These tend to show as two distinct colors: lighter, broader "earlywood" and thinner, darker "latewood." Choose one of these types of rings, and count the number from the pith to the bark for an accurate measure of the age of a tree when it was felled. How much the tree grows each year will depend on the growing conditions, especially the availability of water. The relative amounts of earlywood and latewood give each ring a fingerprint that can be cross-referenced with other species of trees to accurately identify the year that the wood was grown. As the life spans of individual trees overlap, it's possible to construct an unbroken record of climatic information from growth rings evident in cross sections of old timbers found in buildings or buried and preserved in bogs. This is the science of dendrochronology, from the ancient Greek word *dendron*, meaning "tree."

In equatorial and tropical regions, where the weather is more consistent across seasons, trunk cross sections don't show rings strongly in their wood. The exception is when there's a distinct rainy season, which will affect rates of growth.

LOOKING ON THE OUTSIDE

You can also estimate the age of a tree from its external appearance and measurements. Tree height, though, isn't a reliable indicator of age, as the growing conditions for the same species can vary considerably, and some very old trees in harsh environments will remain stunted due to wind strength or lack of nutrients.

» *Branch whorls.* Some types of trees, such as pines, spruces, and firs, produce a new whorl of branches every year after the first two to four years from the seed germinating. If you can see enough of the tree, then counting the whorls from the ground to the top will give a good idea of its age. Getting a good view in dense woodland can be difficult, though, and often the earliest, lowest ring of branches will have died and dropped off.

» *Tree girth.* This can provide an indication of age as different tree species will add wood at different rates. That rate can be looked up in foresters' "growth and yield tables" for the relevant climatic zone. Using a tape measure, calculate the circumference of the tree at breast height, 5 feet (1.5 meters) above the ground. Divide the circumference by the annual growth rate for that species in your area, and you'll have a very rough idea of the age. An oak tree in southern England, for example, will add about 0.75 inches (1.88 centimeters) each year, so a really big oak with a girth of 315 inches or 26 feet (800 centimeters or 8 meters) would be approximately 425 years old. Some trees, mainly conifers like coast redwood, Douglas fir, and western red cedar, can have much larger annual girth growth rates of 2 to 3 inches (5 to 7.5 centimeters).

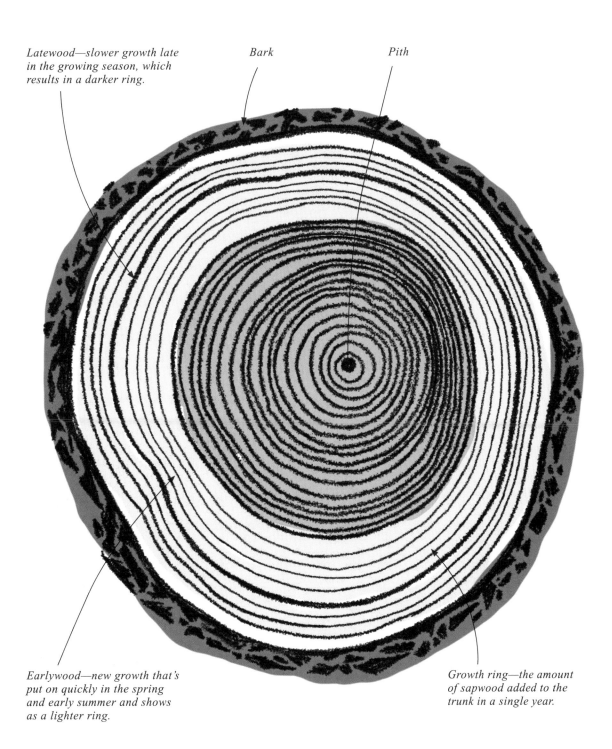

Latewood—slower growth late in the growing season, which results in a darker ring.

Bark

Pith

Earlywood—new growth that's put on quickly in the spring and early summer and shows as a lighter ring.

Growth ring—the amount of sapwood added to the trunk in a single year.

TREES AND THEIR USES

Many of the crafts and projects in this book refer to a particular species or a specific property of a tree or plant. The study of the relationship between people and plants is known as ethnobotany and is the single most important aspect of understanding how humans have met their needs in their chosen environments and how we can all be more self-reliant in the places that we inhabit. Below is a selection of trees from different regions and a summary of their uses—just a start in discovering the multitude of trees in your own area.

» *Hazel.* Found across the northern hemisphere in temperate areas, hazel (*Corylus* species) is a multistemmed shrubby tree that forms the understory of much deciduous woodland. It features heavily in many of the traditional skills in this chapter—its long, straight poles have so many uses that it has been called the "woodsman's friend." All hazelnuts are edible, but squirrels usually beat humans to the harvest. Larger cultivars are a good addition to a forest garden (see pages 182–3).

» *Eucalyptus.* The *Eucalyptus* genus comprises more than 700 species, mostly native to Australia, where they make up around 75 percent of the country's forests. Many eucalyptus make excellent fast-growing timber trees, and their bark—often shed annually—makes great kindling. Eucalyptus oils are used in medicine as decongestants, disinfectants, and insect repellents.

» *Western red cedar.* The most common tree of the Pacific Northwest of North America, the western red cedar (*Thuja plicata*) is also grown for timber in Western Europe, South Australia, and New Zealand. For the First Nations of the cedar's home range, the tree provided planks for houses and bentwood boxes, trunks for canoes, and roots and bark for fibers to make ropes, baskets, mats, and clothing.

» *Ash.* All ash trees (*Fraxinus* species), from the green and red ash in North America to the European ash (*Fraxinus excelsior*)—under serious

Hazel   Eucalyptus   Western red cedar

threat from ash dieback disease—have similar properties. Ash has clean white wood, which cleaves beautifully and is perfect for steam bending. The wood isn't especially durable outdoors and is usually kept for indoor uses.

» *Larch.* Unusually among conifers, larch trees (*Larix* species) are deciduous, dropping their needles in winter. Young shoots can be cooked and eaten, and the cambium (see page 91) can be ground and mixed with flour. Larch needles, like those of pine trees, can be used to make tea, and the roots can be peeled and used as cord. Strong and durable larch timber is particularly useful for outdoor construction.

» *Birch.* The trees of the *Betula* genus, commonly known as birch, circle the globe in the northern boreal forests (known as the taiga in Northern Europe and Russia). This forest biome is one of the biggest on Earth and covers most of Canada, Alaska, Scandinavia, and Siberia, as well as parts of Scotland and Iceland. The thick bark of the birch is perfect for weaving and making containers, as well as for covering canoes and shelters. The wood is a joy to carve and produces wonderful utensils, while the sap makes a refreshing drink when tapped in the spring (see page 47).

» *Scotch pine.* Scotland's national, the Scotch— or Scots—pine (*Pinus sylvestris*) is a pioneer that can thrive on poor, thin soils. Its timber's strength made the tall trunks ideal for ships' masts. The timber was also burned for charcoal and for tar to coat the hulls of wooden boats. Today, the tree is used in building work and to make telegraph poles, as well as pulpwood and chipboard. The chopped fresh needles make a light and refreshing tea, rich in antioxidants and high in vitamin C.

» *Aspen.* The light and durable wood of the aspen (*Populus* species) was traditionally used for roofing shingles in northern Russia, and the tree has a huge range around the world in latitudes from the Arctic to North Africa. Aspen wood is noted for its low flammability, which has made it a popular choice for match and paper production.

» *Douglas fir.* Native to the coast and mountains of western North America, the Douglas fir (*Pseudotsuga menziesii*) is also common across Europe. It's one of the most important softwood timber trees for building work, and its needles make a distinctive citrus-smelling tea. Resin blisters on the bark can be used in wilderness first aid (see page 61).

Birch   *Scots pine*   *Aspen*

USING AN AX

At its simplest, an ax is just a sharpened lump of metal on the end of a stick. The earliest "axes" were no more than handheld lumps of stone, but tool technology has evolved over the last few hundred thousand years to the point where there's now an ax for every occasion: splitting firewood, hewing beams, felling and limbing trees, carving, and even skinning animals.

A RANGE OF PURPOSES

The head of a splitting ax has a wedge-shaped profile, whereas a general-purpose ax has a narrower, tapering profile. Carving axes can be symmetrical or asymmetrical (flat on one side, beveled on the other). If asymmetrical, they're either left-handed or right-handed, since the main bevel needs to be on the outside of the cut when in use.

A long-handled ax is good for splitting wood as the head will travel farther with each swing, allowing it to move faster and impart more energy. For carving, a short handle held near the head allows fine control over the position of each cut. If you only get one ax, it's most likely to be a multipurpose version, with a 2.2 pound (1 kilogram) head and around 19 or 20 inch (50 centimeter) handle that can be put to use for a wide variety of tasks and isn't too heavy or cumbersome to fit in a backpack.

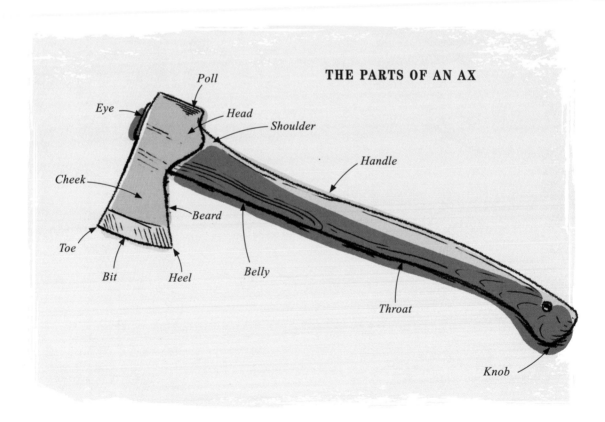

THE PARTS OF AN AX

fig 1

fig 2

AX BEST PRACTICE

An ax should be treated with respect and used mindfully. Any ax accident has the potential to be catastrophic, but used with knowledge and care, the tool can be more helpful than any other. Before using an ax, check that you're feeling calm and that the area you're going to work in is clear of anything that might snag the ax or get in the way. If possible, chop onto a large, heavy block, but make sure that your hands are higher than the ax-head when it hits the block. Ask yourself where the ax might end up if your swing doesn't go as intended, and adjust your feet to keep the ax away from your legs and torso.

» When splitting firewood, take a wide stance and put the log on the far side of the block, so the ax hits the block if you miss the wood (*fig 1*). Don't swing too hard. The mass of the ax-head multiplied by the velocity it hits the wood will determine the energy imparted to split the wood; but if you try too hard and miss, then the effort is wasted, and the ax-head is out of control. Take it easy until your skill develops.

» When making short chops—for example, to sharpen a stake or split kindling—use a higher block or kneel beside a lower block. Keep the work to your side, between your body and the ax, and hold the handle near the ax-head (*fig 2*). Eliminate any potential for the bit to accidentally end up in your body by first thinking through what will happen if it misses the wood, knocks into the side of the wood, or bounces off.

» Filing or grinding out a large nick in the blade is a tedious job, so take care of your ax. Don't set or strike the bit on the ground, and when the ax isn't in use, keep the blade covered with a leather or wooden guard.

» Sharpen your ax regularly with a stone designed for the purpose. Some stones can be used dry; others need lubrication with water. Hold the head steady with the bit pointing away from you, and rub the stone in a small circular motion along the whole cutting edge. When you can feel a burr along the edge, turn the ax over and repeat on the other side. Make sure your fingers stay on top of the stone and behind the cutting edge.

HOW TO FELL A TREE

Humans have laid waste to huge areas of woodland habitat to satisfy a desire for cheap timber, and many of the consequences are felt globally as well as among local people and other living things. Materials for outdoor projects should be sourced in a responsible way, using certified wood where possible, from sources that are sustainably managed. But if you want to work with wood in the forest, then at some point you're probably going to have to fell a tree or two.

First, think for a moment about why you need to fell a tree. Is it part of a sustainable woodland management plan to increase timber, wildlife, or amenity value? Can wood for a project be upcycled from scrap timber or even made from other recycled materials? Is there dead wood around that can be responsibly collected and used without destroying a valuable invertebrate habitat? If not, then you need to find the right tree in the right place and cut it down, following a safe and effective procedure.

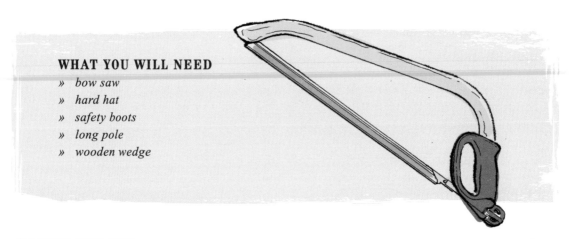

WHAT YOU WILL NEED
» *bow saw*
» *hard hat*
» *safety boots*
» *long pole*
» *wooden wedge*

MAKING THE CUT

The following instructions are based on felling an idealized tree of up to about 8 inches (20 centimetres) in diameter, in winter and in fairly open woodland where there's no chance of damage to other trees, power lines, or neighboring property. Felling trees can be dangerous. Make sure that you understand what can go wrong, and have a plan in place in case you need help. Wear personal protective equipment, and never fell a tree on your own.

1. Choose your tree. Look for the source of the materials you need, and try to pick an example that's unlikely to thrive, perhaps because it stands in the shade of a larger neighbor or has a low fork that will eventually split.
2. Clear the area around the tree of anything that will get in the way. Pull any climbing plants off the lower trunk. Assess where you would like the tree to fall—go with any lean that the tree already shows, if possible.
3. Using the bow saw, make a "gob cut"—also known as a "bird's mouth"—on the side of the tree where you want it to drop. Start with a 45-degree cut about 12 inches (30 centimeters) above the ground that goes about a quarter of the way through the trunk (A).

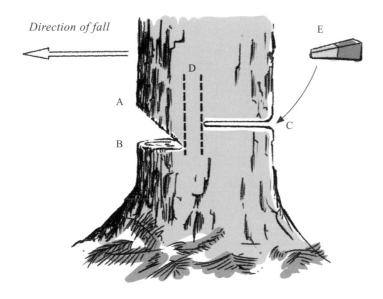

Direction of fall

4. Follow up with a cut 90 degrees to the trunk (B), which meets the bottom of the first cut and frees a wedge of wood.
5. Make the felling cut from the other side (the back) of the tree (C), directly behind and about 0.4 inches (1 centimeter) above the bottom of the wedge. Don't saw all the way through, but leave 0.4 to 0.8 inches (1 to 2 centimeters) of wood to form a hinge that will help control the fall (D).
6. The tree may well start to go by itself. If not, give it a slight push from the side, ideally with a long pole. If the tree needs a helping hand, hammer a wooden wedge (E) into the felling cut. The tree should then lean and fall. As soon as it starts to move, get well out of the way!

MAKING AN ESCAPE

Before you make any cut, make sure you plan an escape route. This should be located behind the direction of fall but also to the side, at an angle of about 45 degrees. Make sure this route is clear, so you can move through it quickly. Never stand or work directly behind the felling cut, since there's always a chance that the butt of the tree will shoot outward or upward, or jump backward off the stump as it falls.

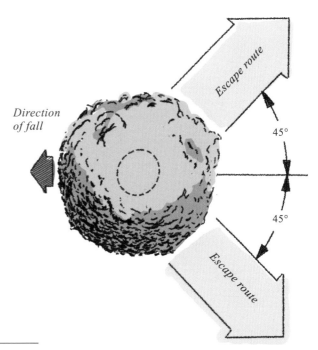

Direction of fall

Escape route

45°

45°

Escape route

CLEAVING WOOD

Why split—or cleave—wood lengthwise instead of ripping it with a saw? Historically, a saw was a much more complex and costly tool than a wedge, and for thousands of years, splitting wood was the most common way to make planks and beams. Cleaving demands more skill than sawing, but it's quicker and produces timber with greater strength because the fibers aren't broken and run intact through the length of the wood. This makes a big difference if you want to steam and bend the wood—as in the tongs-making project on page 165.

Cleaving a large log in two always holds surprises. You can try to read the log in the round and predict how it will split, but you'll never know until it actually happens. Will the split run off, will it twist and corkscrew, or will you end up, as hoped, with two flat, even halves? Logs are heavy, so it's a good idea to wear safety boots. You should also consider safety glasses, especially if using metal wedges, which, when struck, can let loose small fragments.

WHAT YOU WILL NEED
- » *ax*
- » *bow saw*
- » *wedges—metal or plastic, or homemade wooden wedges (known as "gluts")*
- » *long-handled wooden mallet (called a "maul")*

fig 1

fig 2

1. Look for a long length of fairly fresh-fallen trunk with as few side branches as possible, and saw off the piece you want to split.
2. Check the ends to see if there are any natural splits starting to open through the pith (*fig 1*). Use an ax to score and extend a line through one split to divide the end of the log into two equal halves.
3. Scrape off the bark along the length of the log where you would like the split to run (*fig 2*). You can mark this line by repeatedly tapping in an ax along its length.

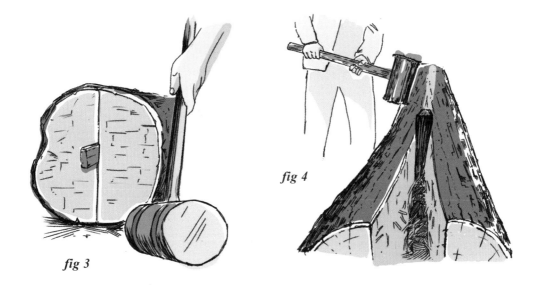

fig 3

fig 4

4. Using a mallet, tap a wedge into the center of the end of the log (*fig 3*). If it all goes to plan, you'll hear and see the wood starting to split along its length.
5. Where a crack appears, tap in a wedge to open it further. Work your way along the log, repositioning loosened wedges farther along the split as you go (*fig 4*). Make sure that you don't hit metal with metal, and never put any part of your body into the split.
6. Use the ax to chop any fibers in the crack that hold the two halves together. Be aware that the heavy log pieces may move toward you as they separate. You should now have two flat timber surfaces to use for building camp furniture, bridges, shelters, or other green wood projects.

SMALL-SCALE CLEAVING

To split long, thin pieces of wood to make gates or fences, you need a special tool called a froe (see pages 116–17), which uses leverage to control the direction of the split. You'll also need a device called a cleaving brake to hold the wood as you work (*fig 5*). The brake allows the work to be moved quickly and held in many different positions.

fig 5

FOREST FAIRY TALES

F airy stories set among woodland and forests—with their myriad species of densely packed trees, flora, and fauna; flying, crawling, and swimming animals; fantastical beasts and magical creatures—reside deep in our collective unconscious. These characters and the challenges undergone in this primal environment echo our deepest desires and fears, hopes, and dreams, providing catharsis and a kind of "psychic roadmap" of our collective unconscious.

The most popular fairy tales, adapted to each new generation, speak to the profound human story that we must all navigate to survive and thrive in the world. From 1812 to 1822, two folklorists, the Grimm Brothers, collected and published some of the best-known anthologies of tales, steeped in the atmosphere of their native German forests. But they were not the first chroniclers: In France, Charles Perrault and Madame d'Aulnoy published anthologies in 1697, followed by Madame de Villeneuve's "Beauty and the Beast" in 1740. By tracing the evolution of these tales, it has been found that some are more than 6,000 years old.

FOREST–LIFE ALLEGORY

Tales set in the forest are some of the most ancient. "Hansel and Gretel" features a brother and sister cast out of their home during a famine by a cruel stepmother and left to fend for themselves in the woods. The siblings leave a trail of bread crumbs to find their way back home, but these are eaten by birds. After an exhausting hike, they come upon a house made of gingerbread and cakes; the starving children are enticed inside to feast by a seemingly caring witch—but soon discover her plans to fatten them up and eat them. Gretel outsmarts the cannibalistic witch and kills her; they return home with the witch's treasure to find that the evil stepmother has also coincidentally died. Thus, the children have navigated the challenges of the forest—of life—and successfully survived.

In "Little Red Riding Hood," a young girl faces a talking wolf on the forest path. Although her mother has cautioned her "not to talk to strangers," Red Riding Hood all but directs the wolf to her grandmother's cottage; the cunning beast lollops ahead and swallows Grandma whole, then tries to eat the girl. Both humans are saved by the grace of a passing woodcutter, but the story could have easily ended in death—perhaps an allegory for the need to be conscious of potential dangers when journeying through any isolated wood? Another tale, "Sleeping Beauty," captures the timeless, ethereal quality of the forest. A princess is cursed by an evil fairy to sleep for one hundred years. To keep Beauty from loneliness when she awakes, a good fairy sends her entourage to sleep as well. Trees and brambles grow up around Beauty's castle, until a comely prince slashes through the thorns, kisses the princess, and releases her from the curse.

NATIVE AMERICAN TALES

Stories of creation and migration abound in Native American fairy tales. Across thousands of American Indigenous cultures, the overarching theme is the Great Spirit and the ways that spiritual forces can be experienced through the natural world, connecting humankind with the earth and gods.

The fascinating character of the Trickster features in many tales. Supernatural and mischievous, he may take the form of animals such as a coyote, hare, ram, or raven. Creating fun or chaos wherever he goes, the shape-shifting Trickster symbolizes uncertainty. A collection published in 1869 by Cornelius Matthews, *The Indian Fairy Book*, offers a selection of tales such as "The Enchanted Moccasins," a coming-of-age story in which a boy with supernatural powers seeks the company of other humans. He escapes dangerous situations on his quest, aided by magical moccasins that can run to the ends of the earth.

STRIPPING BARK

It may look like a simple substance, but bark is complex, an accumulation of layers each with a purpose vital to the health of a tree. The outer bark protects the tree from pests and diseases, is breathable and waterproof, and covers the inner bark, or phloem (see page 119), which transports sugars through the tree. Under this is the thin, living, cambium layer of new wood grown in the current year. Bark is rarely used or valued in modern forestry, but it's an amazing resource, yielding items as varied as string, roofing, pots, containers, mats, clothing, and even emergency food.

HARVESTING BARK

Bark can be peeled and processed from recently felled trees or those that have blown down in spring or early summer.

1. Using a knife, score a line through the outer and inner bark along a section of trunk.
2. Carefully prise a small section away from one end, and then work your fingers along the length of the cut to free a short length of bark. A stick carved to a blunt wedge and pushed under the bark layer will speed up the process (*fig 1*).

fig 1

3. Work back along the trunk to release more of the sheet. Do this slowly and carefully, since it's easy to break the sheet by trying to peel too much at once.
4. Once the bark is released, slide the tube off the trunk so it's ready for use. Sections of bark sheet can be sewn together with split tree roots to make containers and baskets—or even a boat!

To cut even strips of bark from the trunk—for weaving, for example—first make an improvised scribe with a stick and a wood screw.

1. Cut a 12 inch (30 centimeter) long, thumb-thick stick, and saw a stop cut (see page 135) partway through the middle of the stick.
2. Use a knife to cleave down toward the stop cut, and remove a section of wood, so that there is a step in the stick.
3. Screw a wood screw through the rounded top of the stick, so that the sharp tip protrudes on the flat underside (*fig 2*). The distance between the step and the screw will be the width of the bark strips that you cut.
4. Remove the first strip from the trunk as evenly as you can with a knife. A straightedge or ruler can help if you have one and if the log is itself straight enough.

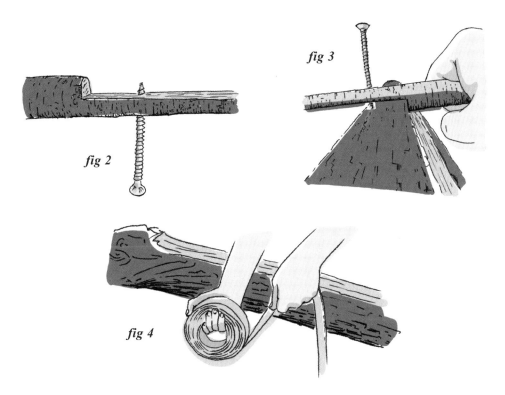

fig 3

fig 2

fig 4

5. Place the scribe on the log with the step sitting on bare wood, butting against the edge of bark exposed in step 4.
6. Press the screw into the bark, and with constant downward pressure, drag it along the length of the log to release a strip (*fig 3*). Peel this off, and repeat until you have processed all the bark.
7. Roll the strips up with the inner bark facing outward, so they dry more quickly on the inside and don't curl into a tube (*fig 4*).

Store your bark in a dry place until needed. You'll need to soak the bark in water to soften it up, so that it becomes workable.

THE VERSATILITY OF BARK
Different types of bark have different properties and provide a versatile material for a variety of crafts. It's worth experimenting with your local tree species to find out which ones produce the bark that's best for making containers or weaving strips. The only commercially harvested bark comes from the cork oak (Quercus suber)*, which—apart from wine bottle stoppers—has many applications because of its sound-absorbing and heat-insulating properties. Large sheets of birch bark, taken from trees in northern latitudes, have long been turned into containers of all kinds and even canoes. Elm bark has traditionally been used for strong and durable woven seating, oak bark for the tanning of leather, and cedar bark for everything from clothing to emergency food in times of famine.*

WHITTLING AND CARVING

It may offend some serious wood carvers, but the terms whittling and carving are used interchangeably here. Carving is about making a thing, whereas whittling is a way of passing the time—making wood shavings and doodling in three dimensions with a sharp knife. For many whittlers, process is everything, and the product isn't particularly important: It's a way of keeping busy and losing yourself in an absorbingly creative task that settles the mind. Whittling also teaches proficiency in using a knife, a vital skill if you want to craft the "stuff of life" and become more self-reliant when living outdoors.

WHERE TO WHITTLE

Whittling can be done just about anywhere, but the best place must surely be by the fireside in the woods. Wherever you are, make sure there's reasonable light, that you're sitting comfortably and safely, and that you leave any alcoholic drinks until after the tools are packed away for the day. There are many safe ways to work, such as leaning forward with your forearms on your knees, sitting upright, and working to your side; or working on your knees with the work resting on a stump. There are also one or two dangerous ways—using the knife anywhere between your legs is a definite no-no, and sitting too close to your friends is better avoided!

Don't get too hung up on "the best knife." To start with, it may be the one you already own. As long as the knife is sharp enough and comfortable to hold, you can start whittling. Eventually, you might find limitations with the angles and curves that your knife is able to carve and think about getting something more specialist such as a tapering "sloyd" knife—from the Swedish word *slöjd*, which roughly translates as "crafts."

KNIFE TECHNIQUES

» *Freehand carving and power cuts.* Holding the wood in one hand and the knife in the other, place the knife on the wood, find the angle where the cutting edge just bites into the wood, and push the knife away from you, or pull the wood toward the knife to make a shaving. This action can jar the elbow if you're trying to remove a lot of wood, so try to push the wood onto a stump or chopping block by your side (*fig 1*). Just make sure that your knuckles don't hit the block as you finish the knife stroke.

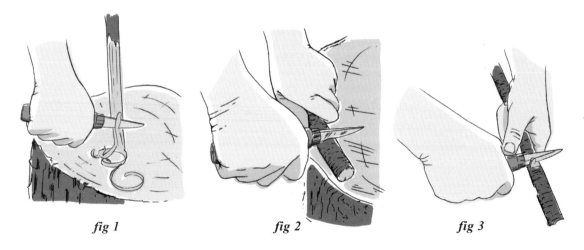

fig 1	*fig 2*	*fig 3*

» *Stop cut.* A stop cut goes across the grain of the wood to literally "stop" a knife cut from traveling any farther. Push the knife down across the wood, and lean on it with a straight arm to exert the most force and slice through the fibers (*fig 2*). There's no point in trying to do this with a sawing action, since your whittling knife won't have a serrated blade.

» *Thumb push.* For short, controlled cuts—especially toward a stop cut—push the knife with the thumb of the hand that's holding the wood (*fig 3*). The hand holding the knife exerts no force, it simply maintains the correct angle of the cutting edge. Pressing on the metal spine of the knife can lead to a sore thumb, so push on the back of the handle instead.

» *Chest lever.* Sometimes known as the scissor (or even chicken wing grip!), the chest lever is an effective way of removing lots of wood quickly. The grip may feel strange to start with, but once you get used to it, it will become a whittling staple. Place your wrists against your lower rib cage, with your palms facing up to hold the knife and the work. When knife and wood are gripped, the knuckles of each

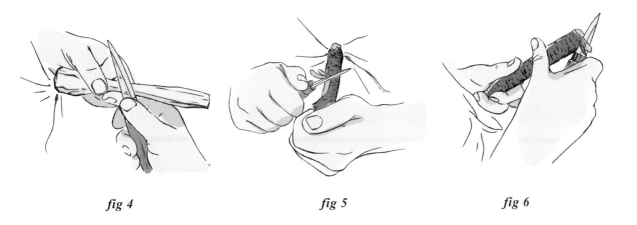

fig 4   fig 5   fig 6

index finger should be touching, the cutting edge of the knife facing outward and your thumb lying along the top of the knife handle, facing up at you (*fig 4*). Once the blade has bitten into the wood, open your shoulders and let your back muscles do the work.

» *Cutting toward yourself.* This technique may seem counterintuitive, but it's extremely useful for getting at angles that you couldn't carve safely otherwise. Brace the knife-holding forearm and wrist against your rib cage, and push the workpiece onto your body with the other hand (*fig 5*). The knife must not travel past your wrist, so keep the wrist clamped to your body and make small, controlled cuts. Don't cut toward the hand holding the work. It's possible to nick loose clothing with the tip of the knife, so wear an apron or old shirt rather than your new breathable waterproof jacket.

» *Paring cut.* This is a cut that's used to round off the end of a stick to a dome. It's like peeling an apple in that the thumb of your knife-holding hand is braced against the work rather than around the knife handle (*fig 6*). Make sure you keep the thumb low and out of the way.

PRACTICING YOUR
WHITTLING SKILLS

It's time to grab a stick and start whittling. Cut a thumb-thick green wood stick that's reasonably straight and knot free and start trying out the cuts on the previous pages. Keep it simple, relax, and don't worry about making a recognizable thing until you feel comfortable with at least the freehand cut, stop cut, and thumb push. If at any point you feel tired or frustrated, take a break before having another go. The project below will help you master the basic techniques, and you can keep making better and better versions of it as you become more confident in this most absorbing of pastimes.

MAKING A "TRY STICK"

This classic project was popularized by Mors Kochanski (1940–2019), a legendary Canadian bushcraft and wilderness living skills instructor, as a way to practice and develop knife techniques. The example here includes some typical practical carving shapes and adds a few decorative ideas. Once these cuts are mastered, you'll be able to combine them to make pretty much anything you can think of—using nothing more than a knife and a chunk of wood.

1. *Pointed end.* Use power cuts to take off large chunks of wood, then keep removing smaller and smaller ribbons of wood until there are so many facets that the surface feels smooth.
2. *Bow nock.* Roll the knife to make an angled stop cut, then thumb push into it to make a rounded slot big enough to hold a bowstring.
3. *One-sided groove.* Make a stop cut all the way around the stick, then thumb push toward it at an angle to make the groove. You can also carve from the other side to make a V-shaped groove.
4. *Flat section.* To leave a flat surface, make two stop cuts, and remove the wood in between with controlled thumb push cuts. Two flat sections on different sticks placed together at right angles and then square lashed (see pages 148–9) make a strong joint.
5. *Concave cut.* Thumb pushing while rolling your wrist allows a steep cut to transition to a gentle cut. Remember that you can't cut uphill, so turn the wood around and carve again from the other direction. Use the tip of the knife and a decreasing amount of force to achieve a flat base to the curve.
6. *Wide hook.* Make an angled stop cut in the stick, and then remove chips of wood by making one side of a concave cut toward it. Deepen the stop cut, then keep carving until the hook is deep enough.
7. *Pointed hook.* Make two vertical stop cuts in the shape of an X. Remove wood from the lower three-quarters of the X, leaving the top triangle as a hook. This can be angled inward to make the hook more effective—useful for making pothangers to hang over a fire.
8. *Bobbin.* Make parallel stop cuts all the way around the stick, then remove wood with thumb push cuts between them to leave a smaller cylinder, which can be used for winding twine. You could also saw this piece off to make a bottle stopper.
9. *Spiral.* A simple but effective decoration that looks good on a walking stick. Begin a stop cut at 45 degrees to the stick, and roll it down as far as you like. Then follow the one-sided groove technique to make the spiral pattern. This looks even more effective if you make a second, parallel spiral starting on the other side of the stick from the first spiral.
10. *Rounded end.* Begin with a paring cut at 45 degrees to the end of the stick. Then make the transition more subtle or dome-like with a gentler paring cut below and a steeper one above.

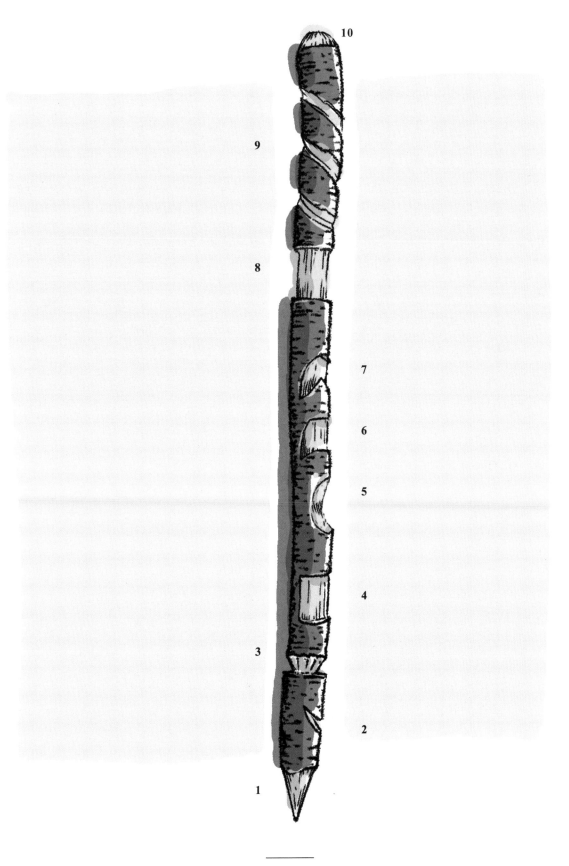

COPPICING

The oldest sustainable method of woodland management, coppicing involves cutting selected tree species in rotation, typically from eight to twenty years between harvests. It's a woodland skill that goes back thousands of years and has been widely practiced across Europe since at least the Neolithic period, providing a constant supply of wood for crafts and building materials. A coppiced tree is one that's cut down to ground level in the winter, so that new shoots will grow from the base or "stool" in the spring and summer. In a coppice rotation, a small patch of the total woodland is cut in year one, then an adjacent area in the next year, and so on, until it's time to cut the first part again. This ensures that there are always areas of woodland with different levels of light and height, which allows a wide range of plants and animals to always enjoy optimal conditions.

AN ANCIENT SYSTEM

At Westonbirt Arboretum, in Gloucestershire, England, a single lime tree, consisting of a ring of stools more than 53 feet (16 meters) in diameter, has been regularly cut for the past 2,000 years. When coppice stools are spaced close together, the new stems grow tall and straight in competition for the available light, resulting in regular-sized, easy-to-work material. Each coppiced tree species yields wood that historically has lent itself to particular products, which in turn influenced local agricultural practices and tools. Coppicing remained a widespread woodland management system as long as there was a market for coppice products, such as tannin-rich oak bark—used extensively in the leather tanning trade—and charcoal (see pages 140–1). It has been said that a "wood that pays is a wood that stays," but the opposite also applies, and when coke, derived from coal, replaced charcoal as a fuel from the eighteenth century, coppicing went into decline. That decline continues today, with very few coppice merchants operating full time and much of the coppicing done in the name of biodiversity rather than as a commercial enterprise.

Tree before coppicing

Coppiced tree

A LIVING PRODUCTION LINE

Dozens of different trees species will coppice. Mostly, these are temperate region deciduous trees, such as ash, hazel, chestnut, oak, willow, black locust, and hornbeam, although the coast redwood (*Sequoia sempervirens*) and monkey puzzle (*Araucaria araucana*) also produce multiple new stems from a stump after cutting. The coppicing of an area of woodland can look pretty devastating, but once the new shoots emerge in the spring and the dormant wildflowers bloom in profusion—thanks to a massive increase in light—the impression is utterly different. And once you know that a regularly coppiced hazel stool can live ten times longer than an uncut hazel, the love of coppiced woodland only becomes stronger.

For a new woodland owner, restoring neglected coppice or instigating a new cycle of growth might be an exciting prospect. But before embarking on such a project, there has to be a long-term plan to keep cutting the rotation, which ideally means finding a use or market for the coppiced wood.

» Coppiced hazel poles can be turned into hurdles, thatching spars, pea-sticks, and beanpoles, used as stakes and binders for hedge laying or wrapped into bundles to reinforce eroding riverbanks.
» Chestnut coppice is especially favored for durable fencing supplies and gate hurdles.
» Alder thrives in wet ground and makes excellent fuel wood.
» Black locust is also a good firewood source, but the tree is invasive in some areas and can root from freshly cut stems, so should be seasoned (see page 118) before use as fence posts.

To coppice a tree, you should cut it close to ground level in winter while it's dormant. The cut should be made at an angle to allow rainwater to drain away and not rot the stump. On multistemmed trees, the angled cuts should drain water away from the center. New coppice needs protection from browsing animals for at least three years. Willow for basketry might be cut every year or two and hazel at around eight years, while oak for tanning might take as long as twenty years. Even if you don't work a coppice rotation yourself, understanding the process and history will enrich your knowledge of woodlands and help you, at the very least, to harvest your own craft materials in more sustainable ways.

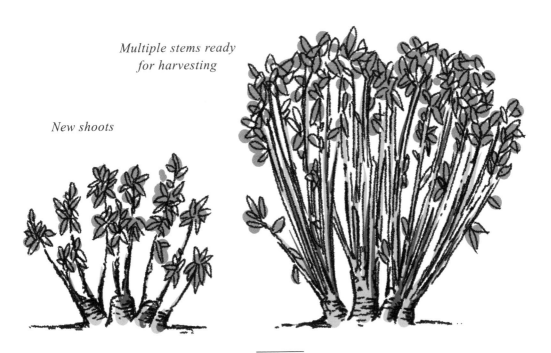

Multiple stems ready for harvesting

New shoots

CHARCOAL BURNING

Charcoal is an ancient forest by-product, and its production—or "burning"—is the oldest of all industrial processes. The light, black combustible material is the result of controlled burning of wood in an oxygen-reduced atmosphere where all the water and volatile organic compounds are driven off, leaving behind pure carbon. A wood fire can typically burn at up to 842 degrees Fahrenheit (450 degrees Celsius), but with charcoal as a fuel—and stoked by bellows—temperatures reach up to 1,832 degrees Fahrenheit (1,000 degrees Celsius). In such intense heat, metals can be smelted from their ores, and it was this discovery at least 5,500 years ago that lifted humans from the Stone Age to the Bronze and then to the Iron Age. Charcoal also yielded wood oils and tars that were vital for waterproofing wooden ships and their rigging.

AN INTENSIVE PROCESS

Charcoal was traditionally made within forests, since once converted, it was much lighter to move than cut timber. Wood was stacked in a pile with a chimney in the middle and then covered in soil and turf to limit the supply of oxygen during the burn. A fire was set in the chimney gap, and as the burn progressed, the volume of the stack would shrink, meaning that gaps in the turf covering had to be covered to keep the whole "clamp" from fully combusting. This required twenty-four-hour human attention for several days, hence the need for the special one-legged charcoal burner's seat (see pages 166–7).

The huge demand for charcoal from the Bronze Age through to the Industrial Revolution, where it was eventually replaced as a fuel by coke (derived from coal), resulted in mass deforestation across Europe and North America. Today, however, well-managed coppiced woodlands (see pages 138–9) can provide sustainable raw materials for charcoal.

MAKING YOUR OWN BURNER

If you're feeling adventurous, you can produce small quantities of hardwood lump charcoal—perfect for barbecues—in an old oil drum. A warning, though—this is a really smoky, smelly process. Make charcoal well away from any neighbors if you want to remain on friendly terms!

WHAT YOU WILL NEED

- *55 gallon (200 liter) oil drum (with all oil residue removed)*
- *cold chisel and lump hammer*
- *angle grinder (plus essential eye and hand protection)*
- *four bricks*
- *earth or sand*
- *round post*
- *seasoned, split firewood*
- *kindling and matches or other firestarter*

fig 1   fig 2   fig 3

fig 4   fig 5

1. Using the cold chisel and lump hammer, punch five or six holes in the top of the drum (*fig 1*).
2. Turn the drum upside down, and using the angle grinder, cut a square hole in that end (*fig 2*). This will be the top of the burner. Grind the corners off the removed square of metal, then set it aside.
3. Raise the drum off the ground on four bricks, and build a ramp of damp soil or sand all the way around the base, apart from a 6 inch (15 centimeter) wide door, which will let air in under the drum (*fig 3*).
4. Stand the round post in the middle of the drum, then stack seasoned wood tightly around it (*fig 4*). Remove the post and light a fire in the gap left behind.
5. Once the fire has clearly caught and is burning well, put the square lid on, rotated slightly so that it sits on the remaining metal and leaves small gaps to act as chimneys to let the smoke out (*fig 5*). Where the square lid touches the drum, seal all the edges well with damp soil or sand.

The smoke will be thick and white. Much of it is steam, and you can carefully feel how wet it is between your fingers, which will also have a tar-like smell from the burned-off aromatic hydrocarbons. If activity in the burner slows, bang the sides of the drum to settle the contents and maintain the burn. If all goes well, the smoke will eventually change color to a wispy blue-gray—the signal that the burn is complete. Close the air intake under the drum and the chimneys at the top to exclude all oxygen, and wait twenty-four hours until the drum is cold before opening. You should now find that the wood you loaded has converted to black charcoal. Don't worry if there are some partially converted "brown ends." These are great for lighting a fire or can be finished off in your next charcoal burn.

———

BASKETMAKING

The world's oldest surviving woven basket is more than 10,000 years old, but some woven patterns discovered in clay deposits suggest that the craft of weaving objects from natural materials may date back at least 27,000 years. For preagricultural societies who hunted for and gathered food, among the most important items they owned would have been baskets to collect food, such as fruit, nuts, berries, roots, and eggs, to carry back to their camp. Baskets are still just as useful, and woods and hedges (or hedgerows) are full of pliable plant stems and leaves that can be bent, twisted, and woven together to make strong and sometimes complex containers.

A UNIVERSAL CRAFT

The variety of basket materials around the globe is enormous, from split bamboo in Southeast Asia to palm fronds in Central America, and from the cedar root and bark styles of the First Nations of the Pacific Northwest of America to the coiled sedge containers of the Ngarrindjeri in South Australia. In Europe, willow and—to a lesser extent—hazel and oak are still popular basket staples, and the same weaving skills are employed to make anything from coffins to giant sculptures.

Willow for basketry is often cut and dried, sometimes with the bark peeled, and stored for a long time. It then has to be soaked before weaving. Hedge baskets made from freshly cut material are quick to make but don't last as long. When they dry out and become brittle, you can just make another one.

EASY WEAVING

As an introduction to basket weaving, a tension tray—a kind of platter with a multitude of uses, from collecting mushrooms to draining vegetables—makes for a simple and rewarding project. Willow or dogwood work well as tree material, although a variety of species with different-colored bark will allow you to make patterns within the weaving.

WHAT YOU WILL NEED
» *bundle of straight, bendable plant stems, free from branches,*
  with a little stiffness and spring to them, about 0.3 to 0.4 inches
  (8 to 10 millimeters) diameter at the butt end and around 3.3 to 5 feet
  (1 to 1.5 meters) long
» *pruning shears—or a sharp knife, used carefully*

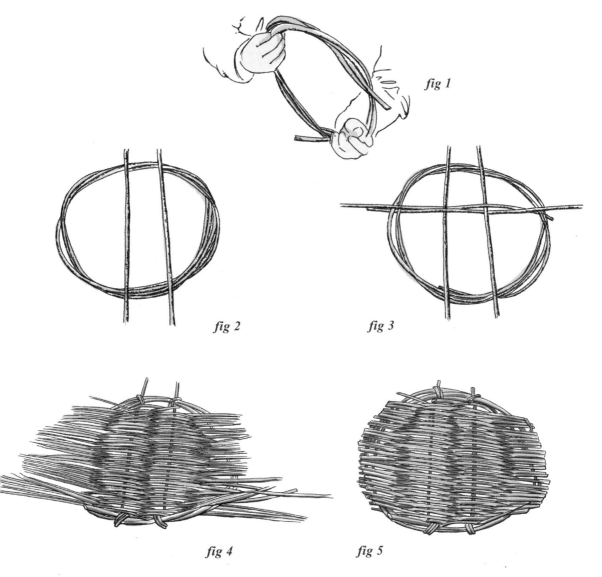

fig 1

fig 2

fig 3

fig 4

fig 5

1. Take one of the longest stems and bend it smoothly into a hoop about 12 inches (30 centimeters) across. Add a second stem to the hoop, so that it's equally strong all the way around (*fig 1*).
2. Use pruning shears to snip off the ends that stick out from the hoop.
3. Cut two pencil-thick rods that are fairly straight and slightly longer than the diameter of the hoop. Lay these parallel to each other across the middle of the hoop (*fig 2*).
4. Take two long stems. Weave the first one perpendicular to the rods, so that it goes over the edge of the hoop, under the first rod, over the second rod, and under the other side of the hoop. Weave the second rod from the other side in the opposite pattern to the first. Push these two rods tight together. This should lock the short rods in place (*fig 3*).
5. Continue to weave more long rods between the hoop edges and center rods in an alternating pattern, until the whole hoop is covered with the woven pattern (*fig 4*).
6. Use pruning shears to trim the long ends off the woven rods on either side of the hoop, until you're happy with the shape (*fig 5*).

HEDGE LAYING

Hedges have been around as long as humans have wanted to protect and demarcate the land. In 57 B.C.E., the Roman general Julius Caesar fought the Nervii tribe in what is now Belgium and described the cavalry-impeding hedges they constructed as "a fortification like a wall, through which it was not only impossible to enter, but even to penetrate with the eye." Hedges also proved a vital defense 2,000 years later in 1944 at the Battle of Normandy, where the dense French hedges, or "bocage," provided excellent cover for German infantry and artillery, and proved extremely difficult for Allied tanks to cross, even with the aid of explosives.

The profusion of hedges in the countryside owes more, though, to agriculture than warfare. Before the invention of electric fences and livestock wire fencing, farm animals were often confined behind living hedges. Maintaining these barriers to keep them dense and effective became a localized skill, with many styles emerging in different places depending on crops grown, animals raised, and tree species cultivated.

CLUES IN THE HEDGES

Some hedges remain as ancient landscape features, not just marking out field and farm boundaries but also the limits of larger district territories. As woodland cover has generally decreased, hedges have become more and more important as wildlife corridors. They are vital nesting places for birds, and they provide navigational aids for bats and cover for small mammals. Ancient hedges are incredibly diverse, with almost the whole vertical structure of a woodland replicated in a thin strip, allowing both shade-tolerant and light-loving flowering plants to find their niche.

If neglected, hedges become overgrown, gappy, and eventually no barrier to animals. But all laid hedges can be regenerated without the need to plant new shrubs and trees. After tangles of brambles are cleared out, individual stems can be "pleached"—chopped and bent horizontally or diagonally, leaving a hinge of bark so the tree stays alive and sends up new shoots in the spring. Side branches are trimmed, and the laid stems held in place with "crooks" or stakes with woven "binders" holding the hedge together at the top.

HOW OLD IS THAT HEDGE?
To date a hedge, you can use "Hoopers Law," which states that if you calculate the average number of tree and shrub species in three different 100 foot (30 meter) lengths of hedge and multiply the result by one hundred, you get the age in years. This is more a hypothesis than an actual law, but it can provide some insight into relative age as well as an appreciation of hedge biodiversity.

HOW TO MAKE YOUR OWN LIVING HEDGE

Hedges require a high density of stems in a long line, so you might need to interplant new trees with existing deciduous trees and wait a couple of growing seasons before laying the hedge. The traditional tool of the hedge layer is the billhook—like a cross between an ax and a large knife (see pages 116–17). The blade typically has a "nose" to keep the cutting edge from hitting the ground and becoming blunt. This also brings the weight of the tool forward for better balance and allows you to lift and move stakes without too much bending down. Billhook-like tools are found around the world in slightly different forms. If you can't get hold of a billhook, a light ax can be used instead.

fig 1   fig 2

1. *Pleaching.* Partially cut through each stem just above ground level, and bend it over at 45 degrees (*fig 1*). If you're working on a hill, always lay the hedge with the branches bending uphill from the cut. Tidy up each cut so that rain water will run off rather than sit in the split and rot the wood.
2. *Staking.* Use stout, straight stakes about 5.6 feet (1.7 meters) long and 0.8 to 2 inches (2 to 5 centimeters) in diameter. These are usually hazel poles, sharpened at one end. Place the stakes in a line every 20 inches (50 centimeters) among the living plants (*fig 2*). Weave the living stems, or "pleachers," alternately in and out of the stakes to create a basket-weave pattern. Use a mallet to secure the stakes in place.
3. *Binding.* Collect freshly cut long (8 feet or 2.5 meters plus), thin (0.8 inches or 2 centimeters) in diameter, and flexible pieces of green wood to act as binders to hold the whole structure together. Weave and twist the binders between the stakes to bind them in place (*fig 3*). In spring, new growth will quickly cover the stakes and binders.

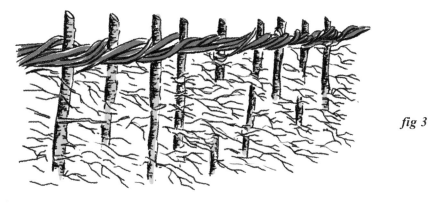

fig 3

Just hanging out in the woods with no particular agenda can be the ideal antidote to a hectic life. But invariably, after awhile comes the desire to get going and make something. It might be an experiment to see what happens "if ". . . , or the need to provide an important item that you haven't brought with you, or simply a way of learning or practicing a new skill.

Making things—as much for the sake of the process as the end achievement—is one way that adults can indulge in forest play and reach a state of "flow," bringing with it feelings of contentment and relaxation. Like children's play, grown-up projects can be messy and chaotic—and hard to make sense of—but above all, you should do them because you feel like it. Don't be afraid to improvise, try new techniques, and lose yourself in the task. Make something again and again and you'll discover your own tricks and tips, gradually becoming more expert through direct experience.

The projects in this chapter employ a wide range of skills, allowing you to construct items for practical purposes or just for fun. Learn new knots or woodworking skills to make a camp chair, or make a tree house where you can sleep up high and watch wildlife at close quarters. Whittle tent pegs or kitchen utensils from green wood, or fire your own clay cup in the campfire. Carve and shoot a simple bow and arrow—or you might unwind on a rope swing. Indulge your creativity with some environmental art, or take action for wildlife by building a birdhouse or planting a forest garden. Many of the skills and activities in this chapter could develop into a lifelong process of enquiry and development. The instructions will get you started. Where you take it is up to you.

6

FOREST PROJECTS

KNOTS, HITCHES, AND LASHINGS

Knots can be confusing. There are hundreds of them, with different names for different places, activities, or sports. Arguments rage about the "best" knot for the job, but the choice should depend on whether it's strong and secure enough for the purpose—and whether you can remember how to tie it correctly. Having a repertoire of a few knots, hitches, and lashings will serve you well for all but the most specialist jobs. Knots are tied in rope, hitches tend to tie rope to other things, and lashings are used to tie other things together. Several projects in this chapter use the examples here.

Tying the knot you need when you need it relies on developing the muscle memory over time. Start by carefully following the instructions, then try without them—and with your eyes closed. Give the tying enough repetitions, and it will become as automatic as writing your name.

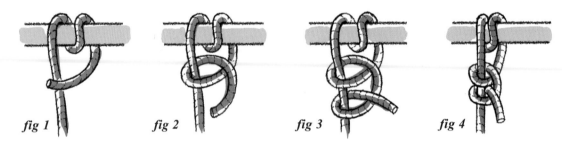

fig 1   *fig 2*   *fig 3*   *fig 4*

ROUND TURN AND TWO HALF HITCHES
A reliable way to make this is to tie one end of a tight line to a tree or other object (see pages 150–1).
1. Wrap the rope or cord twice around the object you want to tie to, and place the working end over the top of the other part of the line to make a triangle (*fig 1*).
2. Bring the line up through the triangle (*fig 2*).
3. Make a second turn over and back under the other line to make a D shape (*fig 3*).
4. Pull tight with the working end to secure the knot (*fig 4*).

SQUARE LASHING
Make a strong lashing that can secure two poles that cross at any angle (see pages 158–9).
1. Wrap the middle of the rope or cord behind the upright pole. Work with one hand on each end of the cord, and bring both ends over the front of the horizontal pole (*fig 1*).
2. Take both ends under the horizontal pole and behind the upright pole, crossing the cords and swapping hands at the back (*fig 2*). Keep as much tension on the cord as you can.
3. Bring the cords over the front of the horizontal pole and around the back of the vertical pole, crossing again at the back (*fig 3*).
4. Repeat one more time—it will look like there are three backpack straps on the horizontal pole (*fig 4*).

5. Cross again at the back of the vertical. Cross in front and wrap the cord between the poles, which will cinch the initial wraps tight. Repeat, so that you have three tightly pulled wraps between the poles (*fig 5*).
6. Tie off the two ends with a square—or reef—knot (*fig 6*).

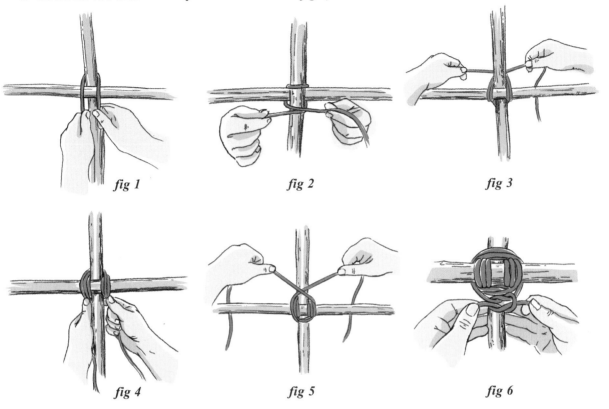

fig 1

fig 2

fig 3

fig 4

fig 5

fig 6

TRIPOD LASHING

Use this fixing to secure the tops of three poles that can then be spread out to create a tripod for many purposes, including a signal fire (see page 55), pot hanger, and smoking rack (see pages 154–5).

1. Lay your poles parallel with each other. Take one end of the string or cord, and tie a clove hitch to one of the outer poles (*fig 1*).
2. Weave the string in and out of the poles four or five times (*fig 2*).
3. Make three tight turns in between two of the poles, and then repeat in the second gap. Tie off the working end with two half hitches—see left—(*fig 3*).
4. Spread the poles so that the outer poles cross below the center pole to create a sturdy tripod (*fig 4*).

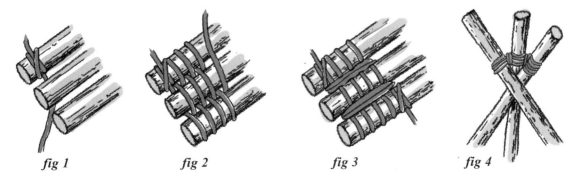

fig 1

fig 2

fig 3

fig 4

PUTTING UP A SHELTER

Shelter is a basic human need. It keeps you dry, shaded from the sun, out of the wind, and insulated from the cold. It also creates a feeling of security and a place to return to after forest activities. Some shelters are straightforward; others require advanced skills in origami. To be dry and comfortable anywhere in the forest, all you need are some sturdy trees, a simple tarpaulin, and plenty of cord for a shelter that can be set up in different ways depending on the weather, group size, and environment. Look for a fairly flat site that won't become a puddle or a stream in the rain, and check for hazards, such as loosely hanging tree branches overhead or insect nests on the ground.

WHAT YOU WILL NEED
- » *cord or rope*
- » *tarpaulin*
- » *metal or wooden pegs*

1. Tie a length of cord between two trees to create the apex, or ridgeline, of your shelter. Make the line as taut as possible.
2. Hang your tarpaulin over the line lengthwise like a sheet hanging on a washing line (*fig 1*). If your tarp has hanging loops on the outside, thread these with the cord before tying the line in step 1. The tarp will then hang from the line rather than over it, which will keep water from tracking along the line and dripping inside the shelter.
3. Using round turn and two half hitches knots (see page 148), tie out the four tarp guy lines to nearby trees. Fix diagonally opposite corners first. You should be aiming for taut edges and as few wrinkles as possible to prevent water pooling if it rains (*fig 2*).

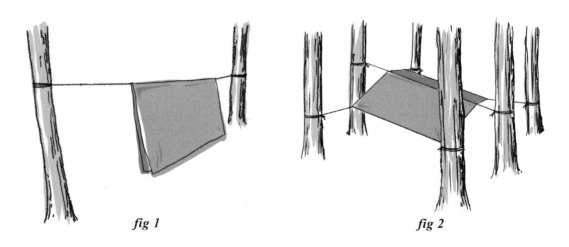

fig 1   *fig 2*

TYING THE KNOT

The Evenk—or Siberian—hitch, truckers' hitch, taut-line hitch . . . There's a bewildering array of securing knots and many different types that you can use to secure ridgelines and tie guy lines. For this project, and in the spirit of keeping things simple, the round turn and two half hitches is as reliable a way as any to tie one end of a tight line to a tree. See page 148 for the knot instructions.

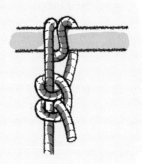

4. Think about where the water will go if it rains. Will it hit the ground and then run through your shelter? If so, rethink your strategy. You can control the flow to some extent by tying down the edges to make a valley or gutter. Alternatively, lift the middle of one edge with a stick or trekking pole, so that water runs toward the corners (*fig 3*).
5. If there are limited anchor points, you can adjust this design to make a diamond-shaped shelter. Hang the tarp diagonally over the ridgeline, so that you can use the ridgeline trees as two of your tie-off points for the corners of the tarp (*fig 4*). You only need to find two other anchors for the other two corners instead of four. This setup works especially well above a hammock or as a sunshade.
6. On a windy day, you can use a "lean-to" design to give more shelter from one particular direction. Follow the instructions for the basic design, but hang more material on one side than the other. Peg the long side as low to the ground as possible.

The large surface area of a tarpaulin can make it behave like a sail. So if you're going to peg the tarp sides to the ground, you could ditch the little wire pegs that might have been sold with it, and make yourself some more effective chunky wooden ones (see pages 162–3).

fig 3   fig 4

MAKING A FIREPLACE

In Old English, the word for "fireplace"—the place on the floor where a fire is made—was *heorth*, which became "hearth." It's a pleasant coincidence that this also contains the word "heart," as it's often said that the fire is the heart of the camp. It keeps us warm, boils our water, cooks our food, and lights the dark nights. If you're able to have a semipermanent or fixed camp in the woods, then it's worth taking the time to plan your fireplace and make it as practical and safe as possible.

Before you start, you need to consider a few points.
» How long are you planning to use the fireplace, and how easy will it be to dismantle and remove all traces when you move on? This question will help you consider how much effort, engineering, and materials are likely to go into this project.
» How many people will sit around the fire? Building a small fire to sit close to rather than a big fire that you have to keep away from makes good sense, since it brings your group closer together and conserves forest wood. A fire built on the ground or in a hollow will warm your feet, but a raised fireplace will radiate heat to your torso and be much more comfortable to cook on.
» What is the ground like underneath? If the earth is high in organic matter, such as partly decomposed leaf litter, there's a risk of starting an underground fire, which can smolder for months. Bare rock as a base can be charred and leave a fire scar for many years. In both these situations, find an alternative site, such as a gravel beach on a river bend, or insulate the base of the fire with soil or sand.
» Is the fireplace mainly for cooking, warmth, or a social focal point? This will determine the fireplace height. Much of the heat from a fire in a hollow or pit will warm the earth rather than the people sitting around it. If people are sitting on chairs, it's best to raise the fire so that it warms more than just feet.
» Concerns are growing about the harmful effects of woodsmoke on human health and the environment, but time spent around an occasional campfire can bring great benefits to community and family. It's all about finding a balance. Burning very dry, small diameter wood on small fires, for example, will mitigate the harm and still allow you to savor your time around the fire.

WHAT YOU WILL NEED
» *four or eight logs, 24 to 31 inches (60 to 80 centimeters) long and 4 to 8 inches (10 to 20 centimeters) in diameter*
» *eight stakes, 2 inches (5 centimeters) in diameter, twice as tall as the height of the fireplace*
» *saw*
» *ax*
» *spade*
» *bucket or wheelbarrow*
» *mallet*
» *soil or sand*

EXPLOSIVE SITUATION

It may seem perfectly natural to surround a campfire with stones to protect the area around it. All too often, though, stones can be a serious hazard. Any porous or stratified rock that has been soaked in water—in the sea or river, or just by rain—can explode when heated. As the water in the pores or between the layers heats up, it expands and may cause the rock to suddenly crack. This isn't an issue with dense igneous rocks or in arid regions, but if you're at all unsure, just don't use stones.

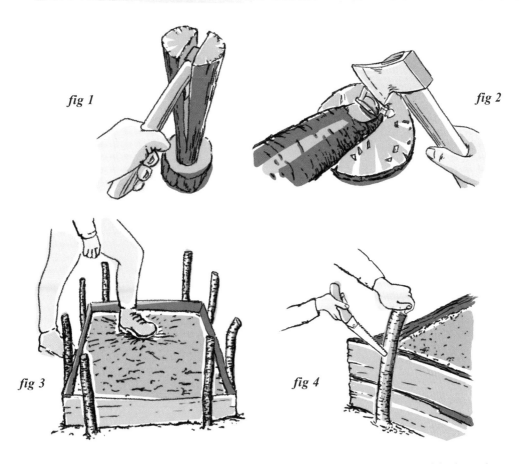

fig 1

fig 2

fig 3

fig 4

1. Identify a site for your semipermanent fireplace. Check the tree canopy and ground for hazards.
2. Decide how big the fireplace will be. Measure the space, and saw the logs to the right length to create the four sides of the fireplace. If you don't have enough big logs, you can double the number by splitting the ones you have in half—lengthwise—with the ax (*fig 1*).
3. Cut long stakes, and using an ax, chop a rough point on one end of each stake (*fig 2*).
4. Lay out the logs in a square or rectangle, and secure them in place by banging in the stakes with a mallet. Fill the inner area of the square with soil or sand, and tamp it down to a firm base (*fig 3*). Avoid using rocks, as they may explode in the heat of the fire (see above).
5. Add a second level of logs on top of the first, and add more soil. Finish by sawing off the stakes—or banging them in—level with the top of the logs (*fig 4*).

BUILDING A
CAMPFIRE SMOKER

Why smoke food? Essentially, smoking meat, fish, poultry, or even cheese and vegetables over a campfire is a way of slow cooking that adds deep flavor to food and helps preserve it. Our Stone Age ancestors were very familiar with both aspects, since they hung spare meat over the fires in their enclosed shelters to be eaten later. If you brine or marinade meat first and then slowly dry it on low heat over a smoky fire, the process will also allow you to store it for longer without refrigeration. This project will show you how to make a smoking rack, but make sure you read about the principles of smoking and curing on page 81 before using the smoker for food preparation.

WHAT YOU WILL NEED
  » *knife*
  » *pruning saw*
  » *string*
  » *three stiff poles, at least thumb-thick and 5 to 6.5 feet (1.5 to 2 meters) long, depending on how much meat you want to smoke—the taller the poles, the greater the number of racks*
  » *a supply of finger-thick green wood poles to make frames and racks*
  » *green foliage, such as conifer branches*
  » *firewood, preferably hardwood—smoke from different woods will impart distinct, characteristic flavors to your food*

1. Light a small fire in your fireplace (see pages 152–3), and burn hardwood logs until you have a good bed of hot, slow-burning embers.
2. Away from the fire at a safe distance, lash the three long poles together with a tripod lashing (see page 149), then fold out into a tripod.
3. Fix two smaller poles to the tripod using square lashings (see pages 148–9) to make a triangular horizontal frame. You can make several frames to vary the height that the food sits above the fire.
4. Move the finished smoker over the fire. Lay peeled green poles on top of each frame to make a rack (*fig 1*). The food can sit on the poles or hang from them.
5. In hot, dry weather, just leave the smoker as it is. The sun will aid the drying process—and the smoke will keep insects away. In cooler weather, thatch the top of the tripod with leafy green boughs to trap the smoke and heat around the drying racks (*fig 2*).

Take care when using the smoker to keep the thatch from catching fire as it dries out. Fat dripping from food can cause flare-ups. Ideally, you should have a constant supply of hot embers producing white smoke, not black. If more smoke is needed, you can add some small chips of freshly cut hardwood.

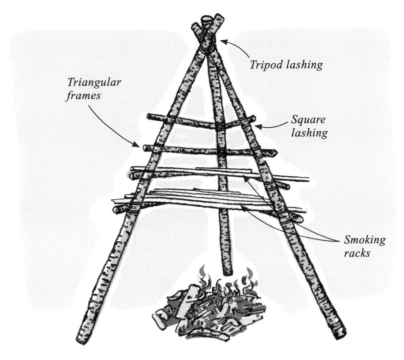

Tripod lashing

Triangular frames

Square lashing

Smoking racks

fig 1

fig 2

LEGENDARY FOREST FOLK

Sometimes, when walking through the woods alone, as you let the cares of the modern world slip away and indulge your senses in the sights, smells, and sounds of the surrounding forest, you may suddenly stop for a moment and sense the presence of something not quite human: a faint whisper on the path, the feeling of being stared at from a copse of trees, a hint of a form dancing by a stream . . .

Depending on where you're walking, you may be trespassing on the territory of supernatural beings, of fairies, elves, nymphs, dryads, gnomes, leprechauns, and other folk who may or may not welcome your company. Fairies are perhaps most associated with Celtic, English, Slavic, and French folklore, where they often take the form of small, magical creatures who live in and guard over natural features, such as trees and flowers. Often attractive with green eyes and butterfly wings, they can either be benevolent—such as the tooth fairy, who brings a gift to humans who have lost a tooth—or cause minor to major annoyances, such as tangling the hair, stealing small items, or requisitioning a child to live in an underworld fairyland when they come of age, never to see family and friends again.

In the Scandinavian countries, Iceland, and Northern Europe, tales of elves are rampant. These humanesque figures are small in stature, twinkle with mischief, and possess magical powers. The story of Santa Claus's helpers stems from Finnish myths of the *tomten*, a type of house elf traditionally associated with pagan Yuletide festivities. They are hard-working, possess superhuman strength, and offend easily. The *tomten* wear red caps and help the Yule Goat distribute gifts door to door at the winter solstice, always enjoying the offering of porridge left out as a "thank you" (think cookies and milk for Santa), so it is easy to see how they have transmogrified into Santa's little helpers.

NATIVE AND ABORIGINAL FOLK

Lurking in the verdant New World forests of North America live beings that are half human, half deer. The Deer People may look like antlered humans, or they may look human with only hooves for feet to identify their true nature. The Choctaw *kashehotapolo* is a mischievous deer man who may frighten hunters in swampy woods. On the other hand, the Deer Woman of the Cherokee, Seminole, Pawnee, Iroquois, and other tribes, appears as a beautiful and seductive young woman. She is benevolent to women, children, and men who follow social norms. But Deer Women can be malevolent toward unruly or promiscuous men!

Identifiable as a cross between a marsupial and a reptile, the Bunyip of Australia is connected to Aboriginal lore and presents a sinister proposition. From their homes near rivers and swamps, they snatch humans—preferably children and women—and feast upon them when their area is invaded.

WILD WONDERS

Tales of the wild men of the woods, also known by names such as woodwose or woodehouse, captured the imagination of medieval Europe and are depicted widely in literature, tapestries, and roof bosses. Naked, with hair covering most of the body apart from the knees, wild men live away from human society in the forest but occasionally try to capture the love of human women, especially noblewomen and queens. Sometimes, a wild man is accompanied by a wild woman and child, but most often he lives on his own.

Myths of wild men and women are endemic in all cultures and date back to ancient times. Enkidu is one such character, described in the Mesopotamian tale *The Epic of Gilgamesh*, dating from around 2100 B.C.E., in which he acts as a foil to the sophisticated warrior king, Gilgamesh. Perhaps our fascination with the untamed, primitive wild man hints at an unspoken inner truth: that we humans are all wild at heart.

BUILDING A NO-NAILS
TREE HOUSE

Why build a tree house? Number one, because it's fun. It's also a great way to spot wildlife, as sitting up high makes you harder to see and smell. And if you need somewhere to rest, it can give you a flat sleeping platform, even on steep ground. Building a tree house, though, uses a lot of wood, so only make it as big as you need to, and ideally—with permission—in a plantation woodland that already needs thinning. The whole structure should be easy to remove, leave no trace, and not interfere long-term with the growth of the supporting trees. Please don't go hammering metal fixings into living trees!

WHAT YOU WILL NEED
- » *three or four evenly spaced living trees, ideally 8 inches (20 centimeters) diameter minimum*
- » *plenty of long, straight poles, at least 3 inches (8 centimeters) diameter*
- » *strong cord—natural fiber or paracord (parachute cord)*
- » *knife*
- » *saw*

For the cord, natural fiber string or rope is more in keeping with the rest of the materials but will eventually rot, so regular checks would be needed to keep it from failing. Paracord will last longer than the wood and so would have to be removed at some point. To secure the poles to each other, use the square lashing technique shown on pages 148–9. You'll need at least a 6.5 foot (2 meter) length of cord to lash two 3 inch (8 centimeter) diameter poles together.

1. Find a site, and decide how high the structure should be. Look for overhead hazards, and check the soundness of supporting trees. If building much above head height, you'll need to climb onto a log or use a ladder.
2. You can lash a frame straight to trees, but it's better to have additional uprights beside each tree to support the frame from below. Cut four poles for a square or rectangular platform. Bang the poles into the ground at the base of your key trees, and lash to the tree (**A**). You can cut a few 24 inch (60 centimeter) long stakes to hammer in flush to the base of these uprights to prevent any movement away from the base of the tree (**B**).

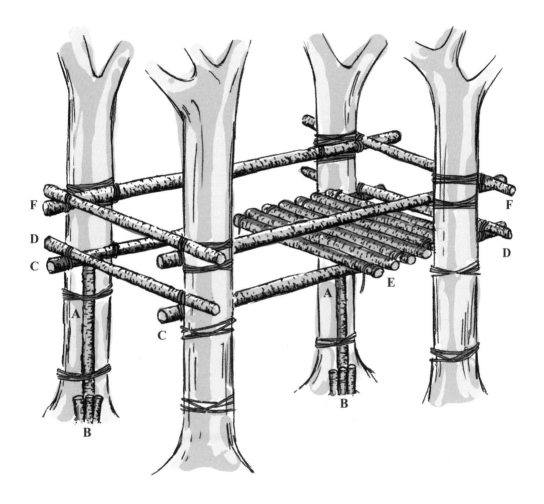

3. Cut two long joists to size—slightly longer than you think you need—to sit on top of the uprights and protrude beyond the trees (**C**). Secure the joists to the trees with lashings, making sure the upright is bearing most of the weight.
4. Complete the other edges of the rectangular platform frame by lashing poles sitting on top of the long joists, on the outside of the trees (**D**).
5. Cut floorboard poles to sit across the joists at right angles without any gaps (**E**). Lay them butt end, and top alternately to keep the floor poles roughly parallel. Weave a long strand of cord under and over the floor poles to secure them to the joists at the edge and keep them from sliding or lifting up.
6. Use long poles lashed to the main trees to create several railings, so that you don't fall out (**F**).
7. Follow the instructions on pages 150–1 to rig a tarpaulin overhead to keep you dry.

MAKING A BIRDHOUSE

Nesting sites for many bird species are disappearing as their habitats are lost, gardens and yards become more manicured, and old buildings are restored. Putting up a homemade birdhouse can help to redress the balance—with the added bonus of allowing you to observe and get to know the avian residents. It's a project for the winter, when you can source freshly felled green wood and put the birdhouse up before the nesting seasons starts in early spring. This rustic round wood design will blend in with a woodland or hedge and will also look great on a wall or fence.

WHAT YOU WILL NEED

» *one straight, knot-free, round log about 6 to 8 inches (15 to 20 centimeters) in diameter—from a tree that will cleave cleanly, such as sweet chestnut or ash*
» *ax*
» *mallet*
» *bow saw or panel saw*
» *sixteen 2 to 2.4 inch (50 to 60 millimeter) long nails*
» *hammer*
» *hand drill—and a drill bit narrower than your nails*
» *brace and an auger bit sized for your chosen bird species (see step 5)*
» *a few 2 inch (50 millimeter) screws and at least one 4 inch (100 millimeter) screw to attach the birdhouse to a tree or wall*
» *fencing wire or synthetic string as an alternative fixing method*

1. Saw a section of log at 45 degrees, so that the longer side is at least 12 inches (30 centimeters) long. The base should be flat, and the top, which will be the roof, is at an angle, so that rain can run off (***fig 1***). Keep the offcut to make the roof in step 6.
2. Use the ax and mallet to split four sections off the side of the log to leave a square core (***fig 2***). The side sections will make the exterior of the birdhouse.
3. Saw a 2.4 to 2.75 inch (6 to 7 centimeter) section from the bottom of the square core for the base.
4. Reassemble the walls of the house tightly around the base section, and fix together with two nails on each side section hammered into the base (***fig 3***). Hammering nails into green wood is likely to make it split, so use the hand drill and a small bit to drill a pilot hole for each nail. Use a single nail in each side to secure the tops of the walls together as well (***fig 4***).

5. Mark a hole 2 to 3 inches (5 to 8 centimeters) from the top of the box on the lower side of the roof slope. This will be the bird's entrance. Drill the hole using an auger bit. The size of the hole will determine which species of birds can access the box. A 1 inch (25 millimeter) hole is good for small birds, such as tits or nuthatches, whereas larger birds, such as starlings or house finches, will need a 1.8 to 2 inch (45 to 50 millimeter) hole.

6. Split the offcut from step 1 to make a rough plank, and fix this to the top of the birdhouse as the roof. Use screws since you'll need to remove the roof to clean out the house each season.

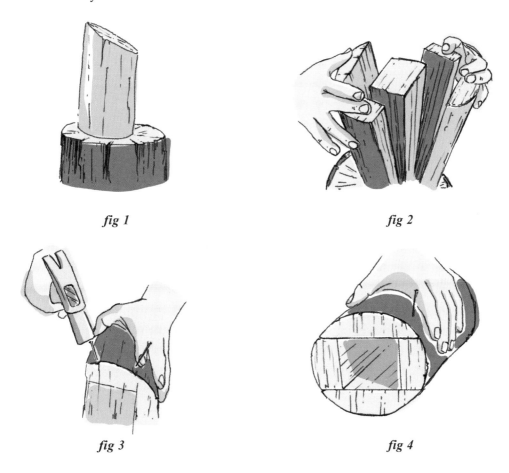

fig 1

fig 2

fig 3

fig 4

WHERE TO PUT THE BIRDHOUSE

Put the birdhouse at least 10 feet (3 meters) above ground, unobscured by foliage and with a clear flight path to the entrance. Make sure the house isn't easily accessible for predators such as squirrels and domestic cats.

You can use a long screw or nail to attach your birdhouse to a tree, the side of a building, or a fence. Avoid steel fixings in trees, as they will corrode, and if not removed, could be a hazard to a chainsaw user. You can also attach the birdhouse to a tree trunk by tying it on with fencing wire or synthetic cord. Any fixings to living trees should be checked and adjusted every year to allow for tree growth.

MAKING TENT PEGS

You've just pitched your tent or tarp for the night when the wind picks up, signaling that bad weather is on the way. You need to batten down the hatches but don't have any tent pegs left to secure every attachment point to the ground. If you want to stay dry and comfortable under your shelter, it's time to make some quick pegs. They can be made directly from thumb-thick roundwood for small tent or tarp guy ropes. Heavier duty, large tent-style pegs can be made from cleft sections of larger diameter wood. These were traditionally handmade in bulk from ash, chestnut, or beech wood using a stock knife—a long-handled knife with a hook at the end. Hundreds of thousands of these pegs were needed by armed forces in World War II, and they were still in production for military use until the 1980s.

WHAT YOU WILL NEED FOR ROUND WOOD PEGS
» *straight plank of relatively hard wood, around 1.2 inches (3 centimeters) diameter and 8 to 12 inches (20 to 30 centimeters) long*
» *sharp knife*

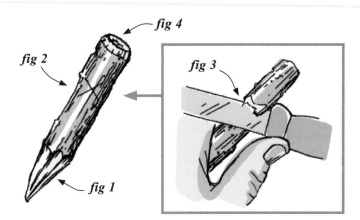

ROUND PEGS
1. Using the knife, whittle one end of the stick of wood into a point (*fig 1*). It doesn't need to be sharp, just tapered enough to drive into the ground.
2. About 1.2 to 1.6 inches (3 to 4 centimeters) from the other end, press down with the knife to make two vertical stop cuts in an X shape (*fig 2*).
3. Use a thumb-push cut (see page 135) to remove wood in the lower three-quarters of the X (*fig 3*).
4. Repeat the stop and thumb-push cuts until you have a hook deep enough to hold the guy rope of your tarp or tent.
5. Chamfer the peg top at 45 degrees to keep the wood from splaying over time when hammered (*fig 4*).

WHAT YOU WILL NEED FOR CLEFT WOOD PEGS

» *12 inches (30 centimeters) long, straight, clean log 4 to 6 inches*
  (10 to 15 centimeters) diameter, from a species that will split cleanly with an ax
» *mallet or hefty stick*
» *pruning saw*
» *sharp knife*

CLEFT PEGS

1. Using the ax and mallet, split your round of log through the pith into six or eight sections (*fig 1*). You can make a peg from each section.
2. Take one of the pieces and saw a groove about 0.8 to 1.2 inches (2 to 3 centimeters) deep on the inward side of the piece (*fig 2*). The cut should be about 2 inches (5 centimeters) from the top of the peg and angled slightly upward. All the shaping of the peg takes place on this side.
3. Invert the peg, and whittle down toward the groove from about halfway along the length (*fig 3*).
4. Turn the peg around, and whittle from halfway toward the tip to make a blunt point (see *finished peg*).
5. Traditional pegs are curved from the hook to the top, so that when hit with a mallet all the force travels directly to the tip. If the top of the peg is too big, the force can split the wood at the saw cut. Carve the wood to taper from the saw cut to the top of the peg (see *finished peg*).
6. Chamfer any rough edges around the saw cut and the top surface.

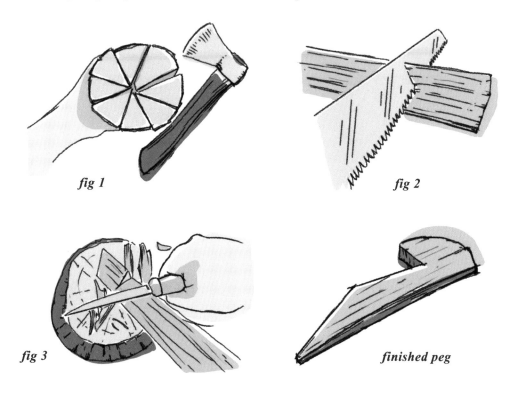

fig 1

fig 2

fig 3

finished peg

DO-IT-YOURSELF UTENSILS

There's a particular satisfaction in being able to provide yourself with the stuff of life—those things that we use every day, especially for cooking and eating. These can be quick, single-use items, where function is more important than form, or carefully designed pieces, pleasing to the eye and kept for many years. The utensils below can fall into either the form or function camp. The materials and initial processes are the same—it's up to you how much finesse you want to add.

WHAT YOU WILL NEED
» *wood for cutting board: freshly cut log, 4 to 6 inches (10 to 15 centimeters) diameter and 12 to 16 inches (30 to 40 centimeters long)*
» *wood for tongs: straight, knot-free stick 0.8 to 2 inches (2 to 5 centimeters) thick, and at least 24 inches (60 centimeters) long*
» *ax*
» *knife*
» *saucepan and water*
» *campfire*
» *string*

CUTTING BOARD
1. Split your freshly cut log in half and then again into a plank.
2. To make a handle, draw your handle shape on the plank, and make two angled saw cuts at the transition from handle to board (*fig 1*).
3. Using an ax, split and remove wood on either side of the marked handle (*fig 2*). The saw cuts act as stop cuts to prevent the wood from splitting along the whole length of the plank.
4. Carve the handle to a shape that you like, and smooth any sharp or rough edges. If you want, you can refine the cutting board by carving the split surface to a smoother finish.

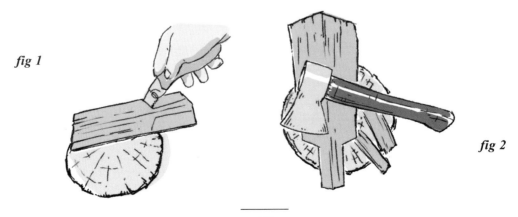

fig 1

fig 2

SPATULA

Use the other half of your split log to make a spatula. The process is the same as that for the cutting board, except that you can make the handle longer and thin the working end to get under food in a pan and flip it over.

TONGS

1. Using the ax, split the stick in half lengthwise, through the pith if you can (*fig 1*). As long as the stick splits cleanly in half and doesn't twist in a spiral, you can make a set of tongs with each half.
2. Mark a 6 inch (15 centimeter) section in the middle of the split stick, and whittle until it's thin enough to flex a little (*fig 2*). If you peel off the bark, try not to cut through fibers on the outside of the stick.
3. Boil a pan of water on the fire, and hold the thinner middle section of the stick over it to heat. As the wood heats up, gradually pull the two ends together—do this too quickly, and you'll break the fibers. In time, the bend will be enough to allow you to plunge the wood into the water to heat further (*fig 3*).

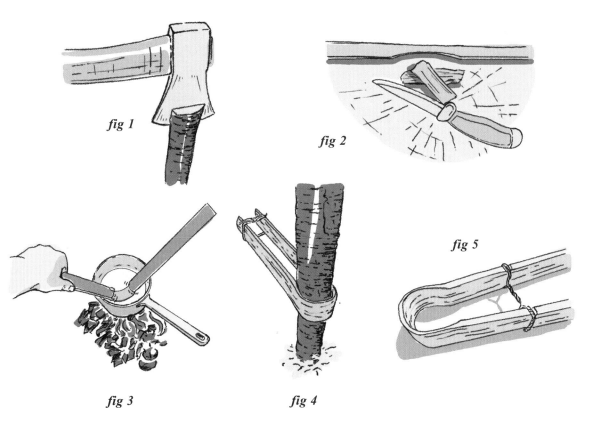

fig 1

fig 2

fig 3

fig 4

fig 5

4. Heat the wood until you can bend it in half with the ends touching. Take the wood out of the water, and bend the middle around a 2 inch (5 centimeter) diameter wooden stake so that it can take on an even curve. Tie the ends together, and let the wood cool and dry completely (*fig 4*).
5. Carve a groove a third of the way along the tongs from the top of the curve, and tie string between the halves to keep them from springing apart too far (*fig 5*).
6. Carve the tips of the tongs into thinner wedges, so it's easier for you to pick up small items. You can also carve grooves on the inside of the tips to improve grip.

MAKING A RUSTIC STOOL

ustic is the key word here, but how rustic depends on what you want from your stool. If you just want a little comfort around the campfire, then a tree stump or log might do. If you're anxious to make something, a one-legged stool is the simplest option. It was the stool of choice for charcoal burners who had to stay up all night to keep their burn under control. If they nodded off, they fell from the stool and soon woke up!

The following instructions are for a one-legged stool, but you can use the same principles and techniques to make a three-legged stool (see bottom of opposite page).

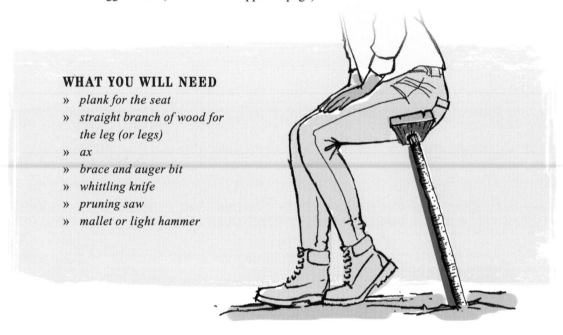

WHAT YOU WILL NEED
- » *plank for the seat*
- » *straight branch of wood for the leg (or legs)*
- » *ax*
- » *brace and auger bit*
- » *whittling knife*
- » *pruning saw*
- » *mallet or light hammer*

1. Split a log around 16 inches (40 centimeters) long in half, using an ax (*fig 1*). The flat surface will be the seat. If the log is big enough and straight grained, you can cleave some wood from the other side to make a plank—or use it to make another stool.
2. With the flat face of the split log uppermost, use a brace and an auger bit to drill a hole through the center, perpendicular to the surface (*fig 2*). Make sure there's a scrap piece of wood underneath to prevent the tool from coming into contact with the earth and becoming blunt.
3. For the leg, find a straight, round piece of branch wood that's slightly larger in diameter than the auger bit used to drill the hole. The leg should be a little longer than the distance from the ground to your knee. You can also make one or more legs by splitting the other half of the cleft log lengthwise into sections.
4. Whittle the end of the leg that you'll insert into the seat to size (*fig 3*). Keep the sides parallel, not tapering like a cone. Take care to leave this end—known as a tenon—a fraction oversized, since the wood will compress as you tap it into the hole—known as a mortise.

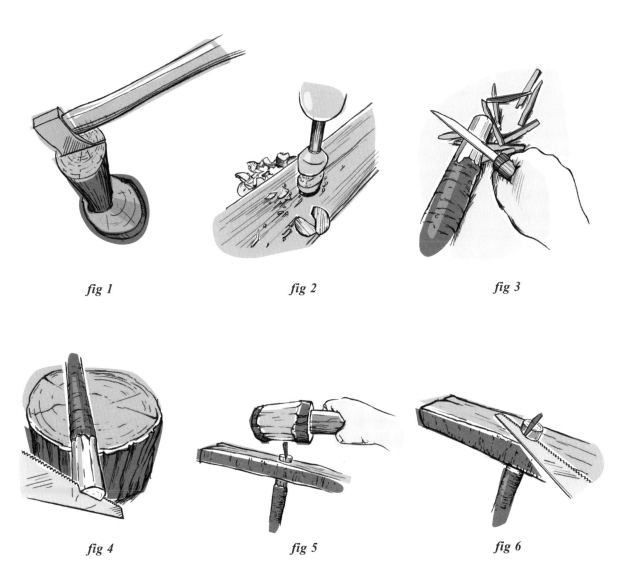

fig 1

fig 2

fig 3

fig 4

fig 5

fig 6

5. Saw a slot into the end grain of the tenon (*fig 4*). The depth of the slot should be a little more than half the depth of the mortise hole. Whittle a thin hardwood wedge to fit into the slot.

6. Align the slot in the leg across the grain of the seat, and firmly tap the leg tenon into the seat mortise. It should be at least flush with the seat and may protrude a little.

7. Tap the wedge into the slot as far as it will go (*fig 5*). This will expand the tenon against the wall of the mortise and keep the leg tight, without the need for any glue or fixings.

8. Saw off any protruding tenon, and wedge flush with the seat to leave a flat surface with a visible wedged tenon (*fig 6*).

9. Test the seat!

To make a three-legged stool, drill three holes in the split log, each at the same slight angle, so that the legs, when inserted, will splay beyond the seat. Make and fit the legs as described above.

MAKING A CHAIR

Hiking, squatting, and sitting on the ground can all take a toll on your body. Knees and backs can especially suffer after years of outdoor activity. But with wood, string, and a couple of simple tools, you can construct a throne worthy of the most wise and seasoned camp dweller.

This classic A-frame design uses a reasonable amount of medium-diameter roundwood, which might be lying around as dead wood in a thicket. If not, you may need to cut fresh wood—in which case, only make the chair for a camp you'll use for several days or as something to be taken home for yard use.

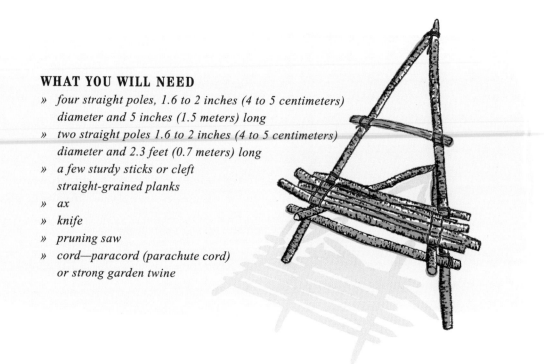

WHAT YOU WILL NEED
- » *four straight poles, 1.6 to 2 inches (4 to 5 centimeters) diameter and 5 inches (1.5 meters) long*
- » *two straight poles 1.6 to 2 inches (4 to 5 centimeters) diameter and 2.3 feet (0.7 meters) long*
- » *a few sturdy sticks or cleft straight-grained planks*
- » *ax*
- » *knife*
- » *pruning saw*
- » *cord—paracord (parachute cord) or strong garden twine*

1. Using the ax, chop one end of each of the four long poles to a wedge (*fig 1*). Check that the wedges of each pair of poles placed against each other make an angle of 45 degrees or less.
2. Cut notches in each pole partway along the wedge, then tie two of the poles together at the notch (*fig 2*). Take a yard or so of cord, and tie a loop with a long tail in one end. Thread the other end through the loop. Pull tight so the cord pulls the two poles together and their wedged faces are flush.
3. Wrap the cord tightly around the joined faces five or six times, and secure the tie-off to the long tail with an overhand knot (*fig 3*). Repeat with the other two long poles to make two triangular frames.
4. On the sturdiest of the two frames, measure about 1.3 feet (40 centimeters) up from the wide end, then tie one of the shorter poles as a cross piece (*fig 4*). Use square lashings (see pages 148–9) to secure.

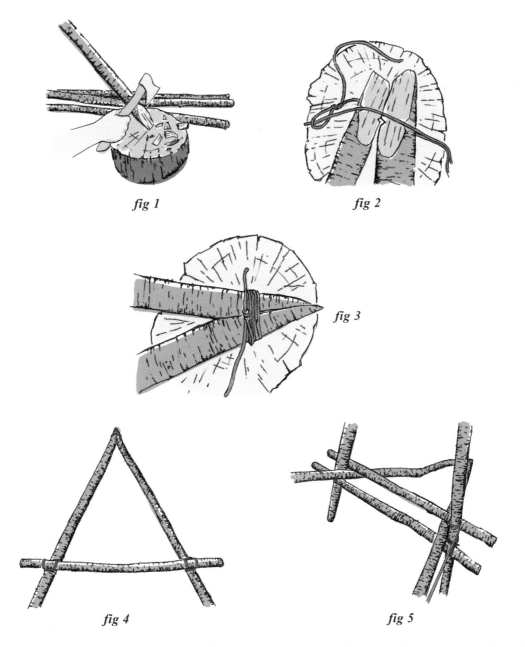

fig 1

fig 2

fig 3

fig 4

fig 5

5. Put the other frame through the frame with the cross piece, so that it rests on the cross piece. Adjust the angles so the back is as upright or reclining as you wish.

6. Lash the other short pole to the back of the first frame, above the second frame (*fig 5*). This provides leverage to make the chair stay in place when you sit on it.

7. Place the sturdy sticks or cleft planks on top of the protruding horizontal lengths of the second frame to make a flat seat (*see main picture*). These should stay in place as they are, but you can tie them to the frame if needed. Lashing on a cleft slat as a backrest will make the chair more comfortable—and keep you from falling through the back (*see main picture*).

Now sit back, relax, and enjoy the campfire and birdsong.

MAKING A BOW

The forest is the natural place for archery. Using the energy stored in a bent stem to propel a straight, pointed piece of wood some distance at great speed is a timeless thrill. Traditional archers say that a bow is a stick that's nine-tenths broken. The trick is to make sure it doesn't bend that extra tenth and snap when you draw it to shoot an arrow. As an introduction to the highly addictive world of traditional archery, we'll make a stick bow that can be cut and shot in the same day. It won't be the most powerful, beautiful, or long-lasting bow in the world, but you'll learn some key principles of bow making—and then you can simply produce another one.

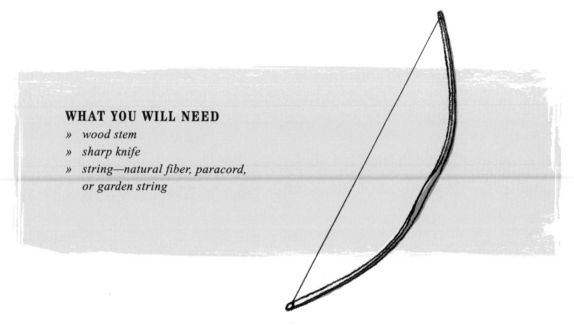

WHAT YOU WILL NEED
- » *wood stem*
- » *sharp knife*
- » *string—natural fiber, paracord, or garden string*

FINDING THE BOW STAVE
The stave is the piece of wood that will become the bow. Usually, bows are made from large-diameter wood that's split into thick pieces (or billets), seasoned, and then shaped. For our bow, the stave will be a freshly cut, small-diameter 1.2 to 1.6 inch (3 to 4 centimeter) stem that has grown in shaded conditions and is fairly straight and knot free. In length, it should be as close to your height as possible. Remember that you can always make the stave shorter but never longer. There are no exact dimensions—it's a matter of experimentation with the materials available.

WILL IT BEND?
The process of getting the bow to bend in a nice, even arc is called tillering. Place one end of your stave on the ground. Holding the other end, push on the middle with your foot with slowly increasing pressure. Look carefully at how the stave bends—can you see any straight parts that aren't bending or "hinges" that are bending too much? The key is to shape the bow stave so it's an even C or D shape when pulled to full draw. This is done by removing wood where the stave is too stiff and leaving wood where there's too much bend.

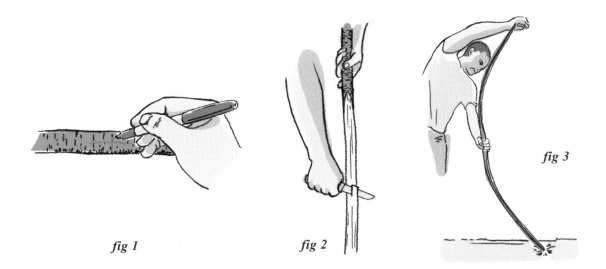

fig 1

fig 2

fig 3

SHAPING, NOTCHING, AND STRINGING

1. Make a mark at the center of the bow where you'll hold it (**fig 1**). Then mark a center line along the length of the bow as a reference.
2. Using a knife, gradually carve out the belly of the bow (the inside of the curve when the bow is drawn), tapering each limb toward the bow tip (**fig 2**). Leave the handle grip as intact roundwood, and be careful to leave the back of the bow (the outside of the curve, which will face the target) intact.
3. Keep bending the bow to check the shape of the curve of each limb (**fig 3**).
4. With a knife, carve two V-shaped channels at each end of the bow, at an angle of about 45 degrees from the back down to the belly. These notches, or nocks, should be deep enough to keep the string from slipping when the bow is drawn. Smooth out any rough edges that might abrade the string.
5. To make the bowstring, twine natural fibers together (see pages 48–9), or use the inner strands from paracord or several lengths of garden string twisted together for strength. The breaking strain of your string will need to be more than 66 pounds (30 kilograms) to keep it from snapping at full draw, which can damage both the bow and the archer.
6. Tie a loop in each end of the string, and slide one loop over one end of the bow (**fig 4**). Place this end on the ground outside one foot, then step between the bow and string with the other foot, so that the bow grip is pushing against your thigh.
7. Slowly pull the tip of the upper limb of the bow toward you until the loop at the other end of the string can fit over the top notch. The gap between the string and the grip should be about one fist and a thumb (**fig 5**).

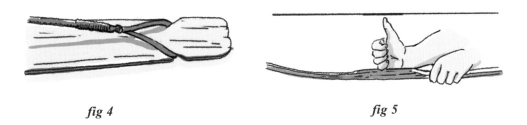

fig 4

fig 5

MAKING AN ARROW

In traditional societies, where hunting with the bow and arrow was essential for survival, local materials were expertly crafted to make highly effective weapons. In medieval Europe, where the long-range longbow was the height of military technology, huge volumes of arrows were made by fletchers (from the French *flèche*, for arrow) from split or sawn straight wood, which was planed and shaped into dowels before being "fletched" with feathers and tipped with sharp points. You can make some pretty effective bow-launched projectiles just by following the instructions below.

WHAT YOU WILL NEED
- » *source of straight-growing shoots or 0.3–0.4 inch (8–10 millimeter) wooden dowel rods from a hardware store*
- » *fine-toothed pruning saw or hacksaw*
- » *sharp knife*
- » *feathers, glue, and thread or duct tape*

1. Cut a selection of straight shoots or saplings that are at least as thick as your little finger. They must be longer than your draw length, or you risk shooting your own hand. A good guide is to cut the shoots as long as the distance from your outstretched fingertip to opposite ear.
2. Peel the bark off the shoots, and bind them together with string to dry for a few days—this helps to keep them straight (*fig 1*).
3. After drying, unbind the shoots. To further straighten the individual arrow shafts, heat any bends over a fire (*fig 2*) or the steam from a boiling teakettle. Brace the area you want to straighten with your thumbs until the wood has cooled again. It should then hold its new shape.
4. Use a fine-toothed saw, such as a hacksaw, to cut a groove in the end of each arrow that is wide enough to accommodate the string (*fig 3*). This is called a self nock.

fig 1

fig 2

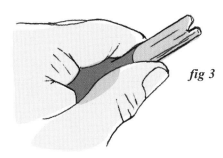

fig 3

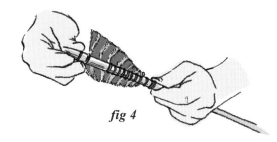

fig 4

5. Sharpen the arrow point with a knife. To harden the point, hold it over a hot fire to bake but not burn. Alternatively, you can experiment with attaching stone or metal arrowheads fitted into the tip and secured with glue and thread.

6. To hit its target, the arrow needs to spin in flight and fly straight. This is achieved by attaching two or three vanes, or fletchings, to the rear of the arrow. Folded duct tape is an easy fix that works fairly well, but for a more traditional-looking arrow, there's no substitute for feathers*. Take some long tail or wing-tip feathers, cut them in half down the quill, and trim to a shape you like. Attach each vane with strong waterproof glue, then bind all three vanes to the shaft with fine thread. Each feather or vane should be about 4 inches (10 centimeters) long and spaced evenly around the arrow shaft (*fig 4*).

Now you're ready to shoot your arrows from your bow (see pages 170–1). Remember that even a simple homemade bow and arrow can be a dangerous weapon, so get instruction from an experienced archer or archery coach. Most of all, make sure you shoot safely and within the law where you live.

Only collect feathers shed naturally by wild birds—and only if it's legal to do so where you live. If not, source feathers from a craft or pet store, or even from a poultry farmer.

THE ARCHER'S PARADOX

When you nock an arrow and hold the bow up in line with the target, it will look as if the arrow isn't pointing at the target. As you pull the string back to full draw, the tip of the arrow should now appear "on target." This visual distortion is called "the archer's paradox." When the string is released, it travels directly toward the bow, but the arrow is propelled around the side of the bow. As the arrow flies forward, it will bend backward and forward. The role of the fletching is to spin the shaft and stabilize the rear of the arrow to keep it on course. Large fletchings give greater stabilization but also slow down the arrow. Try different sizes and shapes of fletchings to find out what works best for you.

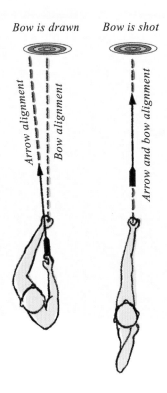

Bow is drawn   Bow is shot

Arrow alignment   Bow alignment

Arrow and bow alignment

THE HAUNTED FOREST

Maybe it's the human or beast-like form that trees take when glimpsed from the corner of an eye, the cacophony of disembodied woodland nighttime noises, or simply a sense of things hidden. Forests have long awakened the darker side of human imagination, eerie haunts for restless spirits in all corners of the world. Some forests, though, are spookier than others . . .

The almost impenetrable fir trees and smothering darkness of Germany's Black Forest made it the perfect setting for the witches, goblins, werewolves, and other creepy creatures of fairy tales. One of the scariest myths involves *der Grossmann* ("The Tall Man"), a disfigured character with white hollows for eyes, who preys upon children who carelessly wander into the depths of the forest.

The Transylvania region of Romania, home to the legendary bloodsucking Count Dracula, also contains Hoia Baciu, possibly the world's scariest forest. The name means "shepherd's forest" and derives from the story of a shepherd who disappeared along with his two hundred sheep among the wild, twisted, and crooked trees that are the stuff of nightmares. People who enter Hoia Baciu speak of a sense of being watched, feelings of anxiety and sickness, electronic devices going haywire, and photos populated by ghostly figures.

AMERICAN APPARITIONS

Forests and woodlands cover more than 40 percent of the land in North America. It's hardly surprising, then, that such dense tree cover has provoked spooky tales for thousands of years. The Native American Lenni-Lenape people called the million-plus acres of the Pine Barrens in New Jersey "the place of the dragon" after a frightening spirit they believed gave the forest its life force. European colonizers dismissed this "superstition," but as they increasingly cleared and harvested the forest, there were ever more sightings of a bizarre horned and winged creature, which became known as the "Jersey Devil."

In southeastern Massachusetts, the Freetown-Fall River State Forest has a legitimate claim to be the most haunted forest in the United States. Part of the ancestral home of the indigenous Wampanoag people, it's said to be haunted by the spirits of Wampanoag men, women, and children who died during the early days of European colonization. Wampanoag folklore tells of a race of tiny, hairy, big-eared humanlike creatures called Pukwudgies, who caused the death and disappearance of people foolish enough to stray into the dense forest. Other strange sightings include huge flying prehistoric creatures and gigantic snakes.

BOY SPIRITS AND A DEVIL DOWN UNDER

Near Darjeeling, in the foothills of the Himalayan mountains, the Dow Hill Forest is one of India's most ghoulish spots. It borders the hill station and lush tree plantations of Kurseong and is said to have been the site of numerous murders. Woodsmen tell of a headless boy who wanders a path known as "Death Road," which leads to the Dow Hill Victoria Boys' School. Locals claim that when the school is closed over winter, footsteps of long-gone pupils drift along the corridors.

In the middle of Australia's Queensland rain forest is a boulder-strewn pocket of water—the Devil's Pool—that looks picturesque but has a deadly reputation. An Aboriginal legend tells of the beautiful young wife of a tribal elder who falls in love with a young man from another tribe. They run away together but are discovered beside a creek. The woman throws herself into the waters, which become a torrent, flowing around huge boulders and so creating the Devil's Pool. Her spirit is said to haunt the forest, crying out to her lover and so enticing young men to their death in the raging waters.

MAKING A SWING

What child doesn't love a swing? And let's face it, what grown-up doesn't? The forest provides the perfect opportunity for indulging this innocent and thrilling pleasure—you just need a sturdy-enough tree, a few rope skills, and a few precautions.

Finding a strong, undamaged horizontal branch on a healthy tree with a clear area below for unobstructed swinging isn't always easy, especially in dense coniferous woodland. Trees will branch sideways where there's available light, so woodland edges, sides of tracks, and riverbanks often yield the most swing-friendly trees.

» Check that your branch is strong enough to take a person's weight and the force of swinging, and that it's far enough from the trunk to avoid collisions.

» Look for signs of weakness, such as dieback in the crown of the tree or bracket fungi—hard, shelflike varieties that stick out from the tree.

SWING SAFELY

» Check the fall zone to make sure it's clear of hazards, such as sharp rocks or stumps and roots.

» If you're swinging over water, check the depth and quality of the water, and sweep it for obstacles.

» Check the rope regularly for fraying and wear. If the rope looks worn, stop and replace it.

» If you swing over a slope, the highest point of the arc of swing can be high above the ground, and the farther you fall, the harder you'll land. Remember, it can be just as much fun swinging 6 feet (2 meters) above the ground as 30 feet (9 meters).

HOW TO TIE A FIGURE EIGHT LOOP

Used often in outdoor activities such as caving and climbing, the figure eight loop is also a perfect knot for setting up a simple swing.

*1. Grab a "bight" or loop of rope in the place where you want your loop to be. Bend this working end completely around both strands to create another loop (**fig 1**).*

*2. Pass the working end through the new loop, and pull tight (**fig 2**).*

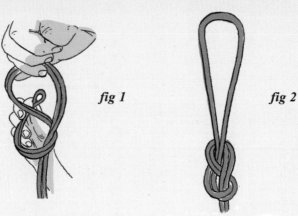

fig 1　　　　*fig 2*

A PORTABLE ROPE SWING

You can make this temporary, removable swing anywhere with just slight variations in the position of one knot.

WHAT YOU WILL NEED

» *thick, natural fiber rope or non-stretch 0.3 to 0.4 inch (8–10 millimeter) static rappelling or blue polypropylene rope, at least twice as long as the height of your branch above the ground*
» *small log for a seat*
» *one or two screwgate carabiners (metal connectors used in rock climbing)*
» *a big, healthy tree with a large, strong horizontal branch*

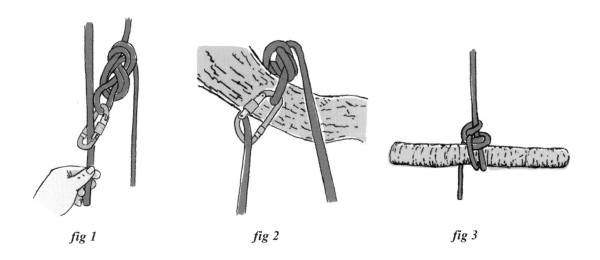

fig 1   fig 2   fig 3

1. Throw your rope over the branch that the swing will hang from.
2. Identify which end of the rope will be the swing. It should be about a yard or so from the ground. Tie a double figure eight knot (see opposite) to make a loop in the other part of the rope.
3. Clip a carabiner into the loop, and tighten the screwgate. Pass the other rope end through the carabiner (*fig 1*). You can leave out the carabiner and just use the loop in the rope, but the carabiner reduces the friction and wear of rope rubbing on rope.
4. Pull on the rope to move the loop up to jam against the branch (*fig 2*). Tie the non-swing end well out of the way.
5. Tie on your seat (*fig 3)* with a round turn and two half hitches—see page 148.
6. Test gently with your weight—then swing!

WILD POTTERY

Pottery—a craft shared by many ancient cultures—was first made in China more than 20,000 years ago. If you can get hold of some natural clay, there's huge potential for experimentation and creativity in making your own pottery and firing it in the wild. These techniques might seem primitive compared to the high-tech world of modern ceramics, but they will allow you to produce something unique, based on your style, your clay, your firewood, and your local weather. You'll be the expert in your field!

WHAT YOU WILL NEED
» *clay*
» *water*
» *wood, kindling, and lighter for a fire*
» *a big can or broken flowerpots*

FINDING YOUR CLAY
Clay is composed of very small, flat particles of certain weathered rocks that slide against each other when wet and lock together when dried. Earthenware clays—which have a slippery feel between the fingers when wet—can be found on floodplains or dug from eroded riverbanks or even plowed fields. First, you need to test the clay to see if it's suitable for making cups and pots.
» Dig up some material that looks promising, and pick out any stones or roots.
» Take a golf ball-sized lump, wet your hands, roll the lump into a ball, and then roll into a long sausage as thick as your little finger.
» Curl the sausage into a doughnut shape. If you can do this without breaking the doughnut, the clay will be fine for making earthenware.

MAKING A CHAI CUP
Spicy, milky tea called masala chai is served all over India in simple terra-cotta cups, which are unglazed and sometimes thrown away after one use. Making your own is a great camp project to work on over a couple of weeks when the weather is fine.
1. Roll a ball of damp clay about the size of an apple into a smooth ball with no cracks. Flatten the ball slightly to make a stable base.
2. Push your thumb into the middle of the flattened ball, and start to pinch up the walls of the cup using fingers and thumb, as you work your way around (**fig 1**).

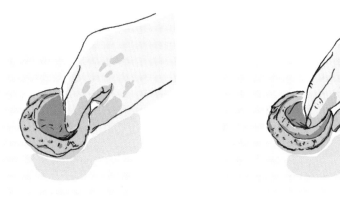

fig 1   *fig 2*

3. The walls of the cup should be a bit less than 0.4 inches (1 centimeter) thick. If you need to build up the walls with more clay, roll out a sausage of new clay and coil it inside the top of the walls. By squeezing, you can work it into the existing cup and make the walls taller (*fig 2*).

4. Dip your fingers in water, and smooth the walls and rim of the cup until you're happy with the shape and finish. Remember, this is rustic earthenware, not fine porcelain!

5. When your cup has dried to a leatherlike texture but not fully dried, you can scratch designs into the surface with a sharpened stick (*fig 3*). Alternatively, rub a rounded pebble or piece of bone against the pot to make the surface smooth and shiny, or add designs using a thin clay slurry made from ground-up soils and rocks.

6. Make a large campfire (see pages 44–5) with enough space at its center to hold your cup. Let the cup warm beside the fire for an hour or two—to avoid any thermal shock from sudden heating of the clay.

7. Put the cup in the center of the fire, making sure that there's airflow around it. Loosely sit a big can or shards of a broken flowerpot over the cup to protect it (*fig 4*). For a blackened finish, surround the unfired cup with very dry leaves, grass, or sawdust. This reduces the oxygen around the clay and also keeps larger embers from damaging the cup during firing.

8. When the fire has gone out, let the cup cool slowly—otherwise, the clay will contract and crack.

A shallow pit fire (see pages 84–5) has advantages over an open campfire. The walls of the pit can provide shelter from cooling gusts of wind and insulate the pots, giving higher overall temperatures—as long as the oxygen supply to the fuel is sufficient. Shelter the fire from gusts of wind with rocks or a log wall.

fig 3   *fig 4*

CREATING NATURAL SCULPTURE

The process of making art from natural materials is based entirely on your relationship with and reaction to a particular place at a particular time, in your own particular state of mind. There are a few things you can do—some technical, some inspirational—to open up the possibilities. However, there's no substitute for just diving in, playing with the materials, and discovering what they can do.

FINDING INSPIRATION

» Wander around the forest and see what catches your attention. It might be a place, a color, texture, or material. If you're open to what you notice and ask some questions of it, then something visual will emerge just by playing with natural forms.

» Collect things as you walk. A profusion of one thing might be the stimulus for a larger-scale work, such as a circle, spiral, or procession of pine cones.

» Look at the work of established artists in this field, such as Richard Long, Andy Goldsworthy, Richard Shilling, James Brunt, Julia Brooklyn, Nils Udo, and Yves Piffard.

» Search for patterns in nature. Spirals, branchings, toothed edges, cracks, and waves all repeat in many organic and inorganic objects and materials.

If you're stumped for ideas, try one of these little exercises to get you up and running.

» Start small—connect two leaves at their stalks, add some more, and see where they take you.

» Lay a trail—repeat rocks, cones, leaves, piles of sand or mud, or whatever else you find to make tracks, lines, or a pattern on the ground.

» Fill in a gap—gather contrasting materials, such as broken twigs or river pebbles, and add them to natural holes and breaks like a buttress root in a tree or even a gap in a wall or fence.

» Clear a path—rather than adding something in a place, make a mark by trampling a deliberate path, cutting or picking a pattern in grass, or moving rocks out of the way to create a geometrically shaped area of land.

Leaf tapestry

Stone and pebble towers

TRYING OUT TECHNIQUES

» Joining objects together is always fun. Try piercing and pinning leaves with thorns, sewing them with fibers or sticking them to rocks and trees with water. Wedge rocks together—or balance one on top of the other. You could use mud, clay, sap, or resin as glue.

» Reshape objects by tearing, cutting, rubbing, cracking—or even smashing. Tools such as knives and scissors, and even hole punches will be useful. Or simply see what you can create with your hands and the natural objects around you.

» Folding and creasing—try some leaf origami with big, fresh leaves, such as maple or sycamore. Test the different leaves growing in your area—you might find that some will work better than others and that there's a perfect time of year to collect them. This kind of enquiry and discovery is an important part of making natural art.

LAND ART

A style of conceptual art that emerged in the 1960s, land art takes the form of large earthwork, timber, stone, or living tree structures in natural surroundings. It's often ephemeral, involving temporary changes to the landscape or the use of natural materials that decay over time. All land artists have a strong connection to the places where their work is made. Some also bring the art into more conventional white-walled gallery spaces or use photography to capture its seasonally changing aspects. Land art and environmental sculpture tend to be abstract rather than representational, often using shape and pattern—and even natural processes—to create works that challenge the onlooker, at the same time as interacting with and celebrating the landscape.

A starburst of massed pine cones

The interplay of art and nature

BUILDING A
FOREST GARDEN

There's much more to making a forest garden than simply throwing together a selection of plants and leaving them to grow. Given the right kind of preparation and investment of time, forest gardening turns into a way of creating food sustainably, mimicking the structure and ecology of a natural woodland to yield a wide variety of edible and medicinal fruits, nuts, seeds, leaves, and roots. Although generally low maintenance, a forest garden needs careful planning and design—and plenty of patience—to work well. Species of plants—some native, some not—are chosen to complement each other, and soil fertility is maximized by a cover of perennial and self-seeding nutrient-rich plants.

PREPARING THE GROUND

The kind of forest garden you create will depend on the site you choose and its particular growing conditions. It's a long-term, multiyear—even multi-decade—project, which is all the more rewarding if you follow some important first steps. And it need not cost a fortune, as you can grow many plants from cuttings and simply add new species each year.

1. Decide how much land you can give over to your forest garden. If you want to plant on land you don't own, reach a long-term agreement with the landowner, and ideally work together on the project. Start small—it doesn't have to be a forest! A simple example might comprise a single fruit or nut tree, underplanted with shrubs, bushes, and low-growing, spreading plants.

2. Do your research. Find out what will thrive and survive on your site. Notice where the sun rises and sets, where the ground holds water or dries out quickly, and where any frost pockets lurk. Also, think about what food species you would actually want to eat!

3. Make a plan on paper. Space out your tallest trees—the canopy needs to be open enough to let light through to the plants growing lower down. Combine plants that will grow well together and have beneficial relationships with each other and the soil.

4. Make connections with other sustainable gardeners in your area. Aside from learning a lot, you'll get to source tried-and-true plant varieties and maybe even trade a few hours' work for some cuttings.

FOOD FOR ALL

If you can't find the land to establish a forest garden, there's always "guerrilla planting." This isn't just about growing flowers and vegetables on unused urban plots. It can also mean planting out a currant bush or a couple of raspberry canes around a crab apple on a path edge that you pass on a daily dog walk. Follow the steps above, and make sure you don't accidentally introduce an invasive species into the wild. Come harvest time, the fruit will literally be there for the picking for any passerby.

5. Plant, mulch, weed, and mow. Eventually, your forest garden will pretty much look after itself, but to start with, you'll need to mow paths, remove perennial weeds, mulch around plants with wood chips or compost, and water young plants in dry weather.
6. Pick and eat! Take a basket and forage for a tasty, healthy, homegrown, organic lunch or dinner.

BUILDING THE FRAMEWORK

A forest garden works best as a series of layers—from trees down to ground cover. The choice of plant will depend on your local conditions, such as climate and soil type.

1. *Trees.* Ideally, choose trees that will yield a nut or fruit crop. Plant with enough space between them to avoid a closed canopy and ensure that full sunlight hits some areas on the ground. Trees can also act as a windbreak and a frame for vines and climbing plants. Some species, such as alder, laburnum, and mimosa, will also fix nitrogen in the soil.
2. *Shrubs.* There's a huge variety of fruit and nut-bearing shrubs that will add variety—and nutrients—and produce abundant crops. Shade-tolerant and sun-loving species should be placed where they will thrive best, either between trees or under the tree canopy.
3. *Herbs.* A diverse range of herbs should be planted, consisting of perennial nonwoody plants as well as self-seeding annuals. You could also plant some annual vegetable crops at the sunnier edge of the garden.
4. *Ground cover.* Anywhere there's a gap, something will grow. Choosing small creeping and trailing plants will create a forest floor mulch that prevents unwanted "weed" species from proliferating. Some species will also produce edible leaves or fruit.
5. *Vines.* Climbing plants utilize all the vertical space by growing up the tall structures of the shrub and tree layers. These are likely to be a later addition, once the taller layers are established.

Trees

Shrubs

Herbs

Ground cover

Vines

MAPPING A WOOD

As you spend more and more time in your local woods, getting to know them really well will prove rewarding in many ways. Learning where natural features and other landmarks are will help you anticipate and understand changes over the seasons and years. You'll get to recognize the natural resources you need for crafts and camp life, such as the location of that alder grove, the place where the straightest hazel poles grow, or where you can find your favorite tea plant when it's picking time. There's no single right way to map woodland, so get creative with your cartography, and use the ideas here for inspiration.

PLOTTING THE FUNDAMENTALS
Mapping some resources that might be useful, without worrying about routes and landmarks, is often a revealing first step in a detailed exploration of a new place. Start at a fairly central point. Walk outward from it for a certain distance or time, collecting things that are particularly common or interesting along the way. When you return, place them in a line in the order that you collected them. This progression of natural objects is actually your first map of the woods.

DRAWING THE MAP
» Start by wandering aimlessly. You need enough time on your hands to freely explore a wood without worrying about what time you need to leave it.
» Follow "desire lines"—the easiest ways from A to B. These may well have already been traversed by animals that have left tracks and other signs (see pages 106–7).
» Look up as well as down. Most of the mass of a woodland is often above head height, so give the canopy some attention.
» Don't overthink the detail—just allow a mental map of the area to form as you explore.

On another day, go for a similar amble, but this time take a pencil and paper, a plant identification guide, and a camera. Note any areas of similar vegetation and rare and intriguing plants. Identify paths made by humans or other animals and eye-catching features, such as rock outcrops, big dead trees, or animal burrows. Draw these on paper as you go, but don't worry about scale and distance—getting things in the right place relative to each other is more important. Often, this rough sketch map is sufficient and will be a good reference for later on.

You can improve this first draft by making use of skills learned in the "Navigation" chapter, such as accurately pacing distances between landmarks and taking bearings to establish direction. You can even go from there to a computer and use satellite photos, open-source digital maps, and Geographical Information System (GIS) software to accurately map your area to share with others.

Maps of forests often play a key role in the worlds of fantasy fiction and role-playing games. Mapping woodland could be an excuse to indulge your imagination and place yourself for awhile in your own version of Middle Earth, Narnia, or Westeros.

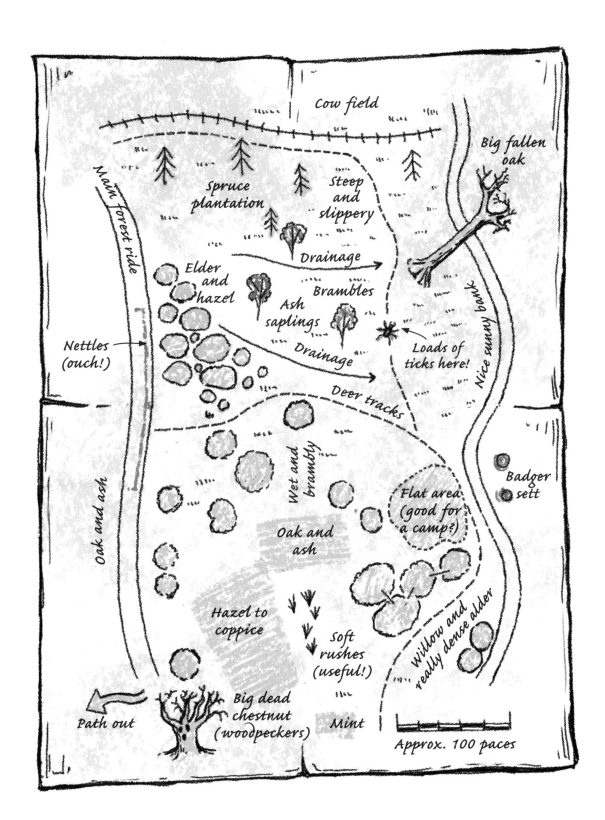

It's easy to over-romanticize living closer to nature, to forget the rain, bugs, mud, and physical effort that's sometimes required. But regular trips to local wild places can have a restorative effect—they can help you switch off for awhile and deal with some of the stresses and busyness of work and urban life in the twenty-first century.

Much of this book concentrates on getting to know the woodland environment, gaining skills, and making and creating. And yet, we can't neglect the effects of all of this new knowledge and exploration on our inner world and sense of self. It's often claimed that time spent outdoors is good for mental health, but why? What is it about being among the trees that makes us feel more relaxed and able to think with much greater clarity? The following pages deal with those psychological aspects of experiencing the woods, exploring techniques you can use to make the most of your time there, and deepen your emotional and even spiritual connection with nature.

Beyond the fundamental well-being impact of woodland recreation, there's also a growing emphasis on nature-based therapy, where trained and qualified practitioners work with their clients in natural spaces and see nature as a co-therapist. Even within this field, there's a wide diversity of approaches and reasons for choosing them, from a general dissatisfaction with the medicalization of mental health, to the desire to weave an ecological perspective into therapy.

Our primate ancestors were, and continue to be, arboreal species, so it's no great surprise that we still feel an affinity for trees and woodlands. Humans may have lost their prehensile tails, but we still feel "at home" in the forest.

7

FOREST IN MIND

YOU AND
THE FOREST

"I went to the woods because I wished to live deliberately, to front only the essential facts of life, and see if I could not learn what it had to teach, and not, when I came to die, discover that I had not lived. I did not wish to live what was not life, living is so dear; nor did I wish to practice resignation, unless it was quite necessary. I wanted to live deep and suck out all the marrow of life, to live so sturdily and Spartan-like as to put to rout all that was not life, to cut a broad swath and shave close, to drive life into a corner and reduce it to its lowest terms . . . "

Walden; or, Life in the Woods
Henry David Thoreau (1817–62)

REALISTIC FOREST EXPECTATIONS

The romantic idea that we're alienated from nature and lacking authenticity in our lives is alive and kicking today. Just as the American essayist, poet, and philosopher Henry Thoreau did in 1845, many people nowadays feel the urge to escape their day-to-day existence and go to the woods in search of "real life," as if it were something that exists elsewhere. There's an idea that time in nature can somehow fix a deep discontentment with the contemporary world, but although it's true that time spent away from traffic, work, and concrete can make us feel good, it's misleading to see it as a cure-all.

So, if forest time can't resolve all our psychological ills, and most of us can't just "give it all up" and go live in a cabin in the wilderness, what can a trip to the forest do for our mental well-being? We need to first ask why the forest is the place to go and what it offers that can't be found elsewhere. Perhaps it's the diversity of plant and animal species as well as variation within them, the irregularity in the landscape, or an unpredictability and yet general familiarity that's both comforting and inspiring.

EMBRACING LIFE'S FUNDAMENTALS

As well as generating a sense of calm from the absence of crowds of people or the trappings of modern life, time in the woods gives us the opportunity to do things that can't easily be done elsewhere. The physical effort required in sawing and chopping firewood or building a shelter is good for our bodies as well as our minds. Stepping beyond our comfort zone by taking risks—for example, by climbing a tree or crossing a fast-moving stream—provides opportunities to extend ourselves. These don't need to be high-adrenaline activities—the goal is to grow our sense of self-worth and confidence by trying new things without too much fear of failure.

By meeting basic needs with a tarpaulin, a knife, an ax, a saw, and a campfire, we learn to be comfortable with very little and so feel much more self-reliant. Identifying and really understanding the difference between our wants and our actual needs can be a powerful way to let go of the stress caused by the pursuit of material things and status in day-to-day life.

THE TRANSCENDENT POWER OF NATURE

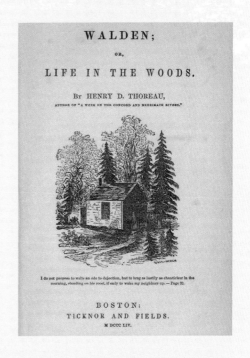

Henry David Thoreau and his friend and mentor, the American essayist, poet, and philosopher Ralph Waldo Emerson (1803–82), shared ideas on the human experience of nature that became part of the philosophy of "transcendentalism" that emerged in New England in the 1830s. Together, they had a profound effect on the Western way of viewing forests and experiences in natural spaces. The two men believed that "uncorrupted" wild places weren't only vital for inspiration and contemplation but offered a chance for individuals to test themselves and reach a deeper understanding of nature through self-reliance. Thoreau put this into practice in 1845 when he built a cabin beside Walden Pond in Concord, Massachusetts, in woodland owned by Emerson. His idea was to live simply and without the obligations of responsibility, although he was hardly a hermit, receiving regular visitors and making trips to town for supplies and materials. Thoreau recorded his observations and philosophical musings in the book Walden; or, Life in the Woods *(1854), which has inspired many to seek out their own place in the woods as a retreat where they can concentrate on the bare essentials of life in tune with the natural world.*

WOODLAND TOGETHERNESS

There's also much to be said of time in the woods with friends, family, and communities of interest. Social dynamics are different when we live together outdoors; people show different strengths and aptitudes than they might do in the workplace or at home. When you're given enough time to slow down, conversations grow and develop in an easy, relaxed way, unconstrained by deadlines or other distractions. Working together on the basic tasks needed for comfort and sustenance can build bonds of community that create a sense of belonging that's hard to find in a busy urban existence.

CONNECTIONS WITH
TREES AND WOODLANDS

Y ou don't necessarily have to go into the woods to find yourself, but stresses and strains are often eased a little by physical forest activity or simply by a slow, mindful stroll in a calming green space. In the 1980s, the American biologist E. O. Wilson introduced the "biophilia hypothesis," which proposed that humans have an innate fascination with the natural world and a deep need to connect with it. Biophilia literally means "love of life," and aside from involuntary interactions with "nature," such as breathing and eating, humans have evolved an attraction to specific natural places for the benefits that they can bring. But is there actually any firm evidence that our affinity with trees and woods promotes good mental and physical health?

ATTENTION RESTORATION THEORY

You might have noticed that time spent in more "natural" as opposed to urban spaces has a restorative effect, perhaps making you better able to concentrate, have more energy, and feel calmer. Taking a walk in a natural environment after a particularly mentally demanding activity or when you're feeling particularly distracted can help unclutter your mind and refocus your attention on the here and now. Over a period of twenty years of research, American psychologists Rachel and Stephen Kaplan explored why this might be the case, and in 1989, they published their findings in *The Experience of Nature: A Psychological Perspective*. This study—which formed the basis for the Kaplans' "attention restoration theory"— identified four states of attention, plotting the route from feeling overwhelmed or unable to concentrate to the point where full attention is restored.

1. Directed attention takes effort and is needed to maintain the focus required to complete a goal-oriented task. This can feel good, especially when we're getting a lot done or are really interested in a topic.
2. When we can no longer maintain focus on the task and become distracted, tired, or stressed, mental fatigue occurs. This can be addressed by switching tasks or moving to an environment that requires effortless attention, as in state 3.
3. When our attention is held by something that's relatively familiar—not too demanding but still extremely varied, such as watching waves, clouds, running water, or leaves on trees, we're in a state of "soft fascination." This allows us to be effortlessly absorbed but not stretched by processing or understanding masses of new information or dealing with risk or uncertainty.
4. Reflection and restoration occur when we've spent enough time in state 3 to reach a state of "fascination," where we're relaxed and able to reflect on the task or situation and approach it again with a renewed ability to concentrate.

In pursuing their theory, the Kaplans also looked at what made an effective restorative environment and found that it should be away from the everyday and from the cause of mental fatigue, and should not be highly stimulating or fully absorbing. You should feel comfortable in that environment and have chosen to be there yourself because you feel an affinity for it or prefer it.

Forests and woodlands fit the bill perfectly as places of fascination. They are familiar and mentally undemanding, yet infinitely varied, making them ideal places of renewal, so long as you take the time to just sit or stand and "be" for a good while before continuing with whatever mentally taxing tasks you need to do.

FOREST BATHING

When, in the 1980s, the Japanese state forest organization started to look into the possible role national forests might play in public health, it coined a new term: *shinrin-yoku*, or "forest bathing," for the age-old practice of mindful engagement with woodlands. Japanese culture has long displayed a reverence for trees, reflected in numerous aspects of life in Japan, including the annual cherry blossom viewing custom known as *hanami* ("flower watching"). Many of the deities of the ancient Shinto religion, called *kami*, are rocks, mountains, trees, and animals, which is why Shinto shrines are often in forests or surrounded by trees. More and more Japanese people have embraced forest bathing as a form of preventative medicine, and researchers are finding increasing evidence for its beneficial physiological effects.

Essentially, forest bathing is going for a walk in the woods—possibly barefoot—in a slow and deliberate way while engaging all your senses. You wander to the places that you're drawn to, sit and meditate, and perhaps undertake some activities with a qualified forest-bathing guide to maximize the benefits. If you're inspired to give it a try, turn off your phone, find a quiet area of woodland, and meander slowly, observing and exploring, with every sense alert to your surroundings. Try to set aside at least a couple of hours to really reap the benefits of a forest bathing session.

Research carried out by Japanese academics, such as Professor Yoshifumi Miyazaki and Dr. Quing Li, suggest that forest bathing may offer a number of potential health benefits.

» Regulation of the nervous system
» Modulation of low and high blood pressure
» Reduction of stress and increased relaxation as the calm forest environment lowers levels of cortisol—the main stress hormone
» Reduction of prefrontal brain activity, leading to physiological relaxation
» Improved sleep by changing to daily walks in the forest rather than in an urban environment

These benefits have been found to work through natural human and forest mechanisms. By avoiding stimuli that activate the human fight or flight responses, the parasympathetic nervous system—which lowers breathing and heart rates and encourages digestion—is encouraged to function properly. Trees give off oils from their leaves and needles that vaporize easily and contain compounds called phytoncides. Exposure to these chemicals lowers stress and blood pressure. Coniferous trees produce the greatest volume of phytoncides, with levels varying between individual species. It's not known if the effects differ between bioregions and their different communities of trees, but you're likely to benefit more from walking in coniferous or mixed woodland than in purely deciduous areas.

CLOSE ENCOUNTERS

Forest bathing is a holistic experience enjoyed within a woodland; not everyone, though, has access to an inspiring, safe, and quiet area of forest. Controlled experiments have shown that many of the activity's benefits can also be experienced around single trees and even houseplants. Encounters with individual trees can be truly inspiring, evoke strong feelings, and depending on your own world view, have a spiritual dimension. Old, tall, or gnarly trees are particularly characterful, but you can choose to connect with any tree. There's no wrong reaction to a special tree—or even a supposedly ordinary one—and no need to be overly analytical, mystical, or reverential about an encounter. You may feel self-conscious or a little silly engaging with a tree, so maybe persuade a few friends to join in, and even clown around as you make your arboreal acquaintance—remember, the tree won't judge you.

» *Listening.* If you can lay your hands on a stethoscope, try listening in on the bark of a tree. In the spring, you might even hear the sap rising. Place your ear on the bark of a thin tree, and give it a gentle shake. The results can be surprising—try it!
» *Hugging.* You don't have to fit the stereotype of the earnest tree hugger to actually hug a tree—just put your arms around it and shut your eyes. Why not, if it makes you feel good?
» *Just sitting.* Sit on the ground, leaning your back against the trunk. Gaze through the canopy, enjoy the shade, and take in all you can with your senses.
» *Climbing.* Get among the branches of a tree, and feel how it moves on a breezy day. This can be a good place to experience the woods at night since you're off the ground and won't spook or be spooked by any nocturnal animals.
» *Looking up.* Lie on the ground and look up at the tree canopy, especially in early spring when the first flush of new leaves is bursting out. In a deciduous woodland, you might notice the phenomenon of crown shyness, where there are gaps like river valleys in between the canopy of each tree. This is great to watch on a windy day—but not so windy that there are twigs dropping from the sky.

A different kind of connection and feeling of positive well-being comes from planting new trees. This is an emotive subject in some conservation circles. Advocates of rewilding might prefer natural regeneration of woodland to tree planting on greenfield sites, but the latter can be an important way for people to get actively involved with trees and woodlands—as long as the right tree is planted in the right place and doesn't replace other, more valuable habitat. However good planting a new specimen makes you feel, don't forget that the tree may well need continued care. Water it in dry weather, mulch it to subdue competing grasses and weeds, and keep the squirrels, rabbits, and deer away.

FORESTS OF THE IMAGINATION

Woodland provides a setting for many of the world's most treasured works of literature, poetry, music, art, and theatre. The forest's rich array of plant and animal life, the human interaction with it, and the allegory of the forest as our inner world supply a canvas for dramatic tension filled with the emotional twists and turns of life and love.

A Midsummer Night's Dream—first performed in 1605—by William Shakespeare (1564–1616) is one of the Bard's most enchanting plays. Set in the forest on the eve of the summer solstice, this romantic comedy features humans and fairies, love and magic, mishap and farce, all the while playing with appearance and reality. Characters include the fairy Puck, who causes chaos when he casts love spells on two couples, making the two men fall in love with the same girl, with ensuing chase through the forest.

One of the most celebrated works in Western art is *Primavera* (or *Spring*), painted by Italian artist Sandro Botticelli (1445–1510) around 1480. The work's tableau takes place under the trees in an orange grove. To the right, Zephyrus, the March wind, blows on wood nymph Chloris, impregnating her as vegetation grows out of her mouth. She then becomes Flora, goddess of flowers and spring, strewing blossoms as she walks. Venus, Roman goddess of love, looks at the viewer with her son Cupid hovering above as the three Graces dance a springtime air, and Mercury, messenger of the gods, reaches up into the branches to dispel the winds of winter. More than a hundred different plant species have been identified in the painting, a fitting and beautiful homage to the natural world.

MUSICAL FRONDS
In 1913, the score for ballet *The Rite of Spring*, composed by Igor Stravinsky (1882–1971), set Parisian society on fire. Stravinsky uses dramatic orchestration and innovative composing techniques, such as harmonic dissonance and jarring rhythms, to express a pagan celebration of the earth's rising vital force in springtime.

Married to the groundbreaking choreography of dancer Vaslav Nijinsky (1890–1950), the score created shock waves in a music world more used to the lyrical woodland fare of French composer Claude Debussy (1862–1918). His composition "Prélude à l'après-midi d'un faune" (1894)—also groundbreaking in its time—portrays a faun's journey through a wood and his desires and dreams of becoming one with nature.

WOODY DRAMA
A more ominous view of the forest is represented in the gothic short story "The Legend of Sleepy Hollow," written by the American author Washington Irving (1783–1859). The action takes place in colonial New York, where protagonist Ichabod Crane—a geeky ladies' man who entices a wealthy landowner's daughter—rides alone through a secluded glen, Sleepy Hollow. Here, Crane is chased by the Headless Horseman, a none-too-pleasant spectre who ends up hurling his severed head at Ichabod.

Perhaps the best-loved imagined forests are those of Middle Earth, vividly brought to life by J. R. R. Tolkien (1892–1973) in his epic fantasy trilogy, *The Lord of the Rings*. Here, woodland and forest create the backdrop against which hobbit characters Frodo, Sam, Merry, and Pippin set out in the company of elves, dwarves, and the wizard Gandalf to save the world from the forces of evil. The elves' homeland is the beautiful and timeless forest of Lothlórien; and in the Old Forest the group meet Old Man Willow, a malignant tree spirit. More helpful are giant walking tree beings, the Ents—led by Treebeard—who dwell in Fanghorn Forest and play a decisive role in the Battle of Helm's Deep against the wizard Saruman.

STORY,
SONG, AND MUSIC

A jester once said, "Light a fire, and everyone's a storyteller!" It's not clear if this was said facetiously or with enthusiasm, but there's no reason why everyone gathered around the campfire shouldn't have a chance to tell a tale or make music. For thousands of years, telling stories and singing folk songs as a community was how people spread news, shared experiences, remembered their ancestors, and kept their culture alive. It might just be one of the main things that makes us human. Today, songs and stories tend to be shared with a global community in live chats, games, streams, and videos, with the help of high-speed internet connections. That doesn't mean, though, that the old ways of sharing cannot weave a magic storytelling spell, especially set against the crackling and flickering magic of a fire.

FIRESIDE TALES
Campfire storytelling can be serious, ritualized, and even a little worthy. At other times, tales are fun and inclusive. In either case, storytelling is still a novelty for most of us who live in homes with four walls and rely on digital media for much of our news and communication. To tell, rather than read, a story and to hold an audience are skills that can be learned. And like most skills, they take effort and practice. To remember a story is tricky at first, but once it has been told a few times, it becomes welded to your memory and will pour forth when the time is right.

» Write a list of easy-to-remember keywords for each part of your story. Memorizing them in order will help you improvise around them if you lose track of your script.

» Practice telling your story out loud without an audience.

THE LIVING ICELANDIC STORY
The history of Iceland, from its settlement more than one thousand years ago, is recorded in stories known as the Sagas, which were originally passed on by word of mouth before being written down in the twelfth and thirteenth centuries. No doubt over time, they became embellished and tilted toward the victors in the island's many battles and feuds. As such, the tales are far from an accurate historical record, but they form an inextricable link between Icelanders of the past and present and their landscape. Reading the tales—or even better, hearing them told—is like no other form of literature and helps to wed the listener deeply to a place and its people.

» Use your voice and body—even if it's just your hands—to add drama at key points.

» Involve the audience. Ask questions like "Have you ever seen a . . . ?" Encourage sound effects, with noises for particular characters or events.

Some tales are kept for particular places or events, some are handed down the generations, some are only to be told with permission, and others are free-form, evolving and changing with every telling. From the humble everyday anecdote to the well-honed tale with its own lineage of tellers, everyone has a story to tell.

WOODLAND MUSIC-MAKING

For some forest-dwelling peoples, singing is an intrinsic part of their relationship with the environment. Central African foraging tribes, such as the Baka of Cameroon and Mbuti of the Congo basin, have deep traditions of highly complex community singing, often improvised and multilayered. Living and hunting in the forest, the Baka people have developed great listening skills and can pick up on subtle changes in forest noises, contributing to their community-wide ability to weave together rhythm and melody.

Singing around the fire isn't for everyone. If you like singing and know a few tunes, then just go for it. Some of the introverts among us will find it difficult to join in but still enjoy the sound of everyone else making a song. It might not feel elemental enough, but singing along to a tune from someone's phone is a perfectly good way to get things started. If you don't feel like you can sing, just start your own "tuneless campfire choir." Tuneless choirs are just for people who want to sing in groups but don't feel confident or have the talent to join a "proper" choir. The final noise is not the point—it's the process of taking part that brings social and emotional benefits. The added bonus is that in the dark, no one can see you sing!

Fun and creativity are likely to play some part in most of our time in the forest. There are often spontaneous opportunities to mess around with no particular purpose, but there's also a case to be made for heading out from time to time with a deliberately playful attitude.

This chapter explores some very different ways to have fun and get creative. Activities such as team games, parkour, and fitness training use the forest's huge variety of woodland terrain and natural obstacles and features to explore physicality, as well as developing strength, stamina, and agility. Lounging around in a hammock, on the other hand, can be the ultimate in relaxation, allowing ideas to flow before you leap into action.

Pursuits like letterboxing and geocaching encourage exploration and participation in a global community of cache hunters and take you to places where you would never otherwise go. You might even convince a reluctant friend or child into spending time in the forest in ways they would never have thought of before.

A more traditional take on creativity is making visual art using only what the woodland provides. There's huge enjoyment and satisfaction in creating your own paints from the soils and rocks underneath your feet and brushes from whatever is on hand. Your creative interpretation of the forest, painted on bark, cloth, or skin, is unique to you, and as always in the forest, normal rules don't apply. It's really all about the process, with the end product a potential bonus.

8

FOREST FUN AND CREATIVITY

LETTERBOXING

If you want to add a layer of fun and purpose to a woodland walk—or entice others who need some outdoor activity motivation—letterboxing could be the answer. The idea is to use clues and grid references from a guidebook or catalog to find preplaced "letterboxes" that contain a logbook and ink stamp and occasionally small trinkets to swap. Many letterbox locations are unpublished, with details passed on by word of mouth. Once you get to know the kinds of places where letterboxes are found, you may simply chance upon them, even in the remotest of places.

The activity dates back to 1854, when James Perrott, a guide on Dartmoor in southwest England, placed a bottle in a cairn at a remote spot called Cranmere Pool. Hikers then placed letters or postcards there to be collected and mailed by the next visitor. As this practice gained popularity, more letterbox locations were established, and the tradition of mailing letters or cards was replaced with the signing of visitors' books and the collection of stamps.

GETTING STARTED

Letterboxing has spread across the world and has well-developed subcultures in some countries. The jargon and etiquette in North America are quite different to those in the UK, for instance, and variations even include letterboxes (usually a stamp and logbook) carried around by a person who will only disclose their whereabouts if you know the password! Rather than signing your name, you might also buy or make a personalized stamp to leave your distinctive mark in the letterbox logbook.

» Search online for letterbox clues near where you are. Download to a phone or print them out to take with you. In some areas, you may be able to buy a printed gazetteer that's updated by enthusiasts.

» Dress for the weather and pack for the terrain that you'll cover. Read the survival and navigation sections of this book before heading out.

» Take a map and compass because some clues require careful wayfinding.

» When you find a letterbox, stamp your own notebook and sign or stamp the logbook. Make sure that you put the box back exactly where you found it and try and leave as little trace of your being there as possible.

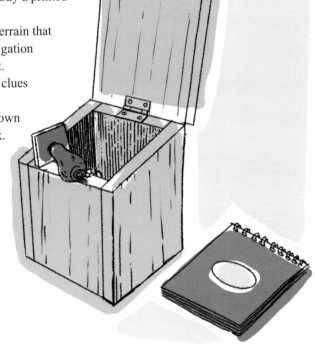

GEOCACHING

With many shared characteristics, geocaching could be seen as letterboxing's twenty-first century, satellite technology enabled iteration. It uses GPS technology, which is based on a network of satellites orbiting Earth and was once the preserve of the military until restrictions on public use were removed in 2000. This change spawned a new pursuit of hiding and searching for caches—which are very similar to letterboxes—by using precise global positioning coordinates. Think of it as a giant, open-world treasure hunt, which you can access through your phone but that also gets the whole family out for some fresh air and exercise.

ON THE HUNT

Getting started with geocaching is cheap and easy. All you need is a free account on geocaching.com and an app for your phone (free and premium apps are available) or a dedicated GPS receiver. Unless you have unlimited data and really good cell phone coverage, it makes sense to download maps and cache data at home before you go out. The great news is that GPS functionality doesn't require mobile data, so this is a free activity.

Once you have a list of caches on your cell phone, select a cache and use the clues and navigational aids to seek it out. Some caches are in regular, plastic lunchboxes, but others can be extremely small and even camouflaged to look like a rock or stuck to a railing with a magnet. Some caches (called multi-caches) have a clue that will lead you to the next one, while mystery caches require you to solve puzzles and cryptic clues to reveal their coordinates. Log your finds on your geocaching app and give the owner and fellow cachers some useful feedback.

LAYING YOUR OWN TRAIL

As you record more and more finds, you might want to make a cache yourself. The first step is to check the requirements of the website that you want to list it on. There are several standard provisos, such as making sure your cache is far enough away from existing caches and that it's not in a dangerous location.

» Put a logbook, pen, and printed instruction note—explaining what this "treasure" is and what to do with it—into a waterproof container.
» Find an interesting place to put your cache and check that you're not on private land—or get permission first.
» Create a little challenge by hiding the box well and maybe even camouflaging it to fit in with the surroundings.
» Finally, record the exact coordinates of the container and submit it to the website for listing. The geocaching community is huge, so you shouldn't have to wait too long before someone finds the cache and leaves a message or photo on the app. Don't forget to check on the cache every once in a while, to make sure that it's watertight and to replace the logbook, if necessary.

Geocaching and letterboxing are addictive activities that will take you to places you would never ever think about going otherwise. From a residential area of Reykjavik to a mountaintop in Scotland or a park in New York, it's also a great way to persuade otherwise reluctant hikers to head out for a ramble in the countryside or an exploration of city streets.

FOSSIL HUNTING

Whether you're inspired by watching *Jurassic Park*, seeing a brontosaurus skeleton in a museum, or finding a strange-shaped rock on the beach, the science of fossils, or paleontology, is more accessible than you might think. There's no more direct and tangible link to the past than finding the fossil of an organism that lived millions of years ago in the place where you collected it. The fact that, at the time, the location might have been at the bottom of a deep ocean and very possibly at a different latitude just adds to the mystery and the urge to discover more.

Any living organism can become fossilized if it's buried in an anaerobic—oxygen free—environment so that it doesn't decay. Usually, it's only the harder parts or imprints of plants and animals that are preserved. You might dream of stumbling across an intact *T. rex* skeleton like the one Montana rancher Kathy Wankel discovered in 1988, but you're much more likely to spot invertebrate fossils such as ammonites, trilobites, belemnites, and brachiopods—or even an ancient shark's tooth. Researching the lives of the fossils you discover is one of the most fascinating parts of this hobby, and as your collection grows, you'll thank yourself for keeping a few notes on the geology and location of your finds.

WHERE TO LOOK

To find any fossils, you'll need to have an idea of where to explore. If you're lucky, there might be a well-known fossil-hunting spot nearby. As the somewhat obvious saying goes, "Look for fossils where fossils have been found before." Otherwise, it's time to learn something about the geography of your local area and where there are exposed layers of sedimentary rock or unconsolidated material such as limestone, mudstone, or shale. A local geological map—usually available online—will show you where different types of rock can be found.

Let nature (or construction workers) do the hard work of uncovering new fossils for you. Erosion by water on the coast and on riverbanks constantly exposes rocks that have been covered for millions of years; finding fossils can be as simple as turning over stones from a fresh rockfall. New rock faces are also exposed when cuttings are made for new highways and railroad lines, although make sure that it's safe to stop and explore wherever you happen to look.

GOOD FOSSIL PRACTICE

» Fossil hunting might take you to some remote places, so go prepared and let someone know where you're going and when you'll be back.

» On beaches, check the tides and exit points from the beach and always go fossil hunting on a falling tide. Search a reasonable distance away from the base of cliffs, not directly underneath them, where you may be in danger from falling rocks.

» Wait until river levels have dropped after heavy rain or snowmelt—fresh sediments may be exposed, and there's less chance of being caught in a flash flood.

» If you're going to try and break rocks gently with a geological hammer, then wear gloves, a hard hat, and good eye protection.

» Get permission from the landowner, and check that it's legal to collect fossils in your area. If you find what you think might be a fossil of a vertebrate, don't try to dig it up yourself: Find a local expert to advise and help, so that you don't accidentally ruin what might be an important specimen.

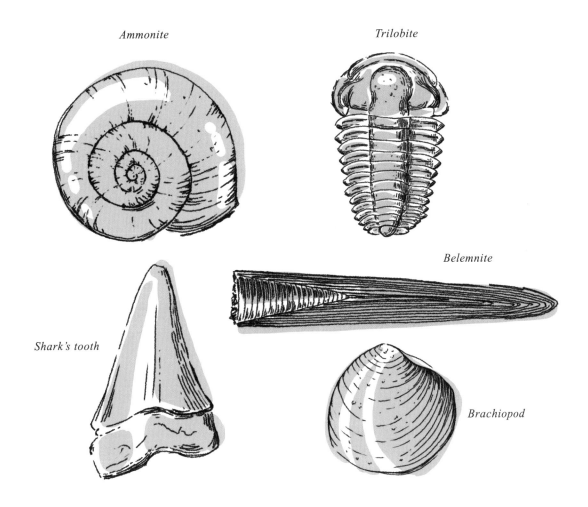

Ammonite

Trilobite

Belemnite

Shark's tooth

Brachiopod

A PIONEERING PALEONTOLOGIST

Mary Anning, one of history's greatest amateur fossil hunters—and the subject of the 2020
movie Ammonite*—lived in the seaside town of Lyme Regis on the "Jurassic Coast" of southern*
England. She was born in 1799 to a poor family and from an early age accompanied her father
on fossil-finding expeditions on the local beaches. Her career involved a string of firsts, starting
when she was twelve years old with the excavation of the 17 foot (5.2 meter) long skeleton of the
first identified ichthyosaur, a marine reptile. Despite also finding the first plesiosaur—another
marine reptile—and pioneering the study of fossilized feces, or coprolites, her work was barely
acknowledged by the male scientists in the field, and she died age 47 after a lifetime of financial
struggle. Today, you can still walk in Mary's footsteps on the beaches of Lyme Regis and
Charmouth, where you barely have to wait five minutes before you find some sign of life from
nearly 200 million years ago.

SETTING UP A
HAMMOCK

No longer just for resting sailors or lounging around on Caribbean islands, hammocks are now the friend of the lightweight hiker, stealth camper, and general fireside loafer. It doesn't matter how steep or bumpy the ground underneath, all you need for your hammock are two trees. You won't wake up gasping for air and a drink of water on a hot day like you might in a tent, and you may have some of the best wildlife encounters imaginable as you peer out from under a tarpaulin in the late evening or early light of dusk.

IN SEARCH OF COMFORT

At their simplest, hammocks are no more than a sheet of strong material held aloft with a rope or strap at each end. There's something of an art, though, to being comfortable, which starts with the proper hanging of your hammock.

» If you're using a rope at each end, simply tie a figure eight loop in one end, then secure the rope to a tree with a round turn and two half hitches (see pages 148 and 176 for instructions on the fixings). Repeat for the opposite end of the hammock on another tree a few feet away, and use metal carabiners to clip your hammock into the figure eight loops. The carabiners will keep the ropes fromwearing on the hammock as it swings gently. The hammock material should be fairly taut, rather than sagging, and at about chest height.

» To get into a hammock without drama, stand with your back to the middle of the material and use your hands to push yourself up as if you were going to sit on a wall. Once sitting, swing your feet up and lie down. For a quick lunch stop, just sit across the middle, lean back, and let your legs dangle.

» If you lie lengthwise, your back will arch like a banana, but if you wriggle a bit and can lie diagonally, you'll be much flatter, which is more comfortable for a night's sleep.

» The second secret to a good night's sleep is to have good insulation underneath you, since the wind can wick heat away quickly through the thin hammock material. A roll mat, a partially deflated self-inflating camping pad, or even a sheet of carpet underlay are all good options. Roll up your coat and clothes and lay them along the sides of the hammock for even more insulation.

» If bugs are an issue, find a hammock with an integrated mosquito net. This can be suspended from a cord between the trees, although for some people it can feel a little claustrophobic.

» To stay dry through the night, follow the instructions on pages 150–1 to put up a tarpaulin over your hammock.

Sleep well—or just enjoy hanging out!

SKIPPING STONES

Much like the primal fascination for fire, there seems to be some kind of natural instinct to pick up a pebble by a river, lake, or the sea and throw it into the water. The satisfying plunk and splash, followed by ripples, never fail to entertain, however many times you do it.

Skipping stones is a rite of passage, like learning to ride a bike—once you can do it, you never forget, but you can always improve with practice. There's a competitive edge to skipping, whether it's how many bounces you can do in a row, how far your stone can travel before sinking, or whether you can accurately hit a target. What's the secret to stone skipping success?

» Find the right site and conditions. An open expanse of calm, flat water on a clear day is ideal. Some form of distance marker will help you know if you're skimming farther as you practice.

» Choose the right stone. Look for an oval one that fits neatly into your palm. It should be flat, thin, and as light as possible.

» Hold the stone between your thumb and forefinger in a backward C shape. Stand sideways to the water and crouch down so that the stone hits the surface at around 20 degrees—ideally, fairly close to you for the first skip (*fig 1*).

» Pull your arm back, and then whip it forward with as much energy as you can muster, spinning the stone clockwise as you release it. A little snap of the wrist will set the stone spinning as it flies off your index finger (*fig 2*). This creates "gyroscopic stabilization," which keeps the stone flat after each bounce.

When the stone hits the water, it creates a wave but will continue traveling faster than the wave and rise over it to take off again. This is repeated for as many times as the stone stays stable and carries enough energy.

fig 2

fig 1

FOREST TEAM GAMES

The varied terrain, trees, and dense undergrowth of forests and woodlands make them the perfect places to play large group games, where sneaking around is a key part of the fun. With a big area to play in and lots of time to roam far from camp, aptly named "wide games" can carry you back to childhood, as you pit your wits and skill against your friends and family. Wide games can involve as many players as want to take part. Some games are fast and furious, others are much more about moving slowly and stealthily. With any of the following contests, you can decide whether to nominate one person as an umpire to settle disputes or to play the game on trust.

CAPTURE THE FLAG

In this classic game, with its endless possible variations, teams try to outflank and evade each other to capture the opposition's flag without getting caught. Decide on the size of the area you're going to play in and agree a finish time or a signal to call everyone back when the game is finished. You can play the game with two or more teams.

» Each team decides on a base in the woods where they want to plant their flag. This can be anything from a medieval banner to an old sock. Team bases should be at least a few hundred feet apart, away and out of sight of each other.

» Use a rope to mark a 20 foot (6 meter) circular boundary around the flag (**A**). This is where players must return when tagged by a member of another team.

» Starting from their own base, each team then tries to reach the other team's base and steal their flag. If anyone is tagged by a member of the opposing team, they must either serve a pre-agreed time-out penalty at their own base or do a forfeit, such as ten push-ups on the spot, before continuing. The game ends when a flag is captured, or it can continue until a team gets their opponent's flag back to their own base.

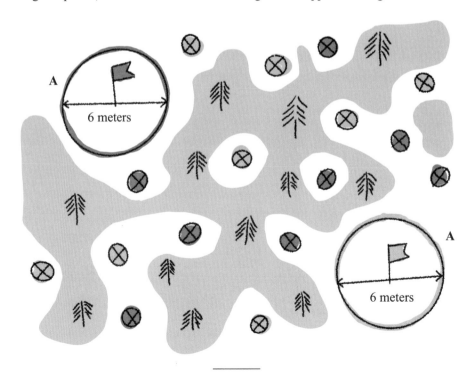

» For a fun twist, you can substitute the flags for frisbees. Once captured, a frisbee must be thrown from player to player on the same team until it lands back at home base. No moving while holding the frisbee is allowed, and it can be intercepted in midair by the opposing team and transferred back to safety in their own base.

PREDATOR

What does it feel like to be a nocturnal animal trying to avoid becoming something else's dinner? Playing predator gives you a chance to find out. The game shares some characteristics with "Capture the Flag" but is played at night. There are two teams and two bases, each illuminated with a different-colored glow stick or lantern. The objective is to creep through the trees and undergrowth and reach the other base without encountering anyone else. No flashlights are allowed. It's best played over a set time, with the winning team being the one with the most members who have reached the opposing team's base.

» Each team nominates one player to be a predator, who's armed with a squirt gun. They alone can catch members of the other team by squirting them with water and then sending them back to their base to start the journey again.

» For added fun and confusion, you can add a "super predator" to the mix. This person can squirt anyone, including the predator from the opposing team.

» This game is better played in stealth mode and is good practice for stalking and hiding as well as developing your senses of listening and night vision.

ON THE RUN

Two prisoners have escaped from a maximum-security prison and are on the run through the woods. Can you follow their trail and bring them back to justice?

» Pick one or two players to be "on the run." They will pick a trail through the forest and try to evade the rest of the group, who will be hunting them down.

» The pursuers should give the fugitives a head start—for example, counting to one hundred or more, depending on how in shape they are!

» There are lots of twists to the game, such as giving the fugitives a bag of flour that they must sprinkle at intervals as they lay a trail with a few minutes' head start on the hunters. Alternatively, find a log that can be dragged on a rope by two people but is too heavy to carry more than about 30 feet (9 meters). The runners must take the log with them, with the dragging log leaving a trail that can be broken only if they carry it. The carrying, however, slows them down, so it's unlikely that the trail will be broken for long. Depending on players' fitness levels, "On the Run" can cover a large area and last quite awhile.

PLAYING SAFELY

All these games carry a risk of injury due to tripping, slipping, falling, and running into obstacles. For this reason, tagging is fine, but grabbing and tackling should be discouraged because things might quickly get out of hand and become hazardous. Playing at night just requires a little safety common sense, such as checking the area for any open water or steep drops that might not be seen in the dark. Have a good, loud signal to call everyone back and do a head count at the end.

WOODLAND PARKOUR

I f skipping stones might be an expression of our hunter-gatherer past, then moving through the forest with ease and grace is a fundamental throwback to our arboreal ancestors. Humans of the twenty-first century are a relatively sedentary lot, and even if many of us do run, go to the gym, or play sports, our movements are fairly similar and far from those our bodies needed to hunt prey or flee from a predator in an undulating wooded landscape. A relatively new way of escaping the physical humdrum—and bringing back the kind of free movement that we all came from in the forest—is the phenomenon of parkour, with its related activity of free running.

Parkour—from the French *parcours*, meaning "route" or "journey"—evolved as an urban pursuit, a way of reimagining and subverting the built environment by moving through it in imaginative and aesthetic but essentially highly physical ways. Free running tends to put more emphasis on theatrics and acrobatics than pure efficiency—a little like a cross between contemporary dance and a Jason Bourne movie. Free running is not just what you do but the way that you do it.

MAKING THE MOVES
» *Jumps.* Practice bending your knees and jumping upward on the spot, then try the same movement but with a forward motion. Finally, practice jumping forward and up onto a stump or fallen tree trunk. Land like a frog—absorb the impact by bending your knees and hold your hands in front for balance.
» *Balancing.* Walk along a horizontal fallen log, one foot after the other, then graduate to narrower beams and even branches in a tree. Practicing on a slack line will build core strength and balance.

Balancing

Bridging

» *Swinging.* Look for horizontal branches just above head height. Spring upward and grab with both hands. You could dead-hang with your arms straight and outstretched, pull yourself up so that your arms are held straight above the branch, spin all the way around the branch on your tummy, or just enjoy swinging backward and forward from your arms.

» *Clinging.* Climb like a koala! Take your shoes off, and see if you can hug a thin tree trunk with your hands and push off with your bare feet. How high can you climb, moving both arms together, then both feet? Can you jump up and grab the tree before working your way up it?

» *Bridging.* This involves climbing a gap between two trunks or a trunk and a rock by pushing parts of your body on either side of the gap. One way is to press outward onto each surface with your hands and feet as if you're in the middle of a jumping jack.

» *Vaulting.* Find a waist-high obstacle like a fallen tree and push down on its top with both arms straight. Then spring off your feet and throw your legs to the side of your arms and over the obstacle.

» *Breakfalls.* Landing safely is critical. To move out of a big downward jump, or if a move doesn't go as planned, a diagonal forward roll on one shoulder and finishing on your feet will take the sting out of the landing—and look pretty cool.

There are many more moves to discover as you practice and play with the different elements you encounter. Free movement in the forest lets you see the environment in a different way—as a place of physical possibilities and movement opportunities to exploit.

SAFETY FIRST

Any of these activities have the potential to lead to injury. Start small and simple and build up to more adventurous movements slowly. Ideally, train with a friend—it's more fun and one of you can get help if needed. It's a good idea to work with a natural movement trainer or experienced free runner, who will help you progress much more quickly. However you choose to play with movement in the woods, remember that it's not about being the fastest, most daring, or strongest: It's about feeling the joy in understanding what your body can do when set free to move.

———

GODS OF THE FOREST

Across the world, forests and groves were the first churches and temples, the natural habitat of the spirits, gods, and goddesses who created and assisted humans on their journey through life and their preparation for death and the afterworld. Their colorful stories are often localized to make sense of events, human characteristics, or natural phenomena attached to a particular place.

For indigenous peoples with animist beliefs— where places, animals, trees, plants, rocks, and rivers all have souls or a spiritual essence— forests, trees, and woodlands have played a primal and fundamental part. There are hundreds of distinct Indigenous American cultures within the United States, each with their own traditional belief system. Some are mingled with modern Christianity, but all have one thing in common: The belief that nature is sacred, with the forest home to an array of spirits, from generous and kind to downright destructive.

Known as "Gitchi Manitou" by the Abenaki, Algonquin, and other tribes, the Great Spirit is an abstract, benevolent deity. He is responsible for creating the world, which he dreamed into being from nothingness—the mountains and valleys; forests with their profusion of plants and animals; waterways and swimming creatures. Countering this divine goodness are malevolent spirits, such as the Northwestern tribes' Stick Indians, who may paralyze, hypnotize, or eat people in the woods. When in a lighter mood, they may simply frighten or confuse travelers by laughing or whistling.

CREATION MYTHS

In Māori mythology, when the world was created, the sky and earth were joined together. But Tāne, god of the forest, knew that the world needed more space, so he separated his parents—the gods Papatūānuku (earth mother) and Ranginui (sky father)—then clothed his mother in plants and trees, and turned his own beads of sweat into stars to help his father.

The origin of mankind holds a fascination for every culture, its mystery often explained using trees as raw material. In Scandinavian mythology, dwarves molded two figures from trees that were found by the god Odin. The figures were named Ask and Embla and became the first human beings. Roman legend imparts oak trees with the role of the first mothers, their children born out of an opening and fed with acorns. In Iranian mythology, the first human couple was an entwined double tree, separated at maturity to become a man and a woman, each with their own individual soul.

STRUTTING THE STAGE OF LIFE

The forest is a favorite backdrop for the gods and goddesses, nymphs, and dryads of ancient Greek and Roman religions. Many tales enact dramas that explain the machinations of the physical world, and the loves and foibles of the human persona. Apollo, Greek god of music, archery, and the sun, got into a spat with Eros (Cupid, in Roman myths), god of love. In a huff, Eros shot one of his arrows at Apollo, causing him to fall in love with Daphne, a river nymph. Eros then proceeded to shoot Daphne with an arrow that made her despise Apollo. Stalked relentlessly through the forest, Daphne cried out to her father, Peneus— a river god—to help save her from Apollo. As she spoke, her limbs became heavy and bark crept up her torso; her arms became branches and her fingers leaves— to preserve her virtue she had been transformed into a laurel tree.

The ancient Celts, who populated parts of continental Europe, Asia Minor, Ireland, and Britain, were deeply entwined with the land. They revered spirits that inhabited local mountains, forests, trees, and springs. Sacred groves and natural landmarks were powerful spiritual symbols and became the stages where the key rituals of life—birth, marriage, and death—took place.

GREEN GYM

The common New Year's resolution to get in shape often means a gym membership that's barely used beyond the end of January. Loud music, pumped-up companions, and hi-tech machines will motivate many people, but some might feel more like a routine that uses the natural gym of the woods. Circuit training on fixed outdoor equipment can combine the benefits of a beautiful forest environment with a great workout.

This kind of outdoor exercise can be no-frills, body-weight training in the forest, using natural movement—as in parkour or free running (see pages 208–9)—or can even replicate some familiar gym equipment. You could design your own workout in a circuit with as many different stations as you want, or simply use what the woods provide and make some apparatus where you need it.

MAKING YOUR OWN FOREST FITNESS TRAIL

» Use simple, low log benches for sit-ups (**A**) and straddle jumps (**B**). Several log benches spaced out can act as hurdles (**C**). A bench set up at waist height is great for vaulting—just put your hands on the raised log and vault from side to side (**D**).

» Lash a log between two trees above head height to make a pull-up bar for chin-ups (**E**). Or, with a little imagination and a few square lashings (see pages 148–9), rig up some monkey bars (**F**).

» Gather a load of sticks to make a grid for hopscotch (**G**), and collect large logs or rocks to provide lifting weights (**H**).

» A cargo net for climbing or crawling under is a great addition (**I**). If you live near a beach, you might find a discarded commercial fishing net washed up after a storm. Getting it off the beach can be a major workout in itself!

» A webbing strap with a ratchet to tighten it between two trees (**J**) is an easy temporary element to add, which is not only great fun to try and walk along (known as slacklining) but also develops core strength and balance. Set up the slackline at about knee height to avoid any hard falls.

If training for its own sake doesn't sound like your thing, why not use as many of the elements of the fitness trail as you can to make an obstacle course. Then race your friends or just the clock.

FARTLEK TRAINING

A combination of two Swedish words, fartlek translates as "speed play" and refers to a type of interval training. Developed in the 1930s by Gosta Holmer, a Swedish Olympic athlete and coach, fartlek involves varying the pace of a run from walking to jogging to sprinting, ideally over varied terrain. Forests are perfect places for fartlek training since you can choose particular trees to run to, jog up hills, sprint for ninety seconds on the flat, and walk quickly to recover without stopping. There are no strict rules or duration, and you can decide how long each phase lasts, using landmarks or music for timing if you don't want to rely on a watch. Athletes use fartlek to make training varied and enjoyable, as well as to practice bursts of speed that might be needed for passing or racing to the line. A typical session might look something like:

1. *Gentle run to warm up—0.5 mile (800 meters)*
2. *Run at race pace—0.25 mile (400 meters)*
3. *Gentle run—0.5 mile (800 meters)*
4. *Faster than race pace—1 mile (1,600 meters)*
5. *Fast walk to recover—0.25 mile (400 meters)*
6. *Fast run—0.5 mile (800 meters)*
7. *Jog to recover—0.5 mile (800 meters)*
8. *Jog uphill—0.5 mile (800 meters)*
9. *Jog to recover—0.5 mile (800 meters)*
10. *Sprint—200 yards (180 meters)*
11. *Gentle jog to recover, then warm down—0.5 mile (800 meters)*

EARTH PIGMENTS

Every hue of color in our clothes, paints, and consumer objects is a result of light reflected from a pigment that has been added to a material. Changing the color of things for decoration has been important to people for millennia, and one good way of doing this is to make paint. Luckily, you only have to look beneath the forest floor for a huge range of colors that you can use to make your own earth pigment paints. As these pigments are really just rock dust, they won't dissolve, which means they have to be added to a binder (see following page) before you can apply them to a surface. To dilute your paint, you need a solvent such as turpentine or mineral spirits, or even water.

THE ORIGIN OF PIGMENTS

The hugely varied geology of our planet is a rich source of red, yellow, brown, and black colors, which have been used to create art for at least 70,000 years. Making earth pigments can be as simple as drying, crushing, and sieving subsoil, minerals, or ores to obtain a colored powder, but there are also many ways, discovered over centuries, to chemically modify minerals to create different colors. Many of the names of colors that are recognized today, such as umber and sienna, are named after the places where the soil for the pigment originated. Reddish-brown umber comes from the Umbria region of Italy and gets its distinctive hue from iron and magnesium oxides. Raw sienna is a yellow ochre from near the city of Siena in Tuscany, Italy. It can be changed to a much redder color by heating at a high temperature and is sold as burnt sienna pigment.

CREATING COLOR FROM THE FOREST

Thankfully, making your own pigments from forest soils is neither difficult nor expensive. This isn't about creating a standard palette, but instead about looking carefully at variations around where you live and travel, then building up a collection where every color has an origin and a story behind it.

1. Dig up some subsoil (*fig 1*) and leave it to dry.
2. Break the soil up into small pieces and crush them in a mortar and pestle (*fig 2*). Use eye protection if you need to use force to deal with large lumps.
3. Pass the material through a fine sieve to remove any larger particles (*fig 3*), and then grind again in the mortar and pestle to achieve a consistency like fine flour. Be careful not to breathe in the fine dust in windy conditions.

| fig 1 | fig 2 | fig 3 |

4. Mix the earth with your choice of binder and solvent.
5. Get painting—but remember that even though the paint is wholesome and homemade, using it on rocks and trees where it won't wash off is still pretty disrespectful to the natural habitat. Respect the local environment and leave no trace, or paint on surfaces that you can take home with you.

WHICH BINDER?

As the name suggests, the binder binds the pigment to the surface. There are plenty to choose from. Try out a selection of the following examples and see which you prefer and which work best with your local pigments.

» *Saliva.* This might sound gross, but saliva is very possibly what was used in much early cave art.
» *Milk.* Casein, the main protein in milk, binds with pigment and hardens, often to a semiopaque finish, which gives a lovely weathered look to wooden ware. Ideally, use milk that's turning sour. A good alternative is powdered milk with a little baking soda added.
» *Flour.* The starch in flour forms a base to which pigments can bind.
» *Egg yolks.* These can be used to make a traditional tempera, which dries quickly and is particularly long-lasting.
» *Oil.* If you want the paint to harden, it's important to use an oil, such as linseed, tung, or walnut, that will polymerize, or harden, over time. These oils can be thinned with mineral spirits for ease of application. Other vegetable oils will turn sticky and rancid rather than harden.

All the above binders can set hard, not fade, and last for decades, if not thousands of years.

STONE AGE EARTH PIGMENT ANIMATION

In 2012, Dr. Marc Azéma, a French filmmaker and specialist in movement in Paleolithic art, presented a theory that delicately overlapping images of animals in cave paintings more than 30,000 years old were ancient animations. Lit by powerful modern lamps, expansive wildlife scenarios in the Chauvet and La Baume Latrone caves in southeast France can be seen all at once in minute detail; however, the warm, yellow, flickering light of traditional tallow lamps create a very different effect. A small area at a time is illuminated, something that might have allowed a Stone Age storyteller to focus on one scene at a time, much like looking at a single panel of a graphic novel. The flickering of the light, especially when shifted rapidly from side to side, would have created the effect of movement and perhaps the first animated images created by humans.

NATURAL BRUSHES

Once you have manufactured or found some pigment (see pages 214–15), you can make marks with it on card, paper, cloth, bark, rock, or even skin. The earliest artists must have used their hands and feet, and getting tactile with natural pigments is about as direct an artistic expression as you could make. Almost anything can be used to apply paint, whether as a form of brush, palette knife, or dot-making stick. It's fun to experiment by exploring the different marks and textures left by a variety of natural materials, such as moss, feathers, leafy plants, pebbles, and fur, but nothing beats the trusty paintbrush, especially when you make it yourself.

THE BUSINESS OF BRUSHES

What brush you choose will depend on the type of effect you want to achieve. Varying the stiffness of the bristles and the shape of the brush will allow for a huge variety of effects. But first, you need to gather the materials to make your paintbrush.

» *Brush handle.* This needs to have a hollow end to hold the brush material. Stiff tree branches or stems with a hollow or soft pith core are perfect, but you can always drill a hole in the end grain of any suitably sized piece of wood. If you want to go full Palaeolithic, a sawn-off hollow bone like a turkey leg will also work.

» *Brush bristles.* Traditionally, brushes were made from animal hair. In the woods, this might mean hair from the winter coat of a large mammal, such as a deer, shed as temperatures rise in the spring. Badger hair can often be collected where animal trails run under fences at field boundaries, although it might take awhile to collect enough for a brush. If you can source some, then hog hair is probably the best in terms of stiffness and ability to hold paint. You could even use human hair from yourself—or a consenting friend!

To attach the hair to a brush handle, take a bundle that will fit tightly into a hollow stem. Tie the end to be inserted tightly with thin thread and dip it into a little glue. Squeeze and repeatedly press the bundle into the core with a long needle or awl until at least 0.5 inch (1.25 centimeters) is held in the handle. If the bristle bundle is a little loose, you can cut a small sliver of wood and push it into the side of the hole to make it tight. Let the glue set well before using the brush. You can trim the brush into the shape of a wedge, fan, or square, or give it a round tip.

THE ONE-STICK SOLUTION

A simpler, rougher alternative can be made by using the same stick for both handle and paint applicator—in the form of a split-fiber brush. As always, you'll need to experiment with local tree species to find those that work best.

1. Cut a green stick about 12 inches (30 centimeters) long—and anything from matchstick to thumb-thick diameter, depending on how widely you want to apply your paint.

2. Carefully and repeatedly bash one end of the stick with a mallet, stone, or lump of firewood until the wood fibers separate and take on a brushlike appearance (*fig 1*).

With small sticks you can sometimes get the same result by carefully chewing the end of the stick—just make sure that it's a nontoxic tree first.

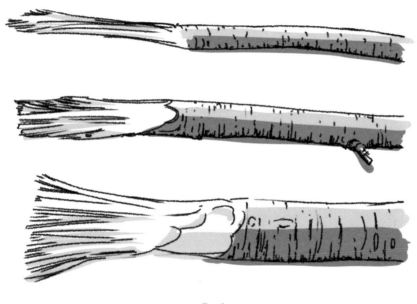

fig 1

PIGMENT HANDIWORK

One of the most obvious and satisfying ways to apply paint is to forget all about the brushes and use your hands and feet as stamps and stencils. This way, you can mark your presence with your own unique handprint or footprint, to be washed away quickly, slowly decay over time, or last for millennia—like those made more than 10,000 years ago by the people who lived in the Cueva de las Manos (or Cave of the Hands) in Argentina. In the late summer and fall, when berry bushes are laden with fruit, fill your mouth with the juiciest examples and press your hand with fingers spread over a smooth tree trunk. Purse your lips, then spray the berry juice over the back of your hand to leave a silhouette artwork that will wash away in the rain.

RESOURCES

The following titles are a selection of books that will help you dig deeper into many of the most rewarding aspects of exploring woodlands and forests, from fishing and foraging to whittling and wayfaring.

SURVIVAL AND BUSHCRAFT
Kochanski, M. *Bushcraft: Outdoor Skills and Wilderness Survival*. Edmonton: Lone Pine Publishing, 2016.

Mears, R. *Essential Bushcraft*. London: Hodder & Stoughton, 2003.

FIRST AID
Schimelpfenig, T. *NOLS Wilderness Medicine*. Mechanicsburg, PA: Stackpole Books, 7th ed., 2021.

FORAGING
Boudreau, D., and Mykel Hawke. *Foraging for Survival: Edible Wild Plants of North America*. New York: Skyhorse Publishing, 2020.

Mabey, R. *Food for Free*. Glasgow: Collins, 2012.

Wright, J. *The Forager's Calendar: A Seasonal Guide to Nature's Wild Harvests*. London: Profile Books, 2019.

Regional Foraging Guides—book series covering California, Midwest, Mountain States, Northeast, Pacific Northwest, Southeast, Southwest. Portland: Timber Press.

GAME
Weston, N. *Hunter Gather Cook: Adventures in Wild Food*. Lewes, UK: Guild of Master Craftsmen (GMC) Publications, 2019.

RURAL SKILLS
Langsner, D. *Country Woodcraft*. Emmaus, PA: Rodale Press, 1978.

Law, B. *Woodland Craft*. Lewes, UK: Guild of Master Craftsmen (GMC) Publications, 2015.

AX CRAFT
Kirtley, P. *Wilderness Axe Skills and Campcraft*. Atglen, PA: Schiffer Publishing, 2021.

WHITTLING
Lubkemann, C. *Whittling Twigs & Branches: Unique Birds, Flowers, Trees & More from Easy-to-Find Wood*. East Petersburg, PA: Fox Chapel Publishing, 2004.

Sundqvist, W. *Swedish Carving Techniques*. Newtown, CT: The Taunton Press, 1990.

FISHING
Stewart, H. *Indian Fishing: Early Methods on the Northwest Coast*. Seattle: University of Washington Press, 2018.

SMOKING AND CURING
Lamb, S. *The River Cottage Curing & Smoking Handbook*. New York: Ten Speed Press, 2014.

NAVIGATION
Forte, C. *Navigation in the Mountains: The Definitive Guide for Hill Walkers, Mountaineers & Leaders —The Official Navigation Book for All Mountain Leader Training Schemes*. Capel Curig, Conwy: Mountain Training UK, 2012.

Gooley, T. *The Natural Navigator: The Rediscovered Art of Letting Nature Be Your Guide*. New York: The Experiment, 10th anniversary ed., 2020.

ANCIENT SKILLS
Elpel, Thomas J. *Primitive Living, Self-Sufficiency, and Survival Skills: A Field Guide to Primitive Living Skills*. Guilford, CT: The Lyons Press, 2004.

The Society of Primitive Technology, Wescott, D. (ed.). *Primitive Technology: A Book of Earth Skills*. Salt Lake City: Gibbs Smith Publisher, 1999.

KNOTS
Boundford, T. *Knots*. New York: Harper Perennial, 2006.

BOW MAKING
Hamm, J., Steve Allely, Tim Baker, Paul Comstock, Ron Hardcastle, Jay Massey, and John Strunk. *The Traditional Bowyer's Bible: Volume One*. Goldthwaite, TX: Bois d'Arc Press, 1993.

POTTERY
Reigger, H. *Primitive Pottery*. New York: Van Nostrand Reinhold, 1972.

LAND ART
Goldsworthy, A. *Wood*. New York: Abrams, 1996.

WOOD WIDE WEB
Simard, S. *Finding the Mother Tree: Discovering the Wisdom of the Forest*. New York: Knopf, 2021.

TREES
Young, P. *Oak*. London: Reaktion Books, 2013.

MIGRATION
Elphick, J. *The Random House Atlas of Bird Migration: Tracing the Great Journeys of the World's Birds*. New York: Random House, 1995.

DEER
Geist, V. *Deer of the World: Their Evolution, Behavior, and Ecology*. Mechanicsburg, PA: Stackpole Books, 1998.

FOREST MEDITATION
Miyazaki, Professor Yoshifumi, *Walking in the Woods: Go back to nature with the Japanese way of shinrin-yoku*. London: Aster, 2021.

INDEX

Page numbers in *italic* refer to photographs and illustrations.

*Thanks to all the forest folk that have generously shared their
skills and knowledge with me over the past thirty years. Special thanks to the
Forest School community in the UK who hold the principles of Forest School dear
and to the European Outdoor Education Network, who have helped me to better
understand why I do what I do, and how I might do it better.*

*John Andrews has steered this project with kindness and sensitivity, for which
I am very grateful. Finally, as always, the biggest gratitude to
Suzie, Jake, and Stan for absolutely everything.*